Healthy Eating in Schools

SCHOOL PSYCHOLOGY BOOK SERIES

Healthy Eating in Schools

Evidence-Based Interventions to Help Kids Thrive

Catherine P. Cook-Cottone,
Evelyn Tribole, and Tracy L. Tylka

American Psychological Association · *Washington, DC*

Published by
American Psychological Association
750 First Street, NE
Washington, DC 20002
www.apa.org

To order
APA Order Department
P.O. Box 92984
Washington, DC 20090-2984
Tel: (800) 374-2721; Direct: (202) 336-5510
Fax: (202) 336-5502; TDD/TTY: (202) 336-6123
Online: www.apa.org/pubs/books
E-mail: order@apa.org

In the U.K., Europe, Africa, and the Middle East, copies may be ordered from
American Psychological Association
3 Henrietta Street
Covent Garden, London
WC2E 8LU England

Typeset in Goudy by Circle Graphics, Inc., Columbia, MD

Printer: Edwards Brothers, Inc., Lillington, NC
Cover Designer: Naylor Design, Washington, DC

The opinions and statements published are the responsibility of the authors, and such opinions and statements do not necessarily represent the policies of the American Psychological Association.

Library of Congress Cataloging-in-Publication Data

Cook-Cottone, Catherine P.
  Healthy eating in schools : evidence-based interventions to help kids thrive / Catherine P. Cook-Cottone, Evelyn Tribole, and Tracy L. Tylka.
    p. cm.
  Includes bibliographical references and index.
  ISBN 978-1-4338-1300-9 — ISBN 1-4338-1300-9 1. School children—Food—United States. 2. Children—Nutrition—United States. 3. Children—Nutrition—Psychological aspects. I. Title.
  LB3479.U6C665 2013
  371.7'16—dc23

                                2012040335

British Library Cataloguing-in-Publication Data
A CIP record is available from the British Library.

Printed in the United States of America
First Edition

http://dx.doi.org/10.1037/14180-000

CONTENTS

Healthy Eating in Schools

INTRODUCTION

Health and well-being are important for children of all shapes and sizes (Daníelsdóttir, Burgard, & Oliver-Pyatt, 2010; Hayes, 2010) and linked to their academic success (Centers for Disease Control and Prevention, 2011a). Children and adolescents ages 5 to 17 spend about 13 years and a majority of their waking hours at school, with many consuming breakfast, lunch, and up to two snacks a day while at school. School physical education, sports, and wellness activities are often the only opportunities that children have to engage in cardiovascular and strengthening activities.

In the wake of high childhood obesity rates, federal policies have mandated schools to address nutritional and environmental factors that promote healthy body weights (Healthy, Hunger-Free Kids Act, 2010). Specifically, schools that participate in federal nutrition programs must establish, conduct, and assess local school wellness policies that include (a) goals for nutrition education, (b) physical activity that promotes student wellness, and

DOI: 10.1037/14180-001
Healthy Eating in Schools: Evidence-Based Interventions to Help Kids Thrive, by C. P. Cook-Cottone, E. Tribole, and T. L. Tylka

(c) nutrition guidelines for foods distributed within the school to promote healthy weight. Yet, given the growing concern about obesity and the concomitant public health mandates, it is important that schools know that dieting and disordered eating behaviors are also harmful to health and can be counterproductive to obesity prevention (Neumark-Sztainer, Wall, Larson, Eisenberg, & Loth, 2011). There are inspiring examples of flourishing schools actively partnering with community to create health-promoting experiences for students. We will be describing these programs in this book as we review best practices for schools. However, despite the clear need and mandates, many schools have a long way to go in their efforts to best support the development of healthy students.

WHERE CAN A SCHOOL BEGIN? A ROAD MAP TO THE HEALTHY STUDENT

To promote positive change in students' health and well-being, school personnel (e.g., school psychologists, teachers, coaches, school counselors, nurses, administrators) need a solid understanding of eating behavior and weight-related disorders. Both obesity and eating disorders (EDs) are weight-related disorders, which are not distinct from each other and share a number of risk factors, including dieting, body dissatisfaction, and teasing (Darby et al., 2009; Haines & Neumark-Sztainer, 2006; Neumark-Sztainer, 2005). Without guidance rooted in empirical support, schools run the risk of implementing ineffective or harmful programming in an effort to do good work. This volume provides a conceptual model and effective interventions that address the prevention of both obesity and eating disordered behaviors within the context of developing healthy and intuitive eating behaviors.

At the most basic level, healthy eating involves *intuitive eating*, which is a firm sense of what, when, and how much food the body needs to be nourished. However, healthy eating also requires interpersonal and social attunement that allows the child or adolescent to remain connected to her or his physical needs and struggles. The culture we create in schools around food and the body can influence these characteristics in our students. When the connection between what the body needs and what, how, and when we eat is disrupted, there is risk for disorder. Eating becomes *disordered* when the primary motivation for and/or function of eating and eating-related behavior is consistently and frequently something other than nourishing the body. Most certainly, school personnel can help create a positive food and body culture in which eating and exercising for health serves growth, development, and academic success rather than increasing risk for physical illness and disorder.

We designed this text to help school personnel develop a healthy eating and positive body culture in their schools. Here, in the Introduction, we provide the profiles of four children who illustrate eating and body acceptance difficulties (Jared, Jacqueline, Kara, and Ben). These four students come from two schools—one urban (City Central Elementary) and one suburban (Bayside High School). We also used other schools, projects, and students as case examples throughout the text to bring the personal into the conceptual. The two schools and the students are composites. The details provided in the case studies were aggregated from actual schools and altered to protect confidentiality. When an example has not been altered, a citation is provided. At the end of the Introduction, we review the definitions, rates, and outcomes of obesity and major EDs so that it is clear about what is at stake.

This book will provide you with ideas and resources for making changes at your school. Part I (Chapters 1 and 2) provides a conceptual framework for fostering healthy students. Specifically, Chapter 1 defines and conceptualizes healthy (i.e., intuitive) eating, and Chapter 2 presents a conceptual model of eating behavior, explaining how personal and external factors influence the way we eat. Part II (Chapters 3–6) presents a three-pillar approach for fostering healthy students. Chapter 3 presents the rationale for the three pillars, and Chapters 4, 5, and 6 present the three pillars, respectively: (Pillar I) intuitive eating and nutrition; (Pillar II) healthy physical activity; and (Pillar III) mindfulness, self-care, and emotional regulation. Part III (Chapters 7–9) addresses school-based interventions and policies. Chapter 7 presents an overview of school-based preventive interventions and addresses program implementation challenges. Chapter 8 discusses screening and assessment instruments and guidelines for supporting students with eating and body image problems. Chapter 9 provides an overview of relevant federal school policies and professional guidelines that address food, eating, and the body; these policies and guidelines are critical to implementing a legally compliant program.

The appendixes provide additional tools for school personnel. First, an overview of less common EDs is presented (Appendix A). Then screening tools are provided to support assessment of children's attitudes toward eating (Appendix B), intuitive eating in adolescents (Appendix C), body appreciation (Appendix D), and sociocultural attitudes toward appearances (Appendix E). Finally, an annotated list of Suggested Resources for school personnel is offered, which includes lesson plans, curriculum, organizations, and authoritative reports, to facilitate the development of a positive school culture for healthy eating and body acceptance.

This volume shares how schools can build a positive environment that enhances student health through encouraging intuitive eating and mind–body attunement. Focusing on health promotion in this manner serves to prevent the type of obesity related to eating in the absence of hunger and low physical activity without running the risk of encouraging disordered eating and food preoccupation among students. Therefore, this book helps develop a plan of action that addresses EDs and obesity concurrently, filling a noticeable gap in the literature left by books that treat EDs and obesity independently of one another. It is our hope that this book provides school personnel with the tools they need to look thoughtfully at their existing school environment, assess what is needed to make changes, and implement changes that will enhance the health of all students.

CASE STUDIES: CITY CENTRAL ELEMENTARY AND BAYSIDE HIGH SCHOOL

The experience of four students is shared in this section to provide a glimpse into what struggles with food and the body look like within the school environment. By exploring the perspectives and challenges of these four students, the conceptual becomes familiar. We hope you will recognize aspects of these students and schools in the students and schools you know.

Jared and Jacqueline at City Central School

Jared is a fifth-grade African American boy at City Central School, which is an urban elementary school located in a northeastern rust-belt city. Jared, like many of the students, lives in a single-parent household well below the poverty level. He is one of the 99% of the children at the school who qualify for free or reduced-price meals. The crime rate in his neighborhood is among the highest in the country, with residents having a 1 in 16 chance of being a victim of a crime and a crime index of 2 (i.e., safer than only 2% of U.S. cities). There is gang and drug activity. Most students are African American or Hispanic. The school is located in what is often called a *grocery store desert*, with the closest fresh foods available 1.5 miles away. For most, this is too far to walk with groceries. Jared and his family shop at the convenience store most nights or eat fast food (e.g., pizza, burgers, tacos).

The school overweight–obesity rates are well above the national average. Since his physical in third grade, Jared has fallen within the obese category. The rates of EDs at his school are unknown. However, Jared, like some of his peers, eats fast food and packaged snack foods too much and too often. He often finds himself eating even when he isn't hungry. At times, Jared eats to soothe emotions and relieve stress. Sometimes he just eats because he is bored or wants to "zone out." His mom has a drinking problem, and he has been told that his dad has a drug problem. He sees his father once or twice a year. Because Jared is the oldest child, he works hard to make sure his little sister is safe and gets to school every day in time for breakfast. He loves breakfast time at school. The school has a breakfast-in-the-classroom program (funded, in part, by the American Dairy Association).

Jacqueline is also a fifth grader at City Central School. She is Hispanic and lives with her parents and older sisters and brothers about four blocks from the school. She is very conscious of her weight. Her older sister is overweight, and her mother and father both fall within the obese range. In second grade, a few kids at school teased her about having breasts and a "booty." She was extremely embarrassed and hurt. This scared her, too, because her mom frequently cries about her own weight and her dad calls her mom "lazy" and "fat" when they fight. Her mom is often jealous of thinner women, and this causes fights between Jacqueline's parents. During a nutrition presentation at school, Jacqueline learned that too much food can make you fat. She started cutting back and skipping meals whenever she could. Jacqueline is small now and falls within the underweight range. She is pleased. No one suspects that she might have some symptoms of an ED. Most people don't think this happens in city schools or to Hispanic girls.

The school and the district are underfunded, and they struggle to meet many educational mandates. Jared and Jacqueline frequently do not have a textbook to bring home. Jared's teacher last year instituted a "no-books-leave-school-grounds policy." There is a high teacher turnover rate (28%) and a low graduate rate for the district (78%). Despite the need, the school has yet to establish a wellness policy and has not addressed many recommended areas of school functions associated with nutrition and exercise. There are some remarkable community attributes, including a community garden, an inconsistent farmers market, and a splash pool. However, crime rates often keep families indoors. For example, Jared and Jacqueline are not allowed to walk to the splash park without a parent. Jared's mom does not like the heat and rarely takes Jared and his sister to the park to play. Jacqueline's mom will not go to the splash park because she is very weight conscious.

Several of the parents active in the PTA (a small but passionate group) have raised a concern in regard to the physical fitness and health of the students. Noting the high rates of overweight and obesity at the school and the limitations of the neighborhood given the high crime rates, the parents feel that the school is the ideal place to address these issues. They worry about the soda and candy machines in the hallways, the limited physical education time for students, and the lack of an outdoor play area. They want a family-oriented and school-based program that helps families support nutritional and physical health of their children. They want to know how to best help their children. They have also raised concerns about the school lunches, snacks, and the use of food for reward in the classroom. They wonder why there is no school wellness policy. They have some ideas but little organized direction. Two of the parents are active in the local garden program and belong to the community center.

Kara and Ben at Bayside High School

Bayside High School is located in a suburban, upper middle class neighborhood in the Midwest, with a wealth of grocery and organic food stores. About 10% of the families belong to an organized farmers' cooperative (i.e., "coop") and have fresh fruits and vegetables delivered weekly. A group of the families get together each year and make jam and tomato sauce to store for the winter. Many families have gardens. There is a local garden tour each June, and about 23% of the residents participate. The youth bureau offers cooking, crafting, yoga, theater, and a variety of other programs throughout the school year and in the summer. The area has a central town park with picnic areas, hiking, and large playing fields for the town-managed youth sports leagues. The crime rate is about average (crime index 48), and residents have a 6.25 chance in 100 of being a victim of a crime. Only 2.6% of the residents live below the poverty level, and 7% of the students qualify for the free or reduced-price lunch program.

Nearly all of the students at Bayside High School are White. The overweight–obesity rates are slightly below average. The prevalence and incidence of EDs are a bit above average, when compared with other high schools. The school is among the best in its region, placing number one or two in school rankings on a consistent basis. The School Wellness Committee was established in 2004, and the first edition of the wellness policy was put into place in 2006. The policies have been updated each year based on teacher and parent feedback. There are no outstanding preventative efforts or programs in place; however, the school follows what are considered to be good general practices. For example, the school has a web page dedicated to education on nutrition, has integrated nutrition education throughout the curriculum at each grade level, is a "Choose Sensibly School" with a strict policy on food and beverages on school grounds, has policies forbidding food as reward and exercise as punishment in the classroom, and has an extensive fitness program open to teachers and families. Despite all of this, there are challenges.

Kara is a Caucasian sophomore at Bayside High School. She lives in abundance, yet she starves herself. She spent this past summer at an inpatient ED treatment center out of state, working to gain enough weight to attend school in the fall. She now sees a psychologist, nutritionist, and a medical specialist once per week. She also attends a weekly aftercare group to prevent major relapse. She feels pressured by an atmosphere that she describes as "perfect is not good enough." As a sophomore, she and her friends are already worried whether their grades will make the cut for the best colleges and universities.

Ben worries, too—about everything. He is a top student, athlete, and has been the lead in almost every school play since sixth grade. His mom is a neurosurgeon, and his dad is a corporate lawyer. Ben's parents expect him to make his own choice but limit his available choices to law or medicine. He is a junior who has many secrets. He is active in sports and looks the part. He has the six-pack abs and broad shoulders of an athlete. Ben has not told anyone that he makes himself throw up dinner every night. He is starving at dinnertime, overeats, and then panics. He is afraid of losing his lean, perfected physique. In his elementary school years, he was labeled as "chubby," and his friends often joked with him about his weight. After a talk with their pediatrician, Ben's mom and dad focused on his food intake and increased his involvement in sports. He lost weight and received a lot of positive social feedback. It was in his freshman year during a workshop on drug use and other problematic behaviors that he heard about people making themselves throw up. After eating too much ice cream one night, he tried it. It made perfect sense. He believed that he could eat whatever he wanted and still remain lean. It was recently that he noticed that the purging, first used to keep the weight off, actually helps him cope with stress. He has considered telling his mom about his eating problem because it is starting to feel out of control. He has also realized that it has become harder and harder to maintain his lean physique because his body is retaining about half of the calories from each binge–purge cycle. His family and friends joke about how he seems to be able to eat anything he wants. He hates these jokes, especially because he is noticing his weight fluctuate.

A group of teachers and coaches at Bayside High School, including Kara's mom, have become concerned with the emphasis on low weight and leanness in the school. Although they agree that overweight and obesity are associated with health issues, they want to focus on nutrition and fitness and move the focus away from using weight, body fat, and body mass index (BMI) as the primary barometers of health. Even though the current wellness policy is not focused on weight and body fat, they believe there is an evolving culture of perfectionism as well as thinness (for girls) and lean muscularity (for boys) as ideals. They also worry that overweight and obesity are conceptualized as bad and associated with laziness or a lack of control. The teachers worry that these stereotypes are reinforced by some of the school coaches and the local dance studios. They feel the students do not have a sense of mindfulness and intuitive eating. Rather, the focus is on staying lean and controlling food intake.

In their presentation to the school's administration, they brought in several student notes that were placed in the school's bully box (a box used for anonymously reporting bullying) that cite fat-related teasing in the locker rooms and in the hallways. They also worry about what they believe are the increasing rates of EDs at the school. Despite good general practice, the school does not have an organized prevention program. Also, despite substantial resources and an engaged PTA, the school has not moved beyond establishing and following policy. Further, there is no protocol for the support of those with EDs or obesity-related health issues, and these students can take an additional year or two to graduate.

HOW COMMON ARE THESE PROBLEMS? DEFINITIONS, RATES, AND OUTCOMES AMONG THE MAJOR EATING DISORDERS AND OBESITY

As seen at both City Central and Bayside, there can be a wide range of struggles associated with eating and care of the body. The first two questions are often, "How do I know if one of my students has a disorder or needs help?" and "How common are these problems?" To answer the first question, more general definitions are provided. To aid in assessment and referral decisions, less common EDs are defined in Appendix A.

The answer to the second question is found in prevalence and incidence rates. Prevalence and incidence are the measures used to report the frequency of particular diseases (Hoek & van Hoeken, 2003). Specifically, the *prevalence* of a disease or disorder is the number of cases in the population, and *point prevalence* is the prevalence at a specific point in time. The *incidence* rate is slightly different; it is the number of new cases in a population over a specific period of time. Incidence is often expressed as the number of new cases within a year per 100,000 members of the population. Hoek and van Hoeken (2003) warned that incidence rates reflect the point of detection. The point of detection might not be the same moment that the disorder reaches a clinical level for the individual. This is especially true for anorexia nervosa (AN), bulimia nervosa (BN), binge-eating disorder (BED), and eating disorder not otherwise specified (EDNOS), as children and adolescents may hide their symptoms (consider Ben and Jacqueline at Bayside and City Central). The *1-year prevalence* rate is the point prevalence rate plus the annual incidence rate. Some researchers and practitioners believe that prevalence rate is most useful as an indication of the demand for care or services (Hoek & van Hoeken, 2003).

Researchers have suggested that like incidence rates, actual prevalence rates for AN, BN, BED, and EDNOS can be difficult to detect for a few reasons. First, there are comparatively low prevalence rates for BN and AN in the general population (Hoek & van Hoeken, 2003). Second, there is a tendency among those struggling with eating disordered behaviors to conceal their struggle. This was illustrated by the secret keeping of Kara and Ben as well as by the secretive food restricting done by Jacqueline. Third, among those who reveal their disorder, only a small percentage seek treatment. In some areas like those near Bayside and City Central, there is stigma attached to seeking out mental health services. Many families try to handle things on their own. Accordingly, reviewing treatment center and hospital records may lead to an underestimate. Fourth, the study of special populations only addresses a specific segment of the population. For example, a special population study would explore the rate of EDs among high school girls, dancers, or adolescents ages 13 to 21.

Given these challenges, researchers have found that the best method for ascertaining incidence and prevalence rates is a two-stage screening approach (Hoek & van Hoeken, 2003) that involves (a) screening a large population for the likelihood of EDs and (b) conducting personal interviews with a randomly selected subgroup of subjects identified as at risk. Although there are also problems with this approach (e.g., poor response rates, sensitivity and specificity of the screening instrument, small size of group interviewed), it is considered an acceptable method for estimating these rates (Hoek & van Hoeken, 2003). For the section below, prevalence and incidence rates are reported using a combination of techniques from various researchers. It is important to note that rates of overweight and obesity are more reliably calculated as pediatricians regularly collect height and weight data as children and adolescents develop. Please note that the diagnostic criteria for all of the major EDs are available in the *Diagnostic and Statistical Manual of Mental Disorders*, published by the American Psychiatric Association (2000; *DSM–IV–TR*).

Anorexia Nervosa

As seen very clearly in the case of Kara at Bayside High School and in the risk factors demonstrated by Jacqueline at City Central School, those who have been diagnosed with AN present with low weight, a fear of becoming fat, an exaggerated influence of size and shape on their overall self-evaluation, a disturbed perception of body shape and size, and clinical denial of the seriousness of their condition (Stice, 2002). For females with AN, amenorrhea (i.e., absence of menstrual cycle for at least 3 months) is also currently a diagnostic criterion (Stice, 2002). Of note, this criterion will likely not be included in the *DSM-5*. Current diagnostic criteria allow for diagnosis with two subtypes: binge–purge and restricting.

Individuals with AN are believed to feel hunger (Kaye, 2008). Paradoxically, a complicating aspect of the disorder is that symptoms are often ego-syntonic. That is, those with AN are not bothered by their constant work to suppress hunger or their preoccupations with food and eating rituals

(Kaye, 2008). Individuals with AN rarely cease eating completely; rather, they engage in severe restriction of calories, fats, or carbohydrates (Kaye, 2008). Many researchers and clinicians believe that the proposed diagnostic changes (e.g., removal of amenorrhea as a criterion) may allow for more accurate diagnosis of children at younger ages. For example, it is expected that fear of gaining weight or becoming fat, a more abstract concept that is potentially difficult for younger children to articulate (Bravender et al., 2010), will also be operationalized as persistent behaviors that interfere with weight gain (American Psychiatric Association, 2011).

AN is a relatively rare disorder occurring in less than 1% of the population (compared with a rate of 5–7% in attention-deficit/hyperactivity disorder; *DSM–IV–TR*, American Psychiatric Association, 2000). In 2003, Hoek and van Hoeken estimated an average prevalence rate of 0.3% for AN among young females. Hudson, Hiripi, Pope, and Kessler (2007) surveyed 9,282 households and found a lifetime prevalence estimate of AN to be slightly higher at 0.6%, with males at 0.3% and females at 0.9%.

The window of risk is shorter for AN than for other EDs, with the earliest cases presenting around age 10 years and lower rates of new onset cases beginning after the mid-20s (Hudson et al., 2007). This places the highest risk at school age and highlights the importance of school-based prevention programs. Incidence rates for AN are the highest among females ages 15 to 19 years, with this age group reflecting about 40% of all identified cases (Hoek & van Hoeken, 2003). Hoek and van Hoeken (2003) also found that the incidence of AN increased from 1930 through 1970, with a stabilization of rates since that time. Although some researchers suggest that increases in incidence may be, in part, due to greater public awareness and the availability of specialized treatment, trends are more aligned with increases in media influence and shifts in the ideal size and shape of males and females (Striegel-Moore & Bulik, 2007). It is believed that AN rates in males are lower than in females. As few studies report incidence rates in males, it is difficult to make an accurate estimate. Hoek and van Hoeken reported that the incidence rate for males is below 1.0 or 0.5 per 100,000 per year. They suggested that the female-to-male ratio may be more than 10:1.

Practitioners often view AN as a treatment-resistant disorder. Kaye (2008) reported that treatment resistance can be partially attributed to the ego-syntonic nature of the disorder, that is, denying being severely underweight and failing to acknowledge the seriousness of one's medical status and risk of mortality. Outcomes range from study to study, with factors such as study design, definitions of recovery and good outcomes, diagnostic criteria used, and sample characteristics affecting the findings. Best estimates can be made by looking at trends or averages; the level of risk or moderating factors associated with the illness; medical complications; psychological comorbidity; and the individual's medical, psychological, and social support systems (Berkman, Lohr, & Bulik, 2007). Factors associated with poorer outcomes (e.g., continued AN diagnosis or longer time for recovery) include extreme compulsive drive to exercise, history of poor relationships, hypochondriasis, paranoia, psychopathic deviance, hostile attitude toward family, extreme compulsivity in daily routines, lower percentage of ideal body weight (IBW), poorer medical status, increased somatic symptoms, and higher rates of laxative use (Berkman et al., 2007).

In contrast, factors associated with recovery include shorter duration of AN episode and higher percentage of IBW, highlighting the need to detect symptoms of AN early to prevent its further development, which could be a responsibility for schools. Berkman et al. (2007) also reported that those diagnosed with AN binge–purge type show higher rates of recovery in the short term than those diagnosed with AN restricting type. Reported recovery rates for clients with AN include 59% at 5 years (Gillberg, Råstam, & Gillberg, 1994), 12% at 10 years (Halmi et al., 1991), and 30% at 12 years (Bulik, Sullivan, Fear, & Pickering, 2000; Sullivan, Bulik, Fear, & Pickering, 1998). Berkman et al. reported that when looking at a series of case studies of clients 5 to 15 years following treatment, between 24% and 82% had no ED diagnosis at follow-up. Interestingly, Eddy et al. (2002) found that over an 8-year period there was diagnostic crossover between restricting and binge-eating subtypes of AN. Specifically, 52% of those initially diagnosed with AN restrictive type later (most within the first 5 years) met criteria for another ED. This phenomenon of individuals shifting from one constellation of ED symptoms (e.g., AN) to another (e.g., BN) has been referred to as *diagnostic migration*, and schools should be on the lookout for this pattern.

Berkman et al. (2007) reported that mortality rates are elevated among those with AN, highlighting the need to intervene and curtail the development of symptomatology early. In a meta-analysis of 36 studies, Arcelus, Mitchell, Wales, and Nielsen (2011) found AN to have the highest mortality rate among the EDs. In fact, Crisp, Callender, Halek, and Hsu (1992) were the first to describe AN as having the highest mortality rate among all mental disorders. Factors that predict mortality, shorter time to death, or both, include very low percentage of IBW at intake, being female, older age at first presentation, hospitalization for affective disorder or AN, suicidality associated with other mental illness, greater severity of alcohol use and abuse, poor social adjustment, history of hospitalization for mental health problems, and a lower global assessment of functioning score (GAF; Arcelus et al., 2011; Berkman et al., 2007). Causes of death associated with AN typically include suicide, complications due to dehydration or electrolyte imbalance, complications related to severe malnourishment, and infection (Berkman et al., 2007; Zipfel, Lowe, Reas, Deter, & Herzog, 2000).

Bulimia Nervosa

As illustrated by Ben's case at Bayside High School, BN is characterized by recurrent, uncontrollable binge eating accompanied by extreme compensatory behaviors such as self-induced vomiting, strict dieting, complete restriction of food intake, excessive exercise, and use of laxatives, diuretics, or both (Fairburn, Cooper, Doll, Norman, & O'Connor, 2000). This disorder also involves an exaggerated influence of size and shape on overall evaluation of self (Stice, 2002).

Individuals who meet criteria for BN often begin their path toward eating disordered behavior by engaging in restriction of food intake (e.g., a diet; Kaye, 2008). Often the restriction becomes too difficult to maintain, and they binge. Not wanting to experience weight gain associated with bingeing, individuals with BN purge via self-induced vomiting or use of laxatives, compensatory exercise, or use of diuretics to reduce fluid retention. The criteria for partial-syndrome BN are much like the criteria for full-syndrome BN with less frequent episodes (McKnight Investigators, 2003). Researchers found that a lower frequency threshold (e.g., once per week rather than twice per week) also has been associated with negative outcomes (Bravender et al., 2010). This behavior becomes clinically relevant as it presents repeatedly and becomes compulsive for the student.

Generally, BN is considered to have a better prognosis than AN in terms of both recovery rate and recovery time (Richard, Bauer, & Kordy, 2005). Nevertheless, the disorder is persistent, and a substantial proportion of those diagnosed may struggle for many years. For example, in a prospective study of those with BN, 15% of participants met criteria for BN at a 5-year follow-up (Fairburn et al., 2000).

Hoek and van Hoeken (2003) cautioned that estimates of the rates of BN can serve only as minimal estimates because of lack of data, lower perceptibility (it can be more easily missed or hidden because the individual may not appear sick) when compared with AN, and the greater taboo associated with purging symptoms. Prior to 1980, what is known today as BN (or perhaps subclinical BN or BED) was labeled *bulimia* in medical records (Hoek & van Hoeken, 2003). The term *bulimia* reflected a range of symptoms that involved overeating.

For BN, rates have been established for both clinical and subclinical presentations. Hoek and van Hoeken (2003) reported that researchers have found the prevalence rates of BN to be about 1% among young females using diagnostic criteria relevant for the time of study. Hudson et al. (2007) had similar findings at 1% lifetime prevalence for BN with rates at 0.5% for males and 1.5% for females. Striegel-Moore and Bulik (2007) suggested that there is some evidence that the incidence of BN has increased, with lifetime prevalence being significantly lower for those born before 1960. In their review of the literature, these authors reported that there were significant increases in the incidence of BN between 1985 and 1995. Of note, this increase may, in part, be due to the introduction of the *DSM* diagnosis in 1980 and the consequent increase in awareness and detection over the following years, as well as social–cultural factors (e.g., media representations of body ideals).

As with other EDs, it is very difficult to reliably assess outcomes for those with BN (Richard et al., 2005). Difficulties lie in the substantial heterogeneity in samples; interval of follow-up; assessment; analyses; and how recovery, relapse, and remission are defined. Studies suggest that those with BN struggle with the disorder from 5 to 12 years (Fairburn et al., 2000; Fichter & Quadflieg, 2004; Hudson et al., 2007). Thus, it would greatly benefit students with BN to be identified, diagnosed, and treated early in their disorder, which could be facilitated through schools. Factors associated with continued BN symptoms or diagnoses include psychiatric comorbidity (e.g., mood disorder, substance use, impulse-control disorders, paternal obesity, premorbid obesity, and lower social adjustment; Berkman et al., 2007). In a recent meta-analysis, Arcelus et al. (2011) found a weighted mortality rate of 1.7 per 1,000 person years of follow-up. Causes of death are indicated as substance-use related, traumatic, medical, and suicide. Studies indicate that those with BN are at increased risk for mortality by suicide (S. J. Crow et al., 2009).

Binge-Eating Disorder

BED, like BN, has the central behavioral feature of binge eating with a sense of being out of control (Allison, Grilo, Masheb, & Stunkard, 2005; Fairburn et al., 2000). Unlike BN, however, those with BED do not engage in compensatory behaviors designed to undo the binge (Fairburn et al., 2000; Stice et al., 2002). The *DSM–IV–TR* does not include BED as a distinct ED, instead classifying it under its Appendix B or disorders that need further study (American Psychiatric Association, 2000). In line with research evidence (Devlin, Goldfein, & Dobrow, 2003), the proposed changes to the *DSM* are expected to include BED as a distinct ED. Until the publication of the *DSM-5*, BED is referred to as a diagnostic category in need of further research (*DSM–IV–TR*; American Psychiatric Association, 2000). Hoek and van Hoeken (2003) reported that prevalence and incidence rates are difficult to report as researchers do not have a unified definition of a *binge*. Therefore, results from study to study may not be fully comparable.

Prevalence estimates have ranged from the lower end at 1% to an upper end of 4.5% (Hoek & van Hoeken, 2003). In 2008, Allen, Byrne, La Puma, McLean, and Davis reported similar findings, stating that estimates of the prevalence of binge eating range from 1% to 5% in community samples and as high as 20% to 50% among those seeking treatment for overweight and obesity. In a national survey, Hudson et al. (2007) found lifetime prevalence rates at 2.8% for BED, 1.2% for subthreshold BED, and 4.5% for any binge eating. Lifetime prevalence rates for males were reported at 0.8% and females at 1.6%.

There have been few outcome studies on BED. In a national survey, Hudson et al. (2007) found that among those with BED, episodes of the disorder were 8.1 ($SD = 1.1$) years in duration. Research suggests that most individuals improve over time, with up to 78% having no ED diagnosis after 6 years (Berkman et al., 2007). A small percentage may have continued symptoms and meet criteria for BED. Fairburn et al. (2000) conducted a prospective study and found that at a 5-year follow-up, 10% of participants met criteria for BED, 18% met criteria for an ED of some form (3% meeting criteria for AN and 15% meeting criteria for BN), suggesting the need for schools to identify and treat students with BED as early as possible. Binge eating has been associated with elevated psychological distress, depression, anxiety, excess weight, poor outcome from weight loss treatment, as well as other ED symptoms (Allen et al., 2008; Berkman et al., 2007). Interestingly, Fairburn et al. found that at a 5-year follow-up those with BED were less likely than those with BN to have received treatment (8% of those with BED as compared with 40% of those with BN).

Eating Disorder Not Otherwise Specified

The diagnosis of EDNOS is given to those individuals who show symptoms of eating disordered behavior but do not meet the criteria for AN or BN (American Psychiatric Association, 2000). It is important to note that although the diagnostic criteria are less specific, EDNOS is a serious disorder with a mortality rate comparable with those of other EDs (S. J. Crow et al., 2009), and these symptoms may develop into AN or BN, highlighting the need for schools to identify and help those who have such symptoms before they develop into disorders that are harder to treat. Examples of individuals who would currently fall into this category include (a) a 13-year-old boy at 90% of his expected weight for his age and height and who has body image disturbance, reports drive for thinness–leanness, and engages in periods of excessive exercise; (b) a 15-year-old girl at 90% of her expected weight and who reports drive for thinness, fear of fat and gaining weight, yet continues to menstruate; (c) an 18-year-old overweight woman who binges and purges once or twice weekly and presents with periods of excessive exercise to control weight; and (d) currently (until publication of the *DSM-5*), those who meet recommended criteria for BED. It is likely that EDNOS will be replaced by "Other Feeding or Eating Condition Not Elsewhere Classified," which will be a residual category for clinically significant problems meeting the definition of a feeding or ED, yet not meeting criteria for another disorder or condition (American Psychiatric Association, 2011).

Obesity

As demonstrated in Jared's case at City Central School, the term *obesity* reflects a weight and height ratio that has been associated with substantial health risk (Flegal, Carroll, Ogden, & Curtin, 2010). To assess whether an individual meets the criteria for obesity, his or her height and weight measurements are taken and a BMI is calculated. There are various formulae for calculating BMI, with the most basic being weight in kilograms divided by height in meters squared (kg/m^2), rounded to the nearest tenth (Flegal et al., 2010). For children in the United States, cutoff criteria are based on the National Center for Chronic Disease Prevention and Health Promotion of the 2000 Centers for Disease Control and Prevention's (CDC) BMI-for-age-growth charts (see Table 1). C. Ogden and Carroll (2010) reported that more recent cutoffs for categories were also based on recommendations of expert committees and reflect an effort to be consistent with organizations such as the Institute of Medicine and the American Academy of Pediatrics.

For children, sex-specific BMIs (BMI-for-age-growth charts) at or above the 95th percentile are currently considered obese. Using these parameters, BMIs associated with overweight and obesity vary. To illustrate BMI, a 10-year-old girl at 4 ft. 8 in. tall and 100 lb would have a BMI of 22.4 and be

TABLE 1
Body Mass Index (BMI) Categories

Age group	Descriptive category	BMI range
Adults (20+ years)	Overweight	25.0–29.9
	Obesity	30.0 or higher
Children and adolescents (2–19 years)	Underweight	BMI-for-age-growth charts: less than the 5th percentile (sex-specific charts are used)
	Healthy weight	BMI-for-age-growth charts: 5th percentile to less than the 85th percentile (sex-specific charts are used)
	Overweight	BMI-for-age-growth charts: 85th percentile to less than the 95th percentile (sex-specific charts are used)
	Obesity	BMI-for-age-growth charts: at or above the 95th percentile (sex-specific charts are used)

classified as overweight. At 120 lb, her BMI would be 26.9 and she "may be obese" (Centers for Disease Control and Prevention, 2010b). These calculations are sex specific, accounting for changes in body fat and muscle mass associated with puberty in adolescence. For example, a 10-year-old boy at the same height and weight calculations (4 ft. 8 in. and 100 lb) would fall in the may be obese rather than overweight category. The CDC offers a web page that easily calculates BMIs for children, adolescents, and adults (http://www.cdc.gov/healthyweight/assessing/bmi/). This web page also offers information for school personnel on the weight categories and interpretation. We strongly advocate against calculating children's BMI in school programs, however, as these public (or even semiprivate) measurement sessions can instigate body shame, weight stigma, and weight-related teasing and bullying within and among children (Bacon, 2010).

Obesity results from a chronic disruption of the energy balance (i.e., energy intake and energy expenditure; Loos & Bouchard, 2003). Current conditions (e.g., easy access to energy-dense foods, increases in sedentary activities) among Westernized cultures have led to rapid increases in obesity rates. One problem with the label of obesity, however, is that it only considers body size and does not account for the reasons behind a child's (or adult's) larger body size. In our book, we aim to help those students who are obese because of eating in the absence of hunger, low physical activity, or both; these children may be able to move from the obese classification to a lower weight by reconnecting to their hunger and satiety cues (i.e., intuitive eating) and engaging in regular enjoyable physical activity. However, if the primary reason that a child is obese is because of genetic build, and the child does not eat in the absence of hunger and does engage in regular physical activity, this child will likely not lose weight. The best thing that schools can do for such students is to have in place a school culture appreciating all body types and disconnecting health from weight. Therefore, in our book, we focus on improving children's modifiable health behaviors (e.g., reconnecting with hunger and satiety cues, regular engagement in enjoyable physical activity), regardless of their weight. Addressing these modifiable health behaviors in lieu of focusing on weight will attend to all children and not shine a negative spotlight on those children who are classified as overweight or obese.

Prevalence of overweight and obesity is monitored using data from the National Health and Nutrition Examination Survey (NHANES; C. Ogden & Carroll, 2010). According to Flegal et al. (2010), the prevalence of obesity in the United States is high (i.e., greater than 30%) in most age groups and both sexes. It should be noted, however, that BMI is a poor estimator of excess body fat because it does not consider muscle mass, which weighs more than fat. For instance, many muscular bodybuilders with low body fat would be considered obese using BMI criteria.

C. Ogden and Carroll (2010) reported that data from the 2007–2008 NHANES suggest that 16.9% of children ages 2 to 19 years are obese. In child and adolescent populations, there are significant racial and ethnic differences in obesity rates. For example, data from the 2007–2008 survey revealed that rates ranged from 16.7% among non-Hispanic White adolescent boys to 26.8% among Mexican American adolescent boys. There were also differences across race and ethnic groups among girls. The 2007–2008 data showed that non-Hispanic Black adolescent girls had the highest rates of obesity (29.2%), with non-Hispanic White adolescent girls showing the lowest rates (14.5%). It is important to note that degree of *adiposity* (i.e., percentage of body fat) associated with any particular BMI varies by age, sex, and racial group (Flegal et al., 2010). For example, compared with White men and women, Black men and women tend to have higher levels of lean mass and lower fat mass (Flegal et al., 2010).

Data trends for each age group (integrating males and females) show an increasing trend toward obesity (C. Ogden & Carroll, 2010; see Table 2). For example, data from 1971 to 1974 indicate that the rate of obesity for children 2 to 5 years old was at 5%, which increased to 10.4% in 2007–2008. Sharper increases were found among children ages 6 to 11, with earlier rates at 4% (1971–1974) and more current rates at 19.6% (2007–2008).

Overall, childhood obesity is seen as a key early risk factor leading to other risk factors as the child ages (e.g., problems with insulin, blood pressure, glucose, and lipid levels; P. W. Franks et al., 2010). Bean, Stewart, and Olbrisch's (2008) review of the literature indicated that overweight youth were more likely to be diagnosed with Type 2 diabetes (TD2), sleep apnea, arthritis, gallstones, and menstrual irregularities. Similarly, Kral and Faith (2009) reported that childhood overweight is a key risk factor for TD2, cardiovascular disease, and orthopedic abnormalities. In a study of the liver tissue of 742 children (ages 2–19), Schwimmer et al. (2006) found obese children to have the highest rates of fatty liver (38%), placing them at risk for poor long-term health outcomes.

TABLE 2
Increasing Trends Toward Obesity Among Children and Adolescents

Age in years	NHANES 1971–1974	NHANES 2007–2008
2–5	5.0%	10.4%
6–11	4.0%	19.6%
12–19	6.1%	18.1%
Overall (ages 2–19)	5.0%	16.9%

Note. NHANES = National Health and Nutrition Examination Survey. Adapted from Table 1 in *Prevalence of Obesity Among Children and Adolescents: United States, Trends 1963–2008* (pp. 1–8), by C. Ogden and M. D. Carroll, 2010, Washington, DC: Centers for Disease Control and Prevention/National Center for Health Statistics. In the public domain.

Childhood overweight and obesity also have substantial implications for children as they negotiate their social and psychological worlds. Bromfield (2009) argued that as long as educational professionals continue to view overweight and obesity only as medical issues, they will continue to be bystanders in the matter of childhood obesity and associated mental health risks and conditions. Individuals who are overweight and obese suffer stigma, prejudice, and social discrimination (Bean et al., 2008). Overweight and obese children suffer increased rates of peer teasing; low self-esteem; depressive, anxious, and ED symptoms; as well as increased risk for suicide (Bromfield, 2009), making a school culture appreciating all body types and disconnecting health from weight imperative. In a study of 4,746 adolescents, Neumark-Sztainer et al. (2002) found that children who deviated from average weight were most likely to be teased, with 63% of very overweight girls and 58% of very overweight boys reporting being teased by their peers. Further, findings indicated that perceived weight teasing is associated with disordered eating behaviors and other unhealthy eating behaviors (e.g., eating in the absence of hunger, eating to soothe emotional distress), possibly placing these youth at risk for additional weight gain (Neumark-Sztainer et al., 2002).

Research has demonstrated that psychological risks associated with overweight and obesity include disordered eating, depression, and suicidality (Bean et al., 2008; Carpenter, Hasin, Allison, & Faith, 2000; Dave & Rashad, 2009). Carpenter et al. (2000) found increased BMI to be associated with major depression, suicide attempts, and suicidal ideation among women, whereas lower BMI was associated with major depression, suicide attempts, and suicidal ideation. In a 2007 study of 5,174 middle school students, Whetstone, Morrissey, and Cummings found that females who perceived themselves as overweight were significantly more likely to report suicidal thoughts and actions, and both perceptions of overweight and underweight were associated with suicidal thoughts and actions in males. These associations appear to be consistent as children reach high school age. In fact, researchers believe that perceived weight status may be a better predictor of suicidal ideation and behaviors than actual weight status (Dave & Rashad, 2009). In a study of 14,041 high school students, both perceived overweight and actual BMI were found to place adolescents at increased risk for suicide attempts (Swahn et al., 2009). Notably, the risk of suicidality associated with overweight and obesity may attenuate as children and adolescents move into adulthood. A longitudinal study of 2,516 older adolescents (high school students, M age = 17.2 years; and young adults, M age = 20.4 years) revealed that extreme weight-control behaviors (i.e., taking diet pills, self-induced vomiting, laxative, and diuretic use) were predictive of suicidal ideation and behavior in women but not in men (S. Crow, Eisenberg, Story, & Neumark-Sztainer, 2008).

Costs of Eating Disorders and Obesity

The costs associated with EDs and obesity are alarming. Beyond the considerable mortality and morbidity rates are the substantial financial costs of the symptoms and treatment. An analysis of insurance claims found the cost per year of treating AN and BN was comparable to that of treating schizophrenia (Striegel-Moore, Leslie, Petrill, Garvin, & Rosenheck, 2000). AN can result in considerable impairment with an average duration of about 6 years, resulting in parental–caregiver distress similar to that seen in parents of children with psychosis (Simon, Schmidt, & Pilling, 2005; Treasure et al., 2001). In a study of the costs associated with bingeing and purging seen in BN, S. J. Crow et al. (2009) found that individuals spend an average of 32.7% of all food costs at about $1,599.45 or up to 5.3% of pretax income per year. Recently, much attention has been paid to the cost of childhood obesity. Children ages 2 to 19 with a primary or secondary diagnosis of obesity were twice as likely to be hospitalized as children of normal weight (Trasande, Liu, Fryer, & Weitzman, 2009). This reflects an increase in cost from $125.9 million to $237.6 million (in 2005 dollars; Trasande et al., 2009). The direct medical cost of adolescent overweight is projected to increase from $130 million in 2020 to $10 billion in 2050 (Lightwood et al., 2009). As these numbers illustrate, the promotion of a positive relationship with food and body will help to reduce not only the human cost seen in illness, death, and psychological distress but also the substantial public cost associated with the progression of illness.

Implications for Your School

The major EDs (AN, BN, and BED) and obesity affect a substantial number of children in schools. Rates suggest that up to 23.9% of students may struggle at some point with clinical-level disorders associated with eating. To illustrate, a group of 1,000 students could include three to six children or adolescents with AN, over 10 children or adolescents with BN, 54 children or adolescents with BED, and 169 children or adolescents whose weight and height ratios are classified as obese. That totals at potentially 239 children per 1,000 struggling with clinical-level eating problems, with hundreds more in subthreshold categories of ED (EDNOS) and overweight. To further illustrate, if children and adolescents in the overweight category are included, well over half of the student population could be estimated to struggle at some point with food, exercise, and self-care.

These challenges are manageable. As you read this book, you will learn what it means to have a healthy relationship with food and what factors put students at risk. Next, this text provides the conceptual and practical framework (i.e., The Healthy Student Approach) for understanding eating behavior and body acceptance within the context of student development and environment. Evidence-based interventions are described that can help your school prevent eating-related problems as well as provide tools for assessment and methods of support for students who are struggling. The text includes several instruments that can be used to assess ED symptomatology as well as its risk factors among children and adolescents, to be able to screen for EDs among your students. Also, in the appendixes you will find descriptions of the less common eating issues that may present at school. To help you ensure adherence to guidelines and standards, we review the federal, state, and sample local policies. Finally, we provide a Suggested Resources section that can guide you to the many rich resources available. With this text as a resource, you can work with your school to build a healthy school environment in which your students can thrive.

I

CONCEPTUAL FRAMEWORK

1

DEFINING HEALTHY AND INTUITIVE EATING

Healthy eating encompasses more than just nutrition. Healthy eating includes having a healthy relationship with food, mind, and body—free of obsession, compulsion, and rigid rules while being attuned to the needs of the body. This chapter describes the components of intuitive eating, which embodies the healthy food–mind–body connection.

During World War II, the federally funded National Research Council created a two-pronged campaign to (a) address food rationing and (b) change Americans' eating habits in order to raise their nutritional status. Led by anthropologist Margaret Mead (Warner, 2010), they placed equal merit on the nutritional and psychological aspects of eating (e.g., how, when, why, and what individuals eat and how they think about food). After the war, however, the psychological component of healthy eating was discontinued, but the emphasis on nutrition remained. Consequently, the importance of cultural and psychological approaches that influence how Americans think

DOI: 10.1037/14180-002
Healthy Eating in Schools: Evidence-Based Interventions to Help Kids Thrive, by C. P. Cook-Cottone, E. Tribole, and T. L. Tylka

about food has largely been ignored. Therefore, we ended up with a wealth of nutrition research and knowledge, without the cultural change to back it up.

Today, the government issues dietary guidelines for public health and updates them every 5 years to reflect evolving research. And for the past 2 decades, there has been nutrition information on nearly every food label, thanks to the Nutrition Labeling and Education Act of 1990. Yet, in spite of the increased availability of nutrition information, the incidence of obesity and eating disorders (EDs) in the United States has risen steadily (Neumark-Sztainer, 2011).

The nutrition research, as reported in the media, easily creates the impression that food will either kill you or make you fat, which contributes to anxiety about eating. This excess "food worry" has not served the health status of Americans. In fact, the preoccupation with eating healthfully may have had the opposite effect, according to the findings of psychologist Paul Rozin and his team from the University of Pennsylvania (Rozin, Fischler, Imada, Sarubin, & Wrzesniewski, 1999). These authors conducted a study in four countries—France, the United States, Belgium, and Japan—to evaluate the psychology of eating on diet and health. Americans were found to worry the most about their health and about the fattening effects of food, but they reported the greatest dissatisfaction with what they ate. The French were found to be the most food-pleasure oriented and the least health oriented; yet, they were among the healthiest of these countries. Compared with France, the United States has twice the incidence of overweight and obesity, for both adults and children (Tribole & Resch, 2012). The French also have fewer EDs and a markedly lower rate of heart disease. Globally, France is ranked third for the lowest incidence of heart disease. Rozin et al. (1999) concluded that the worry and stress over healthy eating may be more detrimental to health than the actual food consumed. Indeed, it is widely accepted that stress triggers a biological chemical assault in our bodies, which is harmful to health (McEwen, 2008).

In tandem with the growing anxiety over food selection, there is a new type of disordered eating called *orthorexia*, which is characterized by an unhealthy and rigid obsession to eat healthfully. Although not officially recognized as a medical diagnosis, orthorexia nervosa appears to be on the rise (Eriksson, Baigi, Marklund, & Lindgren, 2008). Physician and author Steven Bratman (2001) brought national attention to this problem in his book, *Health Food Junkies: Orthorexia Nervosa: Overcoming the Obsession With Healthful Eating*.

Australian researcher Gyorgy Scrinis (2008) described a new paradigm, which he termed *nutritionism*. Nutritionism describes the overly reductive focus on nutrients in food, which can undermine how we think about food and the relationship between eating and our bodies. Ultimately, nutritionism contributes to increased anxiety around eating (Tribole & Resch, 2012).

Eating healthfully should feel good, both physically and psychologically, resulting in a satisfying experience. Because of the food and fat phobia that is sweeping the country with an emphasis on weight, many people have lost sight of pleasure in the eating experience. Research shows that the more a person is focused on external factors, especially body weight and appearance, the more it interferes with the internal process of intuitive eating (Avalos & Tylka, 2006). Furthermore, relying on external eating rules specifying when, what, and how much to eat leads to a disconnection from the body's innate ability to regulate food intake, which is associated with EDs, dietary restraint, higher weight, and decreased well-being (Tylka, 2006).

INTUITIVE EATING: A FLEXIBLE HEALTHY EATING MODEL

An adaptive form of eating that has gained recognition is *intuitive eating,* which is defined as a strong connection with, understanding of, and eating in response to internal biological cues of hunger and satiety as well as low preoccupation with food. The principles of intuitive eating were developed by Tribole and Resch in 1995 and operationalized by Tylka in 2006. Three central and interrelated components of intuitive eating have been identified and empirically supported through their links to psychological and physical well-being (Tylka, 2006; Tylka & Wilcox, 2006):

- unconditional permission to eat when hungry and whatever food is desired,
- eating for physical rather than emotional reasons, and
- reliance on internal hunger and satiety cues to determine when and how much to eat.

Individuals who give themselves unconditional permission to eat do not try to ignore their hunger signals, nor do they classify food into "good" and "bad" categories while attempting to avoid food in the latter category (Tribole & Resch, 1995). They are aware of how their body responds to certain foods; they typically choose foods that help their bodies' function well, and they view taste as only one component of food choice. Researchers have found that people who give themselves unconditional permission to eat do not overindulge in food or engage in binge eating (Tylka & Wilcox, 2006). In contrast, people who place conditions on when, how much, and what foods they can eat (i.e., by restricting the timing, amount, and type of food eaten according to some external standard) often overindulge in their "forbidden" foods when they perceive that their dietary rules have been broken and therefore become preoccupied with those foods (Avalos & Tylka, 2006; Polivy & Herman, 1999; Tylka, 2006).

Eating for physical rather than emotional reasons reflects the tendency to eat to satisfy a physical hunger drive rather than to cope with emotional fluctuations and distress (Tribole & Resch, 1995). Individuals who eat intuitively will eat to quell physical hunger and will stop eating when indifferent or slightly full (Herman & Polivy, 1983). People who engage in dietary restraint, however, tend to eat in a disinhibited manner when they experience emotional distress, especially when they perceive that they have broken their diet (Herman, Polivy, Lank, & Heatherton, 1987).

Reliance on internal hunger and satiety cues reflects an awareness of these cues and the ability to trust them to guide eating behavior (Tribole & Resch, 1995). When individuals do not trust these internal cues and instead replace them with external rules prescribing when, what, and how much to eat, they become disconnected from their internal experience and lose their innate ability to regulate food intake (Birch & Fisher, 2000; Birch, Fisher, & Davison, 2003).

Therefore, intuitive eating is a flexible healthy eating behavior that involves nonjudgmental self-awareness and attunement (see Figure 1.1; Tribole & Resch, 2012). *Attunement* is a form of listening and responding appropriately to the physical sensations of the body. The ability to "hear" these physical sensations is called *interoceptive awareness*, which is the perception of sensations originating from inside the body, including heartbeat, breathing, satiety, full bladder, as well as autonomic nervous system sensations related to emotional feelings (Mehling et al., 2009). Furthermore, interoceptive awareness is the foundation of intuitive eating, where ultimately individuals become the expert on their own body. However, if individuals are too preoccupied by body weight and rigid rules about so-called healthy eating, it interferes with their interoceptive awareness. In essence, individuals' beliefs and thoughts can overrule what their bodies are actually experiencing.

The components of intuitive eating work by removing the obstacles to interoceptive awareness and improving interoceptive awareness as it relates

Figure 1.1. Intuitive eating. From *Intuitive Eating* (3rd ed.; p. 205), by E. Tribole and E. Resch, 2012, New York, NY: St. Martin's Press. Copyright 2012 by St. Martin's Press. Reprinted with permission.

to eating, all while instilling a sense of body wisdom and appreciation (Tribole & Resch, 1995, 2012). Ultimately, intuitive eating is a dynamic attunement process to achieve health and well-being. If a person is truly inner attuned, public health guidelines, philosophical preferences (e.g., eating locally grown food), and dietary guidelines due to medical conditions (e.g., food allergies, diabetes, celiac disease) can be implemented while he or she pays attention to hunger, fullness, and satisfaction.

TEN PRINCIPLES OF INTUITIVE EATING

Since the publication of *Intuitive Eating* (Tribole & Resch, 1995), there has been a growing body of research validating the benefits of the intuitive eating process and its individual principles. This section briefly summarizes the 10 principles of intuitive eating (see Table 1.1), and the last section describes the research.

Reject the Diet Mentality

First is the principle of rejecting the diet mentality. The process of dieting not only interferes with interoceptive awareness but also promotes weight gain and increases the risk for EDs. A study with nearly 17,000 students ages 9 to 14 concluded that "dieting to control weight is not only ineffective, it may actually promote weight gain" (Field et al., 2003). According to a 5-year study, teenage dieters had twice the risk of becoming overweight when compared with nondieting teenagers (Neumark-Sztainer et al., 2006). Notably, at baseline, the dieters did not weigh more than their nondieting peers. This is an important detail because if the dieters weighed more at the onset, we would not be sure whether it was dieting per se or genetic body build that was driving the significant effects. This study suggests that dieting itself prompts weight gain among adolescents. To distinguish whether dieting-induced weight gain

TABLE 1.1
Principles of Intuitive Eating and Interoceptive Awareness

Improves interoceptive awareness	Removes obstacles to interoceptive awareness
Honor Your Hunger Cues	Reject the Diet Mentality
Respect Your Fullness Cues	Make Peace with Food
Discover the Satisfaction Factor in Eating	Challenge the Food Police
Honor Your Feelings Without Using Food	Respect Your Body
Exercise—Feel the Difference	Honor Your Health with Gentle Nutrition

was an issue of genetic propensity, scientists from Finland followed over 2,000 sets of twins (> 4,000 people) from adolescence to young adulthood in a longitudinal study (Pietiläinen, Saarni, Kaprio, & Rissanen, 2011). They evaluated the twins' weight, height, and number of dieting episodes at ages 16, 17, 18, and 25 years. Dieting was associated with a dose-dependent increase in weight, independent of genetics. In other words, the more a person dieted, the higher the weight gain. The researchers believe that dieting "may in part be responsible for the current obesity epidemic" (Pietiläinen et al., 2011, p. 463).

Dieting also is the central predictor of ED onset. Adolescent girls who diet at a severe level are 18 times more likely to develop an ED than those who do not diet, and those who diet at a moderate level are 5 times more likely to develop an ED (Patton, Selzer, Coffey, Carlin, & Wolfe, 1999). Dieting also has been associated with increased food preoccupation, binge eating, and eating in the absence of hunger (Birch et al., 2003; Polivy & Herman, 1999; Tucker, 2008).

Honor Your Hunger

The second principle is honoring your hunger cues. This principle is a basic interoceptive awareness skill that many weight-focused people ignore. Yet, a promising series of studies shows that training people how to recognize and respond to initial hunger cues improves insulin sensitivity and lowers body mass index (BMI; Ciampolini & Bianchi, 2006; Ciampolini et al., 2010). Also, when a person does not eat an adequate amount of calories and carbohydrates throughout the day, it can trigger a primal drive to overeat (Keys, Brozek, Henschel, Mickelsen, & Taylor, 1950).

Make Peace With Food

The third principle is to make peace with food, which helps remove a key obstacle to interoceptive awareness by legalizing foods and provides unconditional permission to eat when hungry, whatever food is desired. Unconditional permission to eat includes attunement to food preferences, rather than choosing foods according to whether the food falls into a good or bad category.

Restricting particular foods increases children's preferences for those foods, heightens responsiveness to the presence of palatable foods, and promotes overeating when restricted foods are freely available (Birch et al., 2003; Fisher & Birch, 1999). It can also lead to *sneak eating*, resulting in decreased attunement to hunger and satiety cues. Unless someone has an allergy or medical condition (e.g., celiac disease), eating one food or meal will not make or break a person's health status or weight.

Challenge the Food Police

This fourth principle aims to eliminate a person's unreasonable and rigid rules about what constitutes healthful eating. Rigid eating rules are an obstacle to interoceptive awareness. Many studies indicate that when individuals break one of their rigid rules, it may lead to overeating (G. A. King, Herman, & Polivy, 1987; Polivy, 1996).

Respect Your Fullness Cues

This fifth principle improves interoceptive awareness by learning how to perceive and respond to the body's *satiety cues*—the cues that inform you that you are comfortably full and no longer hungry. However, if individuals believe that they will never get to eat a particular food, such as candy, they will seize on the opportunity and ignore satiety cues, which can hamper interoceptive awareness (Polivy & Herman, 1999).

Discover the Satisfaction Factor

The sixth principle is to discover the satisfaction factor. The Japanese have the wisdom to promote pleasure as one of their goals of healthy eating. When people are able to eat what they really want, in a pleasant environment, the pleasure derived from eating becomes a powerful force in feeling satisfied and content (Satter, 2005). People are often surprised to learn that it takes much less food to truly feel satisfied. Even the 2011 release of the U.S. "My Plate" recommendations for healthy eating (which replaced the food pyramid) encourages people to enjoy eating (U.S. Department of Agriculture, 2011). Discovering satisfaction in eating also enhances interoceptive awareness.

Honor Your Feelings Without Using Food

The seventh principle is coping with stress and other feelings without using food. This principle has two components. The first step is the ability to distinguish the bodily sensations originating from emotional feelings versus hunger–satiety cues. This involves refinement of interoceptive awareness (recall that interoceptive awareness includes sensations connected to how the body reacts to emotions). For example, if a person experiences the sensation of an empty, churning stomach, he or she will need to distinguish whether it is a biological cue of hunger or perhaps a sensation triggered by an anxious feeling about completing a homework project in a timely manner. The second step is learning to find ways to comfort, distract, and resolve issues without using food. Anxiety, loneliness, boredom, frustration, and anger are emotions we all experience throughout life. Each has its own trigger or triggers, and each has its own means of appeasement. Food will not fix any of these feelings, but eating to cope with feelings will blur interoceptive awareness.

Respect Your Body

The eighth principle is to respect your body, regardless of size. A person who eats based on what they think they should weigh, rather than based on their inner hunger and satiety cues, blunts their interoceptive awareness. An environment that emphasizes and scrutinizes appearance and body size may also interfere with interoceptive awareness and intuitive eating (Avalos & Tylka, 2006). Research shows that appreciating the body is associated with a range of variables related to psychological and physical well-being, such as self-esteem, proactive coping, optimism, and lower BMI, and body appreciation, in turn, is a strong predictor of intuitive eating (Augustus-Horvath & Tylka, 2011; Avalos, Tylka, & Wood-Barcalow, 2005; Tylka, 2011a).

Encouraging research conducted by Eric Stice's team at the Oregon Research Institute shows that having girls and young women challenge the unrealistic thin ideal and eliminate their negative body talk, such as "I'm too fat to go out" or "I can't eat that cookie—it will make me fat," can go a long way at improving their health status (Stice, Rohde, Gau, & Shaw, 2009). Stice's method demonstrated impressive results in a range of ages, from adolescents to college-aged women, with significant reductions in body dissatisfaction and dieting attempts, as well as a 60% reduction in ED symptomatology. Remarkably, the effects were achieved with a relatively short intervention, as described in Chapter 7 of this volume.

Exercise—Feel the Difference

The ninth principle is engaging in physical activities that are enjoyable. Movement is important for physical well-being and should be considered as a way to promote health rather than lose weight (McGuire & Ross, 2011). The emphasis on body weight as the sole indicator of health improvement is misleading because exercise without weight loss has been shown to reduce body fat and increase muscle mass (Chaput et al., 2011). Exercise also aids interoceptive awareness because it improves satiety cues and appetite regulation (N. A. King et al., 2009). When the pursuit of exercise is about feeling good, not about the calories burned or a penance for eating, it becomes enjoyable and sustainable.

Honor Your Health Through Gentle Nutrition

The 10th principle is to honor your health through *gentle nutrition*, rather than nutritionism (which was described in the beginning of this chapter). It is important to make food choices that honor health but also taste good and make you feel well. No one has to eat a perfect diet to be healthy. Nutrition guidelines are intended to be an average, over time, not a rigid mandate (U.S. Department of Agriculture, 2010). A person will not suddenly get a nutrient deficiency or gain weight from one snack, one meal, or one day of eating. It is what you eat consistently over time that matters. This principle requires a dynamic integration between a person's interoceptive awareness and public health guidelines. Gentle nutrition reflects the tendency for individuals to make food choices that honor their health and body functioning (e.g., choosing foods that promote energy, stamina, and body performance) as well as taste good.

INTUITIVE EATING AND TWO CONTINUUMS

Eating behaviors occur along a continuum on which maladaptive behaviors, obsession with food, and disconnection from natural hunger and satiety cues are at the extremes, and healthy behaviors as well as connection with natural hunger and satiety cues are near the center (see Figure 1.2). On one extreme, individuals can be overly restrictive, routinely ignore hunger cues, and be obsessed with food in ways associated with both physical starvation and psychological factors (e.g., food obsessions, attentional biases). Chronic and rigid self-governance of food intake characterizes this end (e.g., anorexia nervosa [AN] and chronic undereating). We saw this kind of eating in Kara and emerging in Jacqueline, who were profiled in the Introduction. At the other extreme, individuals routinely binge eat and ignore satiety cues, either as episodes or as compulsive overeating. Binge-eating disorder (BED), bulimia nervosa (BN), and chronic overeating are examples of this extreme. Food obsession on this end entails both physiological (e.g., physiological reactions to binges, lack of response to satiety cues) and psychological components (e.g., eating as a means of coping with stress or negative feelings). In a mild form, we see Jared eating in the absence of hunger and to negotiate his feelings. This type of eating presents at a much stronger level for Ben.

In the center is *intuitive eating*. Intuitive eating involves a healthy responsiveness to food that lacks obsession, rigidity, and compulsiveness. Instead, eating involves self-awareness, self-care, and attunement with an individual's internal dynamics (i.e., emotions, thoughts, and physiological needs) and external influences (i.e., family, community, and culture; C.

Compulsive Restriction ◄──────── Healthy Intuitive Eating ────────► Compulsive Bingeing

Figure 1.2. Continuum of eating behavior.

Cook-Cottone, 2006a). When an individual is eating in an intuitive manner, natural hunger and satiety cues are respected and followed.

Notably, the distinctions among the various disorders and even variations of normative eating are not always as clear as we would like them to be. For example, individuals may oscillate across this continuum—for example, *AN binge-eating/purging type* (characterized by periods of severe restriction and bingeing) and *yo-yo dieting* (characterized by rigid dieting followed by disinhibited eating). (See the Introduction for definitions of the major EDs, overweight, and obesity, and see Appendix A for definitions of less common disorders of eating.)

Eating behaviors are affected by an individual's relationship with her or his body; thoughts, feelings, and perceptions about the body can direct eating habits (Stice, 2002). Negatively charged thoughts, feelings, and perceptions or apathy toward the body direct more maladaptive eating behaviors, whereas positive thoughts, feelings, and perceptions direct more healthy eating behaviors. At one extreme is an obsessive relationship with the body that can include adherence to a media-constructed ideal body image (e.g., thin, curvaceous, muscular), a distorted body image (see Figure 1.3), or both. Extremes at this end are marked by a tendency to critically judge the body, as well as by rigidity, inflexibility (often viewed as perfectionism), and a mistrust of the body's internal hunger and satiety signals. There is little self-compassion. Negative affect results because individuals cannot attain the media-constructed body ideal, feel that they cannot trust their body's signals, and are left feeling negatively about their bodies. Ben and Kara present many of these features as they relate to their bodies. They both seek what they believe to be perfection. They have lost a sense of an authentic connection with their bodies.

On the other end, individuals are dissociated from their bodies and ignore body sensations (e.g., hunger, satiety, pleasure, pain), as they are apathetic toward their body and unaware of its needs. When Jared eats in the absence of hunger or eats too much as he distracts himself, he has lost touch with his connection to his body as well. For Jacqueline, it is less clear how she feels about and connects with her body. We know she is anxious about weight-related issues. We know she has started to skip meals. As she develops, the function of her restriction will become clearer. For some, restriction is less is about a pursuit of the thin and lean ideal and more about a disconnection from the body. Some may be trying to manage anxiety; others feel too depressed to eat. It all takes a bit of sorting out (see Chapter 8, this volume,

Body Obsessed ◄——————— Mind–Body Attunement ———————► Body Ignored

Figure 1.3. Continuum of body focus.

for screening and assessment information) and knowing that children present with their own unique relationship with food and their body.

The seat of healthy, intuitive eating and body acceptance is found in the center. Here we find *mind–body attunement,* which involves conscious presence and awareness of one's body and is free of judgment. It involves sensing, honoring, and respecting the body by being aware of its needs and regularly engaging in adaptive behaviors to attend to these needs. Mind–body attunement includes interoceptive awareness, a process in which the brain perceives physical sensations arising from within the body, such as hunger, satiety, fast heartbeat, heavy breathing, and so forth. Lack of mind and body integration creates risk. For example, when a person is in the throes of an ED, they are disconnected from their body and override interoceptive awareness—in effect, body sensations are not perceived or are ignored.

Using a conceptual model unique to this text, the three major EDs can be viewed along the extremes of these two continua (see Figure 1.4). For example, those who are body obsessed and compulsively binge eat may manifest BN. Given their body-obsessed stance, they feel they must purge, fast, or compulsively exercise after their binge-eating episodes to prevent weight gain. Another example would be those (typically boys and men) who develop muscle dysmorphia and who feel that they have to compulsively lift weights, overconsume protein, and take anabolic steroids to gain muscle mass. Conversely, those who fall into the lower right quadrant also compulsively binge and may have BED. However, because they ignore physiological cues and/or are dissociated from their bodies, they do not engage in compensatory behaviors in an attempt to rid themselves of calories gained during their binge-eating episodes. Often these individuals struggle with weight

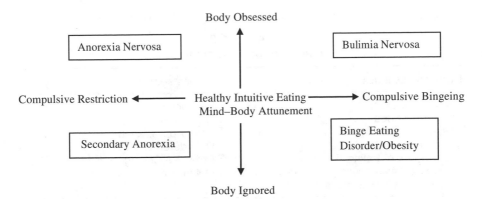

Figure 1.4. Integrated model of healthy intuitive eating and mind–body attunement.

gain and obesity. On the left side of Figure 1.4 are those who compulsively restrict their food intake. This restriction, when combined with body obsession, manifests as AN. Conversely, restriction accompanied by dissociation from the body can be seen in depressive and anxiety-based disorders as a secondary symptom. For these individuals, food restriction is not associated with a desire to be thin, and they often have trouble eating when they are upset or disconnect from their sense of self-care as they work to negotiate their emotional experience. This text addresses issues of diagnostic migration and symptom variability, which may place individuals in different quadrants, depending on their current manifestation of symptoms.

Healthy, intuitive eating behavior involves an attuned relationship with one's body, such as an awareness of when it is hungry and full as well as adaptive eating for nutrition that is free of compulsion and that is based on hunger and satiety cues. In its essence, a healthy relationship with the body and eating is core to an integrated sense of self. Accordingly, understanding what places a student at risk can be best understood in terms of a model of the self (see the Attuned Representational Model of Self section in Chapter 2, this volume).

INTUITIVE EATING RESEARCH

To date, there are over 25 published studies on intuitive eating, with several more currently underway. Together, these studies show that intuitive eating is positively related to many indexes of well-being, with several attributes associated with both physical and mental health, which are summarized in Table 1.2. In this section, intuitive eating scales and key studies are described.

TABLE 1.2
Intuitive Eater Characteristics

↓ Body mass index	↑ Self-esteem
↓ Thin Idealization	↑ Well-being
↑ Variety of Foods	↓ Triglycerides
↑ HDL ("good cholesterol")	↑ Body Appreciation
↑ Body Acceptance	↓ Disordered Eating
↑ Enjoyment of Eating	↑ Proactive Coping
↑ Body Cue Awareness	↑ Optimism
↑ Interoceptive Awareness	

Note. From *Intuitive Eating* (3rd ed.; p. 290), by E. Tribole and E. Resch, 2012, New York, NY: St. Martin's Press. Copyright 2012 by St. Martin's Press. Reprinted with permission.

Two Intuitive Eating Scales

There are two independently developed and validated quantitative measures of the degree to which a person is an intuitive eater, and both are referred to as the Intuitive Eating Scale (IES; Madanat & Hawks, 2004; Tylka, 2006). We differentiate them here by noting the developers of the scale: either the Hawks IES (Madanat & Hawks, 2004) or the Tylka IES (2006).

To assess and validate the key components of Tribole and Resch's intuitive eating principles, Tylka (2006) conducted a series of four studies with 1,300 college women. In the first part of the study, Tylka's IES was developed, and its three-factor structure was evaluated and supported. Then, Tylka's IES was administered, along with a series of other instruments, to evaluate the relationship of intuitive eating to mental health status, body image, and ED symptoms. Women scoring high on the IES were found to have higher body satisfaction, interoceptive awareness, self-esteem, life satisfaction, optimism, and proactive coping as well as lower ED symptomatology. Next, the relationship between BMI and intuitive eating scores were evaluated. Those scoring higher on the IES had lower BMI, which suggests that eating based on biological cues of hunger and fullness is associated with a lower BMI.

Notably, both of the independently created IESs indicate that individuals who eat intuitively are less likely to engage in behaviors that may lead to weight gain—such as eating in the absence of hunger and eating in response to emotions or situational factors (e.g., the sight and smell of food). Intuitive eaters have a lower BMI without internalizing the thin ideal, which indicates that they are less likely to base their self-worth on being thin (Madanat & Hawks, 2004; Tylka, 2006).

The Intuitive Eating Scale for Adolescents

Dockendorff, Petrie, Greenleaf, and Martin (2011) adapted Tylka's (2006) IES in a study with 500 middle school adolescents (both males and females). They identified an additional component needed to be an intuitive eater in this age group—*trust*. Adolescents need to be able to trust their bodies to tell them when and how much to eat, rather than merely being aware of hunger and satiety cues. Given the growing food and fat phobia, trust may be a significant feature of all intuitive eaters, regardless of age. This suggests that it is important for schools to promote healthy behaviors in a manner that fosters trust and flexibility, as opposed to fear-mongering health campaigns.

Adolescents who scored high on Dockendorff et al.'s (2011) version of the IES for Adolescents had (a) lower BMI levels, without internalizing culturally thin ideals; (b) lower body dissatisfaction; and (c) fewer mood problems. These findings are consistent with Tylka's (2006) results on college women. Adolescent intuitive eaters also had better life satisfaction scores and experienced a greater positive mood. This is a noteworthy finding, as adolescents are particularly vulnerable to hormone fluctuations and peer pressure to fit in, which can influence mood and life satisfaction.

Males

Although the majority of research on intuitive eating has been conducted with females, emerging research indicates benefits for males. A preliminary study with 181 college men showed that men scoring high on the Hawks's IES had a lower BMI compared with men having low IES scores (Gast, Madanat, & Nielson, 2012). The men also placed more value on being physically fit and healthy rather than on an ideal weight. The researchers suggested that intuitive eating seems ideally suited for men because it builds on men's antidieting views (men often perceive dieting behaviors as feminine), and it builds on self-care fitness beliefs that appear to be more likely held by men. In addition, Tylka recently updated her version of the IES (to the IES-2) and also found it to be valid with college men and associated with similar health benefits as women (Tylka & Kroon Van Diest, 2012). On average, men had higher IES-2 scores than women.

Impact of Intuitive Eating on Health and Well-Being

Feeling positive represents the pleasant end of emotional states, which include feeling upbeat, happy, appreciative, and has been shown by several studies to predict future levels of health and well-being. Moreover, these effects accumulate and compound over time, making people healthier, more socially integrated, effective, and resilient (Fredrickson & Losada, 2005). In addition to these positive mental health benefits, there are documented physical health benefits, which include lower levels of the stress chemical, cortisol, and lower biomarkers that indication inflammation. Both stress and inflammation increase risk for chronic health diseases.

A study by Tylka and Wilcox (2006) with 340 college women showed that two core constructs of intuitive eating, that is, eating for physical rather than emotional reasons and reliance on internal hunger and satiety cues to determine when and how much to eat, uniquely contributed to many indexes of positive psychological well-being, including optimism, psychological hardiness (an indicator of resilience, or the ability to recover from adversity), unconditional self-regard, positive affect, proactive coping, and social problem solving. These findings validate many of the intuitive eating principles, such as honoring hunger, respecting fullness, coping with feelings without using food, and rejecting the diet mentality.

Health and Properties of Intuitive Eaters' Food Choices

Some people express concern about one of the core intuitive eating principles, unconditional permission to eat. They worry that if people are "allowed" to eat whatever they want, it would result in unhealthy diets and weight gain. To address this contention, T. S. Smith and Hawks (2006) designed a study involving nearly 350 male and female college students and evaluated the health-related properties of the food choices made by intuitive eaters. Contrary to the expectation of critics, students scoring high on Hawks, Merrill, and Madanat's (2004) IES ate a more diverse diet and had a lower BMI. Furthermore, there was no association between intuitive eating and the amount of junk food eaten in the diet. In other words, intuitive eaters were not eating an unhealthy diet. Intuitive eaters also reported taking more pleasure in their eating. Another study led by Hawks showed that intuitive eating was associated with reduced BMI, lower triglyceride levels in the blood, and a reduction in the overall risk for heart disease (Hawks, Madanat, Hawks, & Harris, 2005).

Gentle Nutrition

Tylka and Kroon Van Diest (2012) updated the IES (to the IES-2), to reflect another component of intuitive eating, honoring health or practicing gentle nutrition. Individuals who practice gentle nutrition may ask themselves, "How does this food make my body feel? Do I like this feeling?" and "Does this food give me lasting energy? How do I feel after I eat it?" and use this information to guide their future food choices but not in a rigid way. This new subscale incorporated into the IES-2 was labeled Body-Food Choice Congruence because it measures and reflects the extent to which individuals match their food choice with their body's needs. Tylka and Kroon Van Diest evaluated this subscale and the total IES-2 on over 1,405 women and 1,195 men over three studies. The factor structure of the IES-2 was upheld, and their research further demonstrated that the IES-2 yielded reliable and valid scores with women and men. To be specific, IES-2 scores were (a) positively related to body appreciation, self-esteem, and satisfaction with life; (b) inversely related to ED symptomatology, poor interoceptive awareness, body surveillance, body shame, BMI, and internalization of media appearance ideals; and (c) unrelated or negligibly related to social desirability. IES-2 scores also garnered incremental validity by predicting psychological well-being above and beyond low levels of ED symptomatology, suggesting that intuitive eating is more than the mere absence of ED symptomatology and worthy of study in its own right.

Factors That Interfere With Intuitive Eating

Although the ability to eat intuitively is inborn, the likelihood of remaining an intuitive eater is influenced by the environment, which includes family, friends, and culture. Intuitive eating can be thwarted by an environment that lacks acceptance or imposes rigid rules for eating that ignore a person's inner experience (e.g., hunger, satisfaction). These studies are described below.

Parents' Feeding Practices

Galloway, Farrow, and Martz (2010) evaluated the impact of parental feeding practices on intuitive eating and BMI with a novel study design. Nearly 100 college-age students and their parents completed retrospective questionnaires of parental feeding practices in regard to the college students' childhood. An example of the questions asked is, "Did your parent keep track of the sweets (candy, ice cream, cake, pies, and pastries) that you ate?" Similar items asked about consumption of snack foods (e.g., potato chips) and high fat foods. Next, the researchers measured the students' current BMI and assessed their intuitive eating level by using Tylka's (2006) IES. The results showed that parental monitoring and restriction of food intake had a significant impact on college students' BMI, emotional eating, and IES scores. Moreover, parents that monitored and restricted their daughters' eating, had daughters who (a) reported significantly more emotional eating, (b) had a higher BMI, and (c) were less inclined to eat for physical reasons of hunger and satiety. The association was slightly different for the male college students. Parents who recollected restriction of their son's food intake had sons with significantly heavier BMI levels, but sons did not report higher emotional eating. They also found that intuitive eating was associated with a lower BMI, a finding that is consistent with other studies. The researchers concluded that controlling feeding practices by parents has potentially long-term consequences and may contribute to the development of emotional eating.

Kroon Van Diest and Tylka (2010) reported similar findings from a study with college-age men and women. They created and validated a questionnaire that asked students to rate the degree to which their parents–caregivers emphasized restrictive behaviors while growing up (e.g., commenting that children were eating too much, talked about dieting or restricting certain high-calorie foods, and telling children that they shouldn't eat certain foods because the foods will make them fat). Kroon Van Diest and Tylka found high levels of critical and restrictive eating messages from caregivers were associated with low intuitive eating scores and higher BMI scores.

These intuitive eating studies on parental feeding practices adds to the plethora of studies by Leann Birch, who showed that when parents attempt to restrict children's eating, it backfires by disconnecting them from their natural hunger and satiety cues (Birch, Parker, & Burns, 2011). These studies also support many principles of intuitive eating, including rejecting the food police, making peace with food, honoring hunger, and feeling full.

Self-Silencing

Self-silencing is the suppression of one's thoughts, feelings, or needs (Shouse & Nilsson, 2011). Self-silencing is a gendered phenomenon that influences women's mental health, in particular, and appears to begin in adolescence. Because adolescence is a particularly vulnerable time for girls (e.g., body dissatisfaction and social pressures emerge), when they silence their voice they also may concurrently ignore or suppress their physiological or hunger cues that are inconsistent with societal ideas of thinness. However, expression of thoughts, feelings, or needs appear to be a critical aspect of healthy eating behaviors (Tribole & Resch, 2012).

Shouse and Nilsson (2011) evaluated the relationship between disordered eating, intuitive eating, and self-silencing and found that intuitive eating is maximized when a woman has high levels of emotional awareness, combined with low levels of self-silencing. However, when high emotional awareness was coupled with more self-silencing, participants had more disordered eating and less intuitive eating. The researchers believe that when women have clarity about their thoughts and feelings, but silence their voice, hunger signals may become confused, which may decrease trust of internal signals of hunger and satiation. Therefore, the most intuitive and the least disordered eaters in the study displayed high emotional awareness and low self-silencing. The results of this study validate the intuitive eating principles of challenging the food police and coping with emotions without using food.

Body Criticism

When an environment encourages others to be critical of their bodies, girls especially learn to eat in a disconnected manner in an attempt to regulate their appearance instead of listening to their body (Fredrickson & Roberts, 1997). In addition, pressure to lose weight by family, friends, school, and culture (in lieu of body acceptance) contributes to focusing on appearance-related eating. Many people are surprised to learn that body compliments can be a form of judging a person by their appearance, such as, "You look great—how much weight did you lose?" or "I wish I had a body like yours" (Calogero, Herbozo, & Thompson, 2009).

A series of studies by Tylka and colleagues (Augustus-Horvath & Tylka 2011; Avalos & Tylka 2006), with nearly 600 college women and 800 women ages 18 to 65 years old, respectively, found that emphasizing body function and body appreciation is a key way to translate body acceptance into intuitive eating behaviors. When women emphasize the functionality of their body over appearance, they are more inclined to eat according to their body's biological cues. Tylka's research indicates that it is important to promote a positive body orientation, which focuses on body appreciation and body functionality (rather than appearance), which in turn facilitates intuitive eating.

Westernization

Fascinating multicultural studies from Asian countries and Jordan have indicated that as Western definitions of beauty (i.e., thinness) became internalized, eating styles gradually evolved away from intuitive eating and toward external cues, which can prompt both obesity and EDs (Hawks et al., 2004; Madanat & Hawks, 2004).

Eating Disorder Prevention and Treatment

Until recently, research on EDs has been pathology- and symptom based, without considering positive eating behaviors. However, Tylka and Wilcox (2006) evaluated the constructs of intuitive eating by administering the IES and several mental health assessment measures that reflect proactive coping, self-esteem, positive affect, and ED symptomatology. Their results indicated that intuitive eating contributed uniquely to psychological well-being—and that intuitive eating is more than the absence of ED symptoms. This finding was replicated when the IES-2 was examined (Tylka & Kroon Van Diest, 2012). These studies indicated the importance of individuals' ability to detect and attend to their emotions and biological hunger–satiety signals because it is significantly and uniquely connected to well-being.

Tylka and Wilcox's (2006) findings indicated that intuitive eaters are less likely to develop EDs because they have greater interoceptive awareness, are more optimistic, are more likely to use adaptive coping strategies, have higher self-esteem, and are less likely to internalize Western cultural appearance ideals. Also, unconditional permission to eat, reliance on hunger and satiety cues, and eating for physical rather than emotional reasons have been found to be inversely related to disordered eating symptoms. Therefore, helping individuals learn how to discriminate between hunger signals and emotional needs would serve to promote healthier eating and reduce the likelihood of future ED symptoms. Tylka and Wilcox also recommended that intuitive eating be part of both the prevention efforts and educational process for treating EDs as it could contribute to the patient's ability to flourish and thrive in recovery.

Indeed, a promising study has indicated that implementing an intuitive eating program on a college campus increased adaptive eating practices and reduced ED risk factors in women (Young, 2011). Furthermore, emerging studies have indicated that intuitive eating is effective in the treatment of BED (Kristeller & Wolever, 2010; Smitham, 2008). One advantage of using intuitive eating as an ED prevention effort is that it removes a student participation barrier—stigma. Students don't want to be identified (or perceived) as having an ED and are less inclined to participate in a program with an ED label. In contrast, intuitive eating is rooted in positive psychology with many far-reaching health benefits and is less threatening for voluntary student participation.

CONCLUSION

A growing body of research indicates that compared with nonintuitive eaters, intuitive eaters eat more diverse and often nutritious food as well as have higher well-being, healthier weights, and reduced ED symptomatology. Thus, intuitive eating can be the unifying solution for the prevention of both EDs and obesity. Schools may be ideal for these preventative efforts and can play a positive role in fostering an environment that supports intuitive eating. Ultimately, for a student to achieve authentic health and well-being, dynamic attunement is needed, and intuitive eating is the path for that process (see Figure 1.1). Intuitive eating is an empowering process, which not only promotes psychological and physical health but also is a gateway for students to truly be the experts of their own bodies, as no other persons can better know their physical hunger, fullness, thoughts, feelings, and experiences.

2

WHY WE EAT THE WAY WE DO: THE ROLE OF PERSONAL AND EXTERNAL FACTORS

The relationship between eating behavior and the body is deeply affected by the environment. Factors such as food quality, quantity, and availability; an increasingly sedentary lifestyle; food advertising and marketing; and body teasing or acceptance all affect this relationship (Story, Kaphingst, Robinson-O'Brien, & Glanz, 2008). Given the known impact of environmental influences, the school is the opportune place to make changes and educate today's students. To support the most effective school practices associated with the development and maintenance of healthy student bodies, this text brings together the latest research and knowledge.

Healthy eating involves the food that you eat, how often and when you eat, how much you eat, and why you eat. In regard to quality, most agree that we need to eat food that is rich in nutrition so that our body is nourished (Willett & Skerrett, 2005). There are guidelines that address the frequency with which we should eat. Most agree that to fuel our body over the course of

DOI: 10.1037/14180-003
Healthy Eating in Schools: Evidence-Based Interventions to Help Kids Thrive, by C. P. Cook-Cottone, E. Tribole, and T. L. Tylka

the day, we should eat three meals, with perhaps one or two snacks in pleasant, distraction-free environments (Satter, 1995; Willett & Skerrett, 2005). The next issue is quantity. There are generally accepted guidelines for calorie intake and healthy weights (Willett & Skerrett, 2005). Basically, individuals are meant to eat enough to maintain a healthy weight—no more and no less. However, what is a healthy weight for one child may be different for another child who is the same age, gender, and height, because of their different genetic constitutions (Bacon, 2010; Satter, 2005). The most challenging questions remain: Why do we eat unhealthy foods? Why do we skip meals or eat too often (e.g., grazing all day)? Why do we eat in the absence of hunger? Why do we eat less or more than we need to?

Most professionals and researchers agree that it is these *why-we-eat* questions that get complicated. Of course, we eat for nourishment and energy. However, the challenge and complications lie in all of the other reasons we eat. Your own experience can illustrate this point. The next time you are eating, take a moment and ask yourself, "Why am I eating this right now?" This simple exercise can provide a little insight into the challenge. The answers can be many and can vary greatly. You might have answered, "I am hungry" which would ideally be code for "I need to be nourished with nutrient rich foods" and "I need energy to complete the tasks required of me today, to build and repair my body, and to defend my body against disease." However, many of us can honestly say that there are times that we answer the question "Why I am eating this right now?" with other reasons. This is not a reflection of lack of character or good intention. Things have changed. Food has never been so plentiful and accessible or tasted so good (Kessler, 2009). Given our current food environment, it is no surprise that we eat for many reasons other than nourishment and fuel, for example, "It's Jerry's birthday," "I love pizza (cookies, fudge, cheesecake, cheeseburgers, French fries, etc . . .)," "I can't pass up Chloe and Maya's homemade cookies," "It's low fat (sugar free, low calorie, natural . . .)," "My sister, Anne, made this for me. She'll be hurt if I don't eat it," "I'm bored," "I was craving chips," "We broke up," or "I always eat ice cream before bed." Among those reading this book, there will be some who cannot even ask themselves this question in the near term because they are dieting or skipping meals (neither of which is recommended). The external distractions (e.g., relationship demands, busy schedules, unnaturally lean media ideals) sidetrack so many of us from what our bodies need that we can no longer feel our own true hunger or satiety. For most, the eating, exercise, and self-care struggles continue throughout life at a normative or subclinical level. However, for those at risk for eating disorders (EDs) or the type of obesity that results from eating in the absence of hunger or low physical activity, this struggle can evolve into a complicated, self-perpetuating, treatment-resistant disorder resulting in high emotional, physical, and financial costs.

This chapter explains why we eat the way we do. Specifically, we present the personal and external factors that inform an individual's eating behavior.

RISK, MAINTENANCE, AND PROTECTIVE FACTORS IN EATING DISORDERED BEHAVIORS

What placed Jared, Jacqueline, Kara, and Ben at risk in the first place? The answer to this question involves understanding risk, maintenance, and protection. Each of the major EDs and certain types of obesity share core, as well as disorder-specific, risk and maintenance factors. McKnight Investigators (2003) defined a *risk factor* as "a characteristic, experience or event that, if present, is associated with an increase in the probability (risk) of a particular outcome in the general (unexposed) population" (p. 248). A *maintenance factor* predicts symptom persistence over time among those who initially have symptoms of the disorder (Stice, 2002). In contrast to risk and maintenance factors, a *protective factor* mitigates the adverse effects of a risk factor, modifying, ameliorating, or altering a person's response to an environmental hazard (Rutter, 1985). Researchers are working to identify the specific risk and maintenance variables that serve to increase or amplify the risk of disordered eating and obesity as well as the protective variables that steer individuals away from these conditions and toward body appreciation and intuitive eating (Story et al., 2008; Striegel-Moore & Bulik, 2007). Because the research is ongoing, the knowledge base is evolving (Stice, 2002).

THE SELF: A REPRESENTATIONAL ATTUNEMENT MODEL

For many years, eating disordered behaviors have been conceptualized as disorders of the self (Skårderud, 2009). As early as 1962, Bruch identified several self-regulatory deficits as the central underlying features in EDs: inaccuracy in the perception and control of body sensations (e.g., hunger, satiety, fatigue), confusion of emotional states (e.g., alexithymia, or difficulty articulating inner emotional experience), inaccuracy in language and concept development, and fear of social disapproval. In theory, eating becomes disordered as the individual works to address other struggles, some cognitive and neurological, some relational, and some physiological. Essentially, eating (restrictive or excessive) and the focus on the body (obsessive or neglectful) begin to serve functions other than nutrition and health maintenance. The attuned representation model of self (ARMS; C. Cook-Cottone, 2006a) illustrates the individual and ecological variables that can lead to maladaptive eating behaviors (see Figure 2.1).

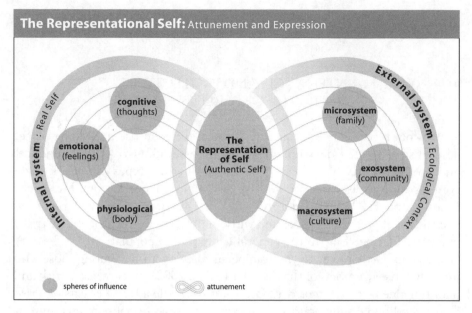

Figure 2.1. The attuned representation model of self (ARMS). From "The Attuned Representation Model for the Primary Prevention of Eating Disorders: An Overview for School Psychologists," by C. Cook-Cottone, 2006, *Psychology in the Schools, 43,* p. 224. Copyright 2006 by Wiley-Blackwell. Reprinted with permission.

The *internal self* negotiates what happens inside of a person (i.e., thoughts, feelings, and the body's needs) and what is going on outside of a person (i.e., friends, family, school, and the culture; C. Cook-Cottone, 2006a). Specifically, the internal arm of the self is composed of an individual's thoughts (cognitions), feelings (emotions), and physiological status (the body's needs). It incorporates an individual's genetic predispositions as well as his or her evolving cognitive and emotional functioning. The external arm of the self negotiates family, friends, school, community, and culture. There is much for the self to negotiate, both inside and out, each day. The true challenge lies in each individual's ability to negotiate thoughts, feelings, and physical needs while successfully adapting to and functioning within the community and the culture while maintaining healthy relationships. The *healthy self* (*authentic self*), or healthy student, can meet this challenge. The healthy self can internally regulate thoughts and feelings as well as effectively represent and meet internal needs through behavior and communication among the external systems.

Disorders of eating are believed to reflect ineffectiveness in this process. Suitably, disorders of eating are generally considered psychosocial. That is, both internal (i.e., within the individual) and external (i.e., familial and sociocultural) factors have been implicated as causal, risk, and maintenance, and protective factors (Loos & Bouchard, 2003; Stice, Presnell, & Spangler, 2002; Story et al., 2008; Striegel-Moore & Bulik, 2007). Investigators exploring internal and individual influences have implicated genetics, neuroanatomical and neurochemical differences, personality characteristics, as well as psychological factors (e.g., Loos & Bouchard, 2003). Others have embraced sociocultural models that emphasize external factors, such as Westernized beauty ideals and the objectification of the physical self, and environmental factors, such as highly palatable low-cost food and technology that facilitates a sedentary lifestyle (Loos & Bouchard, 2003; Story et al., 2008; Striegel-Moore & Bulik, 2007). For some time now, researchers have described the process this way: "Genetics loads the gun and the environment pulls the trigger." Aimee Liu, an author and activist against EDs, accounted for negative emotions in her slightly modified version of the metaphor. Specifically, she stated that genetics creates the gun, environment loads the gun, and extreme emotional experiences fire the ED bullet (Liu, 2007).

Factors Associated With the External System

According to C. Cook-Cottone's (2006a) ARMS model, the external arm of the self involves the interface with friends and family (e.g., parental and peer weight teasing, parental dieting), community (e.g., ballet schools, crew teams), and cultural factors (e.g., media, food availability).

Macrosystems (Culture)

Western consumer culture presents several risk factors that contribute to both disordered eating and obesity: the ultra-lean and happy ideal, rich and plentiful food, an increasingly sedentary lifestyle, and lack of effective policy that addresses food and body issues. First, media images and messages to be lean and eternally happy create a tension inconsistent with healthy weight and the normal fluctuations in mood inherent in living a fully present and mindful life. In addition, these media images and messages encourage us to try to change to this ideal by regulating the physical self (body) as well as both the cognitive and emotional self (our thoughts and feelings). Researchers have identified specific areas that appear to substantially contribute to risk.

Consumer culture provides an abundance of triggers for those with a genetic risk for maladaptive eating. As advertising pervades the seemingly exponential growth of new media platforms, nearly every demographic and ethnocultural group in America is inundated with images of food. Undeniably, the media market idealizes images and brands all specifically designed to inspire product purchase. The sociocultural risk inherent in such media exposure is nearly universal: Practically everyone is exposed to increasingly refined and modified foods specifically designed to be enticingly savory and rich (Story et al., 2008), and collective taste sensations have shifted as the food industry mass manufactures—and individuals repeatedly mass consume—products designed to trigger cravings (Kessler, 2009). Ultimately, this environment serves up the tastiest food humankind has ever experienced (Kessler, 2009) while at the same time exposing us to unattainable images of excessively thin women and mesomorphic men as ideals. Schools are taking on this challenge and implementing effective policies to regulate foods with little or no nutritional value and to encourage healthier foods and physical activity (Kessler, 2009).

Pressure to be thin can come from family members, friends, relationships, and the media (Tylka & Subich, 2004). Media ideals are exceedingly unhealthy. For example, researchers have found that the Miss America pageant winners and Playboy centerfolds of recent decades fall into the underweight categories, with a substantial percentage having a body mass index (BMI) that meets or is below the weight criterion for anorexia nervosa (AN; Ahern, Bennett, & Hetherington, 2008). Western beauty ideals also can impact girls from non-Western cultures who traditionally prefer robust female bodies (e.g., Fiji). In a prospective multiwave study conducted by A. E. Becker, Burwell, Herzog, Hamburg, and Gilman (2002), Fijian schoolgirls' eating behaviors were measured right before television was introduced to their culture and again after 3 years of exposure. Girls' rates of disordered eating were higher after this exposure, with 12.7% reporting symptoms at the first administration and 29.2% reporting symptoms 3 years later. Narrative data further revealed girls' interest in weight loss as a means of modeling themselves after television characters.

Perhaps because of genetic vulnerability, excessive exposure, appearance-related pressures from others, and the lack of media literacy, some individuals internalize these socially defined ideals for appearance. In a meta-analysis, Stice (2002) found that thin-ideal internalization predicted increases in body dissatisfaction, dieting, negative affect, onset of binge eating and bulimic symptoms, and increases in additional ED symptoms in adolescent girls. More recently, a similar process was documented for young adult men: Internalization of the mesomorphic ideal predicted their muscularity dissatisfaction, body fat dissatisfaction, and engagement in potentially dangerous muscularity-enhancement behaviors (Tylka, 2011b).

Self-objectification is another way of considering the internalization of media messages and pressures. *Objectification theory* (Fredrickson & Roberts, 1997) posits that life experience and gender socialization, for women in particular, include regular experiences of sexual objectification in which they are viewed as valuable only in terms of their body, body parts, and ability to sexually serve men. According to this theory, the media act as socializing agents that persistently and repeatedly present women as sexual objects. Others who internalize societal messages then treat women as sexual objects, so women are being objectified within both the media and their daily encounters with others. Girls and women internalize the objectified gaze, conceptualizing their whole self in terms of an object that is valuable only in terms of how it appears and sexually entertains others (primarily boys and men; Fredrickson & Roberts, 1997; Moradi, Dirks, & Matteson, 2005). This process is referred to as *self-objectification*. Moradi et al. (2005) suggested that such self-objectification can lead to body surveillance (i.e., constantly watching, monitoring, and measuring the size and shape of the body), body shame, reduced concentration, appearance anxiety, EDs, depression, anxiety, and reduced awareness of internal body states and needs. Empirical research shows that objectification theory fits the experiences of females more so than those of males (S. Daniel & Bridges, 2010). Without doubt, both Kara and Ben feel these external pressures to be lean and thin. Even Jacqueline in fifth grade has begun to worry about, maybe even internalize, the social pressures.

Since the 1970s, marketing has increasingly targeted children and adolescents (Story et al., 2008). Marketing targets infants and toddlers in an effort to engender brand loyalty and to influence the purchasing behaviors of parents. According to Harris et al. (2010), the fast food industry spent $4.2 billion on advertising in 2009. Studies of advertisements suggest that children view thousands of ads per year for foods high in fat, sugar, and/or sodium and low in nutritional content and few, if any, ads for fruits and vegetables (Story et al., 2008; Strasburger, 2011). In a policy statement from the American Academy of Pediatrics, Strasburger (2011) stated,

> To illustrate the power of marketing, compare the commitment of the Robert Wood Johnson Foundation to spend $100 million per year to try to decrease childhood obesity with the fact that the food industry spends more than that every month marketing primarily junk and fast food to young people. (p. 203)

David Kessler (2009), a former U.S. Food and Drug Administration commissioner, highlighted the substantial influence of changes in food manufacturing, food marketing, and the restaurant industry in the United States.

The major culprit in the rise of obesity rates is the changing environment that encourages excessive caloric intake, makes available low-cost and highly palatable foods, and discourages physical activity (Loos & Bouchard, 2003; Story et al., 2008). For Jared, the cross between his genetic predisposition and the types of foods he eats places him at high risk for obesity. It is believed that the human genome has evolved in entirely different environmental conditions that involved periods of food scarcity, required high levels of energy output in the pursuit and preparation of food, and favored the survival of those who could effectively store energy. Furthermore, low-income and rural neighborhoods often have limited access to supermarkets and healthy, fresh food (Story et al., 2008). These areas, like the neighborhood around City Central Elementary, have been referred to as *food deserts*. The smaller grocery stores in these neighborhoods often offer fewer healthy choices and stock foods with extended shelf life and higher profit margins (e.g., soda, junk food). Finally, although school food policy is changing (see Chapter 9, this volume), many schools, like City Central Elementary, continue to permit and support the availability of competing calorie-dense food with little nutritional value as they cut athletic and sports programs.

Ethnoculture (i.e., the culture of an ethnic group) and race are difficult to disentangle when understanding risk for obesity. Childhood obesity is increasing in all ethnic and racial groups (Caprio et al., 2008). However, its prevalence is higher in non-White and non-Asian populations (see Introduction, this volume). The reasons for these differences are complex and involve genetics, physiology, culture, socioeconomic status, environment, and interactions among these variables (Caprio et al., 2008). Physiological processes and overall awareness of health risk and tendency to access health care can vary by race, increasing risk for some groups and decreasing risk for others. Cultural practices associated with exercise, breast-feeding, meal preparation, and other food-based cultural practices can also place certain groups at risk. For some groups, food is an expression of cultural identity and is believed to be a means of preserving family and community unity. Culturally based family meals may serve to lower the risk of obesity in some children (e.g., Asians) but increase that risk in other children (e.g., African Americans). Moreover, there are substantial differences across cultures associated with body acceptance and what is considered beautiful and desirable. Traditional family foods as well as other cultural influences have played a role in both Jared's and Jacqueline's cases.

Exosystem (Community)

At the community level, larger cultural pressures can be exacerbated and emphasized or even offset by the individuals in children's lives. Children at school, friends, and adults can provide additional support or negative influence, leading to resilience or risk. The research detailed next has focused on teasing and bullying, childhood abuse, sports culture, and social support.

A child's weight may place him or her at increased risk for teasing. As our case study shows, children at school teased Jacqueline about her body and may have triggered her food-restricting behavior. Ultimately, some researchers believe that the most common and immediate consequences of being overweight or obese are psychosocial (e.g., peer-to-peer teasing; Robinson, 2006). Unfortunately, teasing is associated with increased risk. For example, weight-related teasing has been associated with increased body dissatisfaction and eating disordered behavior (Sweetingham & Waller, 2008). For some children and adolescents, like Jacqueline, who engage in eating disordered behavior, it is not about trying to be the prettiest girl or handsomest boy in the room, it is about trying to self-protect, to not be teased or bullied about their bodies.

Childhood abuse may be a risk factor. For many years, it has been theorized that children who have been abused are at increased risk for an ED (Rayworth, Wise, & Harlow, 2004). It is believed that childhood abuse can lead to a dissociative coping style that can evolve into binge eating or increase the general risk for psychopathology, thereby increasing the risk for bulimia nervosa (BN) and AN (e.g., Rayworth et al., 2004). Research trends suggest that childhood physical abuse is associated with increased risk for an ED. However, in regard to childhood sexual abuse, findings have been inconsistent, with some studies reporting a relationship with EDs and others reporting no relation (Rayworth et al., 2004; Stice, 2002).

Although exercise is critical for physical health, there are risks associated with some sport cultures. Given the importance of exercise for both physical and mental health, researchers are working to understand exactly what sports place athletes at the most risk and why. Sports that appear to be associated with the most increased risk include aesthetic sports (e.g., cheerleading, ice skating, dance) and weight-class sports (e.g., wrestling, crew; Sundgot-Borgen & Torstveit, 2010). For some previously less risky sports, there has been a sea change. For example, tennis and volleyball may be increasingly risky as more emphasis is placed on outward appearance. Research has yet to sort out whether the pressure to be thin and lean comes mainly from the media, the sports community, the expectations of spectators, or from coaches. For Ben, these pressures are very real. He and his teammates often compare their abdominal muscles, and he has used his workouts as a form of purging or to compensate for his binges.

The role of social support is not well understood, and there have been conflicting findings across research studies. Higher levels of social support are thought to increase perceptions of self-worth and reduce negative emotionality and eating disordered behavior (Hirsch, 1999). However, other studies have detected no relationship. For example, a study conducted by McKnight Investigators (2003) did not find social support to be associated with the onset of eating disordered behavior. Furthermore, Stice's (2002) meta-analysis exploring risk for EDs did not find social support to be associated with risk.

Community environments also play a role in access to nutritional foods and opportunities for active play and exercise (Story et al., 2008). Typically, low-income neighborhoods have less access to affordable, healthy foods because there are fewer grocery stores and supermarkets with large produce sections nearby (Story et al., 2008). Researchers are exploring the relationships between access to safe playgrounds, parks, and green areas for active play and exercise and obesity rates within communities (e.g., Weiss et al., 2011).

Microsystem (Family)

The influences of family may serve to enhance or protect a child from cultural pressures. The fundamental work of identity, or development of the self, occurs within the family. For many years, researchers and theorists have posited that parents can protect their children through a process of attunement between the needs of the child and the parental responses (Bruch, 1973; Skårderud, 2009). It is through the ongoing parent–child interactions that children begin to develop a sense of self. A healthy understanding of one's self arises from a parent–child dynamic in which the parent accurately mirrors the child's affective states (Rothschild-Yakar, Levy-Shiff, Fridman-Balaban, Gur, & Stein, 2010). Children who do not experience an accurate or consistent affective mirror may be at higher risk for disordered eating (Rothschild-Yakar et al., 2010).

As seen most clearly in Jacqueline's case, ongoing interactions with family members also help children define themselves within the broader cultural context (Haworth-Hoeppner, 2000). From every direction, we who live in consumer cultures are told that being thin (for girls and women) or mesomorphic (for boys and men) will make us happier (e.g., media messages for diet products, exercise programs and machinery, the general endorsement of thinness and leanness across most advertisements). Family dialogue helps children and adolescents establish the groundwork for the construction of an individual set of shared beliefs that can ultimately protect the child or place the child at risk (Haworth-Hoeppner, 2000). For example, if an unrealistically thin or muscular media image is presented on the television, a parent might say, "He or she looks fantastic," or the parent might say, "It is so sad and angering how the media continually present unhealthy images in an effort to make us feel bad and manipulate our purchases." It would be wonderful for Jacqueline to hear the latter type of message at home.

Neumark-Sztainer, Bauer, et al. (2010) highlighted the family environment as a critical influence on weight-related outcomes in children and adolescents. As seen in the tensions between Jacqueline's mother and father, weight-related family behaviors include parental encouragement of dieting behavior, parental modeling of dieting behavior, parents talking about their own weight, and weight-related teasing. Weight teasing by family members may be one of the strongest and most consistent correlates of problematic weight-related outcomes. The researchers reported that the girls who reported being teased by family members because of their weight had a higher BMI, increased body dissatisfaction, and were more likely to engage in unhealthy and extreme weight-control behaviors and binge eating in comparison with girls who were not teased. Parental comments about their own weight, encouragement of their daughter to diet, and maternal dieting were associated with problematic weight-related outcomes (Neumark-Sztainer, Bauer, et al., 2010; Patel, Wheatcroft, Park, & Stein, 2002).

Striegel-Moore et al. (2005) found that familial eating problems (e.g., family dieting, maternal or paternal overweight, family history of EDs, and family overeating) were a reliable and specific risk factor for eating problems. Mealtimes can be especially sensitive. Increased parental control, conflict, and negative moods or feelings during mealtimes place children at additional risk (Patel, Wheatcroft, Park, & Stein, 2002). An effort should be made to keep mealtime a pleasant and social experience for families (Satter, 2005). Parental wishes for the child to be thinner and the consequent withholding of food has been found to be problematic (Birch, Fisher, & Davison, 2003). Specifically, parental preoccupation with food, body shape, and weight may interfere with attunement with the child, making weight and food intake interactions supersede more important relationship interactions, such as caring and connecting. We have seen some of this in Ben's case. Instead of talking about a child's experiences and reflecting and supporting those experiences, the parent is engaged in weight-control dialogue and criticism of the child. The first set of interactions (reflection and support) can enhance the child's development, the latter (weight-control dialogue) can increase risk. Parents can act as poor role models to the child in relation to eating behaviors (Patel et al., 2002). Conversely, parents can enhance positive development by modeling healthy food choices and body acceptance and accepting their child's body. Indeed, perceptions of body acceptance by family predicted body appreciation among young women and men (Kroon Van Diest & Tylka, 2010). Furthermore, adolescent girls and boys with a positive body image felt that their families accepted their body (Frisén & Holmqvist, 2010).

Factors Associated With the Internal System

As conceptualized by C. Cook-Cottone (2006a), the internal arm of the self includes physiological (e.g., genetic, physical), emotional (e.g., feelings, moods), and cognitive (e.g., perceptual biases, attention, memory, attribution biases, cognitive distortions) aspects of the self. Bruch (1973) described the sense of ineffectiveness and lack of awareness of one's own life often experienced by those with maladaptive eating as originating from a failure to rely on thoughts, feelings, and bodily sensations to guide behavior. Even these early conceptualizations viewed the person with maladaptive eating as capable of thinking, feeling, and being, yet not able to distinguish and identify these inner experiences and use them to express needs within the context of his or her world (Skårderud, 2009).

Physiological Factors (the Body)

The body presents with its own set of challenges. Some of these may be present at or even before birth, whereas others may evolve as a child or adolescent develops.

Assessing genetic risk is an important task. The process of determining a genetic link to disordered eating behavior and obesity is complex. The research has progressed along two distinct trajectories. The research on EDs has taken a disorder-specific orientation similar to those of other psychopathologies. The research exploring the genetics associated with obesity has looked at the pathway to being heavy, as well as at evolutionary theories such as the "thrifty genotype" hypothesis, and more complex multifactorial explanations (Loos & Bouchard, 2003).

To understand genetic links to disorders, researchers have explored the rates of related individuals suffering from the same or similar disorders. Currently, researchers suspect familial transmission of eating difficulties associated with AN, BN, binge-eating disorder (BED), and obesity (Baker et al., 2009; Klump, Suisman, Burt, McGue, & Iacono, 2009; Patel et al., 2002). For example, Strober, Freeman, Lampert, Diamond, and Kaye (2000) reported a 7- to 12-fold increase in the prevalence of AN and BN among relatives of individuals diagnosed with EDs as compared with controls. Strober et al. suggested that the cross-transmission of AN and BN that occurs with families reflects a shared family vulnerability. Researchers are also working to understand a general risk or predisposition for ED-related attitudes (Patel et al., 2002). Within this line of research, ED-related attitudes and symptoms are explored in terms of an individual's genetic risk. For example, researchers are exploring the rates at which EDs share genetic transmission with other psychiatric traits (e.g., high levels of harm avoidance, stress reactivity, negative emotionality) and disorders (e.g., major depressive disorder, obsessive–compulsive disorder, obsessive–compulsive personality disorder). Obesity is also believed to have genetic roots (Loos & Bouchard, 2003).

These increased risks among family members are concerning. However, these trends do not help us sort out whether the increased risk comes from factors associated with living in the family environment (e.g., family eating patterns, meal preparation, family attitudes about weight and eating) or from genetic predispositions for EDs that have nothing to do with what it is like growing up in a particular home (Klump et al., 2009). To differentiate family and genetic influences, twin studies have been conducted. Twin studies compare similarity for a disorder or trait between both dizygotic (DZ) or nonidentical twins and monozygotic (MZ) or identical twins. Disorders with a strong genetic etiology should present more frequently in MZ twins than DZ twins (Patel et al., 2002). Also, researchers study twins who have been reared apart so that they can differentiate between genetic and environmental influences (e.g., Stunkard, Harris, Pedersen, & McClearn, 1990).

In general, heritability for EDs (AN, BN, and BED) appears to be on par with that for other forms of psychopathology that are considered biologically based (e.g., schizophrenia, bipolar disorder; Klump et al., 2009). Specifically, results of twin studies have suggested that AN may have a substantial genetic influence, whereas findings for BN are much less clear, with some studies finding less genetic influence and other studies finding heritability comparable to that for AN (e.g., Klump et al., 2009, Patel et al., 2002). In a review of the literature, Baker et al. (2009) found that twin studies reported heritability for AN to vary between 22% and 76% and estimates of BN to range between 54% and 83%. Researchers believe that shared environmental factors do not appear to provide main effects (Klump et al., 2009); however, they may interact with genetic risk to increase susceptibility. For example, family conflict or family stress might interact with genetic risk in all siblings or with nonshared influences (peer group) in creating risk. Moreover, Klump et al. (2009) warned that the lack of shared environmental effects does not explain much about the role of culture in the development of EDs. They noted that strong cultural pressures (e.g., the thin ideal, media messages to be thin and lean) may increase risk among genetically susceptible siblings and therefore strengthen the findings of studies such as theirs. According to these findings, Ben, Kara, and Jacqueline likely presented with genetic risk factors creating a unique vulnerability to external risk factors.

Studies have found that risk for obesity is about 2 to 3 times higher for those who have a family history of obesity, with risk increasing along with the severity of the obesity (e.g., 95th percentile; Loos & Bouchard, 2003), and this perhaps plays a role in Jared's case. It is well accepted that lifestyle and environmental factors are major determinants in the manifestation of obesity. However, current models include genetic correlates known to interact with environmental and lifestyle effects to increase obesity risk. According to Loos and Bouchard (2003), there has been substantial variation in heritability estimates (5%–90%), depending on the study's design (e.g., MZ or DZ twins, twins reared apart).

As the tools used by researchers become increasingly sophisticated, so can the questions they ask. Researchers are now able to study specific genes and their influence on individuals following two methods. First, researchers can use *association studies*, in which they examine the relative influence of specific candidate genes on the manifestation of EDs (Patel et al., 2002). Candidate genes are selected according to their perceived role or function in the biochemical pathways related to the regulation of eating and eating disordered behaviors (Loos & Bouchard, 2003). Second, they can use another method, termed *linkage analysis*. Using linkage analysis, researchers examine allelic sharing among family members by scanning the genome in affected pairs of relatives (Patel et al., 2002). ED researchers in this area have explored candidate genes that encode proteins believed to be involved in the regulation of feeding, weight, and energy expenditure (Das, 2010; Patel et al., 2002). To date, research on candidate genes associated with obesity has been inconsistent, and the associations found were weak (Loos & Bouchard, 2003). However, candidate genes have been implicated in both the regulation of energy expenditure and the regulation of energy intake (Das, 2010; Loos & Bouchard, 2003). More research is forthcoming as the genome-wide studies are published.

Alterations in the brain structure and function of individuals with disordered eating behavior have been noted, although chronic malnutrition and starvation can complicate the interpretations of these findings (Kaye, 2008). For patients like Kara, sorting out behaviors associated with starvation is difficult. The long-term effects are less clear, as researchers have reported varied findings on studies of weight-restored individuals. For those with AN, cerebral atrophy, enlarged ventricles, and increased cerebrospinal fluid volume (associated with deficits in gray and total white matter) have been observed using a variety of methods (e.g., computed tomography, magnetic resonance imaging; Kaye, 2008). For those with BN, brain abnormalities including decreased cortical mass have been reported. Obesity has been associated with ventromedial hypothalamic lesions and dysfunction, as well as with changes in vagal nerve mediation (Das, 2010).

Although there appears to be substantial circumstantial evidence for a neurobiological vulnerability to eating problems, a direct causal pathway has yet to be identified. For example, Kaye (2008) described the substantial discrepancy between the nearly universal media endorsement of the thin (for girls–women) and mesomorphic (for boys–men) ideals and the relatively low prevalence of EDs. For example, if everyone at Bayside High School experiences the pressure to be thin and lean, why is it that only a few students, like Kara and Ben, are struggling? Historical accounts of binge eating and AN existing before the present era of media saturation, heritability findings, and the age-specific onset of the some EDs also suggest biological, rather than environmental, vulnerabilities in etiology. In a review of the research, Kaye (2008) reported evidence of disturbance in the neuropeptides, serotonergic systems, dopamine, and insular functioning. However, we cannot ignore research that has indicated that media and image-conscious pressures to be thin create body dissatisfaction and subclinical (but still dangerous) disordered eating behaviors among many girls and women (A. E. Becker et al., 2002; Stice, 2002).

Central and peripheral nervous system neuropeptides may play a role in EDs (Kaye, 2008). Specifically, abnormalities in the central nervous system's neuropeptide regulation may contribute to poor functioning of some hormones (i.e., gonadal hormones, thyroid hormones, and growth hormone). Kaye (2008) also reported that dysregulated neuropeptides may also play a role in peripheral systems that are involved in gustation, gastrointestinal peptide secretion, and vagal nerve response. The neuropeptides implicated in animal studies include corticotropin-releasing hormone, leptin, and endogenous opiods. Several neurotransmitters have been implicated in eating difficulties. For example, some evidence suggests that the dopaminergic functioning in the limbic and executive-associative pathways may be altered for those with AN (Kaye, 2008). There are several hormones and peptides implicated in obesity (for a review, see Das, 2010).

Serotonergic (5-HT) neurotransmitter systems are known to play a role in the modulation of appetite, feeling, mood, and impulse control (Kaye, 2008; Patel et al., 2002). Kaye (2008) reported that there is some evidence that 5-HT disturbances may be associated with dysregulation of appetite, anxiety, abusiveness, and impulse control problems. Along this same line of thinking, there is a body of evidence that suggests that the L-tryptophan needed for the synthesis of 5-HT is lowered by dieting (Patel et al., 2002). Carbohydrates are known to increase tryptophan and consequently increase serotonin synthesis (Patel et al., 2002). Many believe that diets, in particular, low-carbohydrate diets, lead to problems in the synthesis of serotonin. Further, tryptophan is only available through diet; the content, amount, and frequency of food digested can affect levels of this important precursor (Kaye, 2008). There are several implications for those at risk for BN. For those who have recovered from BN, decreased levels of L-tryptophan may lead to a return of depressive symptoms, concerns with weight and shape, and fear of loss of control over eating (Patel et al., 2002). Researchers have theorized that perhaps this is one pathway of risk (Patel et al., 2002). That is, dieting may reduce L-tryptophan levels, triggering those individuals already at risk for BN, and binges in this disorder are triggered by carbohydrate craving.

Normal eating involves eating in episodes (i.e., meals and snacks) during which individuals eat until they are comfortably full or feel satiated (de Graaf, Blom, Smeets, Stafleu, & Hendriks, 2004). After a meal or a snack, the drive to eat decreases and gradually builds up again until individuals eat again. The cues that trigger the next episode of eating are both internal and external (de Graaf et al., 2004). They include time of day (e.g., lunchtime), smells, visual triggers (e.g., pictures of food, a friend eating lunch), boredom, and a need for sensory stimulation or tension reduction. Individuals at risk for eating problems may be more susceptible to, or neglectful of, such internal and external cues. With Kara's more persistent difficulties with restriction, these issues may be playing a role.

There have been conflicting findings in regard to the influence of puberty on the onset of EDs (Culbert, Burt, McGue, Iacono, & Klump, 2009;

Stice, 2002). Some researchers believe that those with higher genetic risk for eating disordered behavior experience the highest risk period during mid-to-late adolescence (Culbert et al., 2009). Various explanations have been used to explain the increased risk at this age. One model is the cumulative risk model (Smolak, Levine, & Gralen, 1993). This model posits that adolescence is a time of exceptional risk due to the accumulation of stressors: puberty-related weight spurt, cognitive growth, increased academic demands, and the onset of dating behavior. Stice (2002) suggested that the increased adipose tissue associated with puberty moves female adolescents away from the normative body shape of younger adolescents and the thin ideal. As a result, it has been theorized that adolescent females may experience more body dissatisfaction, dieting, and eating disturbance. Puberty is complicated by other adolescent developmental challenges. For example, the development of sexual identity and gender-type identification can influence risk. Specifically, some researchers believe that identification with a traditional gender role may add to risk for EDs among girls (Mussap, 2007). Further, males that identify themselves as gay may be more likely to internalize the mesomorphic ideal and more likely to engage in disordered eating (Striegel-Moore & Bulik, 2007) and muscularity enhancement behaviors (Tylka & Andorka, 2012). Body dissatisfaction (both with musculature and body fat) fully account for (i.e., mediate) the relationship between internalization of the mesomorphic ideal and muscularity enhancement and disordered eating behaviors (Tylka & Andorka, 2012).

Researchers are working to understand the relationship between overweight and obesity and other EDs (Stice, 2002). Claus, Braet, and Decaluwe (2006) theorized that increased BMI, overweight, or obesity status combines with other risk factors. Stice (2002) reported that children and adolescents at higher weights (due to more to excess body fat and not muscle) may experience increased pressure from family and peers to be thinner, as seen with both Ben and Jacqueline. For example, others may make negative comments about an individual's body or attempt to limit their caloric intake. Research suggests that increased BMI has been associated with increased perceived pressure to be thin, body dissatisfaction, and dieting behavior among adolescent girls and young women (Stice, 2002). Furthermore, there is some empirical evidence that higher body mass can predict onset of bulimic pathology, binge eating, and a general increase in ED symptoms in adolescent girls and young women (Stice, 2002).

Dietary restraint is the strict restriction of food intake or adoption of strict rules about food intake and is one of two pathways to bingeing or overeating (Allen, Byrne, La Puma, McLean, & Davis, 2008; Gagnon-Girouard et al., 2009). Researchers have theorized that dieting involves a shift away from eating in response to physiological cues (i.e., hunger and satiety cues) to eating according to cognitive control (i.e., diet or meal plan rules; Claus et al., 2006). As we all know, cognitive control can waver within the context of negative emotions, fatigue, and life stressors (Claus et al., 2006). As seen in Ben's case, binge eating occurs in response to transgressions from dietary rules with an "all-or-nothing" response, sometimes referred to as the *abstinence-violation effect* (Allen et al., 2008; Stice, 2002). The counteraction may, in part, serve to replenish key neurochemicals or may be a psychological response to deprivation (Stice, 2002). Binge eating may evolve out of these episodes as the individual loses control of eating. Although compelling, the dietary restraint model does not explain eating disordered behaviors for all eating disordered individuals. More research is needed to better understand these relationships.

Cognitive Factors (Thoughts)

There are several risk factors associated with the cognitive domain of the self. There is a growing body of work on the neuropsychology of disordered eating that implicates functions such as cognitive rigidity, obsessive–compulsive tendencies, and impulsivity as risk factors (C. P. Cook-Cottone, 2009). Although they may be associated with neuropsychological tendencies, the cognitive factors that are reviewed here are body dissatisfaction and surveillance, body image disturbance, overvaluation of shape and weight, and perfectionism.

Body dissatisfaction refers to an individual's negative evaluation of her or his own physical body (i.e., figure, weight, stomach, and hips; Brannan & Petrie, 2008). We see this in the cases of Kara, Ben, and Jacqueline. Body dissatisfaction is believed to promote dieting and negative affect leading to an increased risk for eating pathology and obesity (Brannan & Petrie, 2008; Gagnon-Girouard et al., 2009; Stice, 2002). Body dissatisfaction may vary by ethnicity, although much more research is needed. For example, a meta-analysis conducted by A. Roberts, Cash, Feingold, and Johnson (2006) showed that Black females were significantly more satisfied with their bodies than White females. Many believe that it is the degree of identification with Westernized ideals that mediates the relationship between ethnicity and body dissatisfaction (C. Cook-Cottone, Jones, & Haugli, 2010). Body dissatisfaction presents as an important risk factor for prevention work. However, because most individuals experience some degree of body dissatisfaction, it is less helpful when trying to understand why certain individuals go on to develop ED symptoms. In some cases, dietary restraint, negative affect, or both, may lead those who are already dissatisfied with their bodies to overeat or restrict food intake (Gagnon-Girouard et al., 2009). For others, body dissatisfaction may interact with body surveillance, a continuous monitoring of the size and shape of the body; those who engage in body surveillance are at increased risk for unhealthy, even dangerous, behavior to control the size and shape of their bodies (Tylka, 2004). Also, body surveillance strengthened the relationship between body dissatisfaction and eating disordered behavior in females, even after controlling for BMI (Brannan & Petrie, 2008).

Body image disturbance can be defined as body dissatisfaction, body shame, and a preoccupation with the size and shape of the body (Tylka & Subich, 2004). Tylka and Subich (2004) reported that body image disturbance has been consistently identified as the strongest predictor of eating disordered behavior. Kaye (2008) indicated that there may be a neurobiological explanation for the distortion of body image that occurs among those with disordered eating. Specifically, distortion of body image may reflect a disturbance of the neurological networks responsible for a felt sense of self. Similarly, those who engage in disordered eating tend to overvalue the shape and weight of their bodies (Grilo et al., 2008). Because of the consistency of this finding, overvaluation is included in the diagnostic criteria of both AN and BN, although it is not specific to individuals who have bona fide EDs (Tylka, 2004).

Perfectionistic individuals set very high standards for themselves in action, emotion, and appearance. Some of these individuals may set high standards for themselves that are realistic and achievable; these individuals are high on adaptive perfectionism (Slaney, Rice, Mobley, Trippi, & Ashby, 2001). However, others set high standards for themselves that are unrealistic and unattainable and therefore consistently perceive a discrepancy between their high personal standards and their ability to live up to these expectations; these individuals are said to be high on maladaptive perfectionism. Maladaptive, but not adaptive, perfectionism, as seen with Kara and Ben, is consistently associated in a negative manner with body dissatisfaction and disordered eating behaviors (C. Davis, 1997).

Many of those with EDs report working toward perfect behavior, perfect regulation of mood, perfect appearance and within that state of perfection everyone will like and accept them—all unrealistic and unachievable goals. They hold a belief that if they are perfect enough, they will be happy and protect themselves from uncomfortable emotions. Although maladaptive perfectionism is a well-organized psychological construct, it may have its actual basis in genetically driven neuropsychological tendencies, such as anxiety, rigidity in thinking, and obsessional behaviors targeting symmetry, exactness, and order (Kaye, 2008). Although associations exist, the exact role of maladaptive perfectionism in ED risk is not quite clear.

Maladaptive perfectionism may interact with other variables (e.g., body dissatisfaction), thereby increasing risk (Brannan & Petrie, 2008; Stice, 2002). For example, Brannan and Petrie (2008) theorized that although many women are dissatisfied with their bodies, without perfectionistic drives they are unlikely to engage in unhealthy behaviors to achieve media ideals. Other researchers believe that it is the subtype of maladaptive perfectionism that matters. Brannan and Petrie explained that AN has long been known to involve self-imposed standards of perfectionism that are associated with rigidity and restraint. Individuals with self-oriented perfectionism can feel strong negative feelings, even self-disgust, when they believe they are not living up to their own strict standards of appearance. It is theorized that to feel okay about themselves, they work very hard to control what they think is controllable about their appearance (e.g., shape, weight). Brannan and Petrie further explained that the media's constant message that body shape and weight are controllable (given the purchase of the right product, procedure, or diet) can strengthen these belief systems and encourage maladaptive behaviors.

Researchers have suggested that women with these tendencies will skip meals, self-impose rigid and difficult exercises schedules, and begin a self-perpetuating cycle of rigid control and extreme and negative self-assessment. Socially prescribed perfectionism (i.e., believing that others will value you only if you are perfect), however, may moderate the relationship between body dissatisfaction and bulimic symptoms (Brannan & Petrie, 2008). Individuals who hold socially prescribed perfectionistic attitudes are more inclined to aspire toward social ideals for appearance and attractiveness. Those holding socially prescribed ideals may be on a self-imposed strict diet, experience a slip or binge, experience consequent shame and self-disgust, and manage and dissipate these emotions through purging (i.e., vomiting, laxative or diuretic use, excessive exercise, or a combination of these). These individuals are striving toward an unattainable ideal, yet they are unable to maintain the dietary restraint and increased exercise associated with excessive thinness or leanness.

Emotional Factors

It is well accepted that emotions play a role in risk for eating disordered behaviors and nonnutritional eating (e.g., emotional eating). In each of the student cases presented (i.e., Jared, Jacqueline, Kara, and Ben), emotional factors play an important role. Jared struggles to regulate his emotions and eats instead. Jacqueline appears to manage her anxiety associated with her self, family, and peer relationships through restricting food intake. Kara feels very little outside of hunger and physical discomfort. Finally, Ben has fallen into regulating his emotions through a binge and purge cycle. The research associated with this aspect is detailed here. There are three general areas relevant to addressing eating issues in the schools: interoceptive awareness, negative affect, and emotional regulation.

Interoceptive awareness has been defined as the ability to perceive physical sensations originating from within the body, including emotions, signals of hunger and satiety, and other muscular and visceral sensations (Kaye, 2008; Mehling et al., 2009; Tylka & Subich, 2004). It is central to self-awareness because it facilitates the link between cognitive functioning, emotional processing, and the physiological state of the body (Kaye, 2008). Many reviews have implicated lack of interoceptive awareness as a risk for disordered eating (Kaye, 2008). Those who struggle with disordered eating are less connected to the feelings associated with emotions and the process of eating. They may engage in more extreme or frequent eating to compensate for reduced sensation, or, due to lack of awareness, they may be unable to properly regulate these behaviors. Neurological processing may play a role, as there is some evidence that the insula (part of the cerebral cortex) may be associated with the processing of interoceptive information or a subjective sense of the inner body (Kaye, 2008). Also, if we do not practice certain behaviors, our ability to perform them is compromised. Thus, chronically responding to external cues (e.g., diet rules) to govern when and how much to eat may interfere with the ability to detect subtle changes in hunger and satiety (Tribole & Resch, 1995; Tylka, 2006). Fortunately, awareness of these cues can be improved (Johnson, 2000).

Negative affect reflects both neuroticism and low self-esteem, and it subsumes depression, anxiety, irrational cognitions, maladaptive coping, and lack of impulse control (Tylka & Subich, 2004). Negative affect may help explain the relationship between body dissatisfaction and disordered eating (Gagnon-Girouard et al., 2009). Research evidence indicates that many individuals with AN and BN have demonstrated a lifetime history of negative affect that predates the onset of their disorder (Kaye, 2008). It is believed that individuals may engage in disordered or emotional eating to experience comfort and/or distraction from negative affect (Stice, 2002). Purging may also be associated with negative affect, as those who are distressed about what they have consumed are not able to tolerate the negative affect and purge to feel better (e.g., Stice, 2002).

Emotional regulation is the ability to moderate negative emotions (e.g., sadness, anger, anxiety, frustration, loneliness, boredom; Allen et al., 2008). It is theorized that eating disordered behavior (e.g., bingeing, purging, excessive exercise) can dull these emotions, providing temporary relief (Allen et al., 2008; Kaye, 2008). Some research suggests that dietary restraint and binge–purge cycles may help reduce dysphoria (or difficult or uncomfortable mood states; Kaye, 2008). Some evidence from brain imaging studies on patients with AN suggests that images of food and food intake may activate areas of the brain known to be involved in emotional regulation (Kaye, 2008). Kaye (2008) suggested that those with AN may work to overcontrol emotions, whereas those with BN may vary between overcontrol and undercontrol. Increased emotional regulation is, therefore, believed to be protective.

CONCLUSION

This chapter has provided an overview of healthy eating and the pathway to a disordered or dysfunctional relationship with both food and body. Furthermore, this chapter has set the stage for school personnel to cultivate a positive food and body culture in schools. The goal is healthy, mindful eating within the context of a positive and supportive environment. Helping students develop a functional and effective sense of self is critical. Research suggests that the three internal domains of the self (i.e., emotional, cognitive, and physiological) as well as the three external domains negotiated by the self (i.e., family and friends, community, and culture) must be addressed and supported. The risk factors relevant to each domain were clarified so that the supports and the interventions detailed in this text can be understood within the context of risk, maintenance, and protection. The school can be a powerful agent of change in helping to provide nutrition, best practices in body acceptance and education about and practice in experiencing a healthy relationship with both food and the body.

II

THE HEALTHY STUDENT
APPROACH

3

RATIONALE FOR A THREE-PILLAR APPROACH

In our conceptualization of intuitive eating (see Figure 1.4), we encourage school personnel to guide students toward intuitive eating (i.e., establishing and maintaining a connection and responsiveness to their natural hunger and satiety cues) and mind–body attunement (i.e., sensing, honoring, and respecting the body by being aware of its needs and regularly engaging in adaptive behaviors and activity to attend to its needs). But how is this accomplished? Consumer culture is at odds with intuitive eating and mind–body attunement. Media often promote mixed maladaptive messages: Compulsively restrict your food intake (e.g., NBC's *The Biggest Loser* program) but eat to soothe your emotional distress (e.g., Arby's slogan, "It's Good Mood Food"). Be obsessed with your appearance (e.g., E!'s *Keeping Up With the Kardashians*), but don't take care of your body (e.g., tempting children with TV and video games so that they engage in less physical activity). These media messages illustrate the maladaptive ends of the continua

DOI: 10.1037/14180-004
Healthy Eating in Schools: Evidence-Based Interventions to Help Kids Thrive, by C. P. Cook-Cottone,
E. Tribole, and T. L. Tylka

of eating behavior and body focus (see Figure 1.4), rather than the adaptive center, or core. It can be challenging for adults, including school personnel and parents, to combat these messages and guide children toward this core. Fortunately, there are models rooted in theory and science that adults can use to promote intuitive eating and mind–body attunement in children. This chapter reviews three such models.

Although these models are discussed separately, their themes are interrelated. At the end of this chapter, we discuss three interlocking themes that schools can use as a foundation for building a healthy school community. This foundation consists of three pillars: intuitive eating and nutrition (Pillar I); healthy physical activity (Pillar II); and mindfulness, self-care, and emotional regulation (Pillar III). Each pillar adds incremental and necessary support to the construction and maintenance of a positive, healthy school community.

GUIDING PRINCIPLES FOR THE HEALTHY STUDENT APPROACH

Before we discuss the foundational models in this chapter, we first turn to the mind-set and modus operandi that school systems need to adopt to bolster the effectiveness of the healthy student approach.

Develop a Transcontextual Approach

First, it is imperative that schools adopt a *transcontextual approach*, or one in which adults within schools, families, and the community work together to implement the policies, procedures, activities, and structures required to promote a healthy body image and eating behaviors for children and themselves. All adults who regularly interact with children (e.g., parents, teachers, coaches, cafeteria personnel, school psychologists and counselors, school administrators, school nurses, community agency personnel) need to be able to discriminate between adaptive and maladaptive eating, physical activity, and media messages and then teach children how to discriminate between them as well. Because various adults work together to promote healthy body image and eating behaviors in children, they are, in fact, caregivers to these children. It also is important that these caregivers "walk the walk" themselves by taking part in the same activities and practices that they prescribe to children that are in their care (O'Dea, 2007).

To ensure that a transcontextual approach is followed, all educators need to be consistent in the content of their messages, which need to be embedded in the school ethos (i.e., mission and philosophy) and disseminated to children's families as well as community partnerships and services. Schools are encouraged to recruit an interested member of the school system (e.g., school psychologist, administrator, teacher, coach) to organize this task and act as a liaison between the school, family, and community. The liaison would need to be an ambitious, creative, and organized person who is able to make connections with parents and community resources and who is grounded in health promotion rather than weight management. Because of the anticipated workload and time commitment involved, the liaison should be compensated for this role if funds allow.

First, the liaison would work with the school to develop a clear ethos about health rather than weight (e.g., one that emphasizes healthy behaviors, body appreciation, intuitive eating, enjoyable physical activity, and zero tolerance for weightism and teasing about weight). Second, the liaison would need to ensure that all school personnel are informed about this ethos, educated on research that supports its tenets, and committed to following the ethos. One of the most critical elements of this stage is addressing and challenging the myths and inaccuracies that are held by many individuals about health and eating. These inaccuracies include (a) that it is most important to focus on weight and/or body mass index (BMI) as a proxy for health, (b) that dieting is effective, and (c) that weight-related teasing is innocuous. Personnel training programs, or inservices, that review the myths and inaccuracies and provide tools for combating false beliefs are recommended. These programs should focus on adults' own issues with food, weight, and body image and, if necessary, adjust their attitudes toward eating disorders (EDs) and obesity to ensure they are not harming students.

An excellent example is provided as a 12-week teacher training program in *Everybody's Different* (O'Dea, 2007). This program helps educators get on board with the transcontextual approach to physical and psychological health promotion and fills in the gaps from inadequate training in nutrition and prevention, which will raise school personnel's self-efficacy when delivering these programs to students (Neumark-Sztainer, Story, & Coller, 1999). In this program, educators learn about using a holistic approach to teach students about health, well-being, social support, self-esteem, self-understanding, interpersonal skills, communication of feelings and needs, conflict resolution, and physical development and growth. They review case studies (positive and negative) of the ways educators have approached weight issues in the classroom, the dangers of using BMI as an index of health, the various other ways health can be measured (e.g., heart rate, blood pressure, glucose), and how to teach media literacy to children. Educators explore their own body image, such as factors that damage it and factors that promote it. (For educators who continue to struggle with their body image, we recommend they consult *The Body Image Workbook* by Thomas Cash, 2008. This self-help workbook contains useful exercises that promote enduring and gratifying changes in body image.)

Third, the liaison would work with each school personnel member to develop lesson plans for implementing the ethos in their classroom or area. The liaison, being educated about the ethos and the research (contained in this book), and the school personnel member, being educated about his or her line of work, should be able to mutually come up with ideas for implementing the ethos in the classroom. Many specific examples, which are grounded in the models presented in this chapter, are provided in the summary of this chapter.

Fourth, the liaison would discuss with each school personnel member how they can best disseminate this information to parents (e.g., through parent–teacher orientation day meetings and conferences). The liaison (in conjunction with school personnel) would need to devise handouts to provide to parents that describe (a) the ethos, (b) clear steps that the school is taking to follow the ethos, and (c) suggestions for how the family could apply the ethos within their home. Handouts should be at a sixth- to eighth-grade reading level to cover all levels of parental education, and they should be available in various languages for non-native English-speaking families. These handouts could cover the fundamentals of intuitive eating, mindful eating, enjoyable exercise, and media literacy, noting how they are grounded in research, as well as discuss how to practice these skills with their children. For instance, while watching television, parents can challenge the content of commercials, for example,

> Dove chocolate does indeed taste good, but it doesn't make all your problems go away, like that commercial suggests. There are better ways to deal with problems, and chocolate should be reserved for times when you are hungry, a healthier food won't satisfy you, and you can really savor and enjoy it.

Families could practice intuitive eating during family meals. Parents can help children appreciate their bodies through unconditional body acceptance (e.g., messages such as "Who you are on the inside is more important than what you look like," and "You're beautiful just as you are," rather than "You could lose a few pounds; then maybe you could get a boyfriend" and "You're too scrawny; bulk up").

Reserving a night at school in which families are introduced to this information may also be beneficial as a more hands-on approach (interpreters and transportation should be available as needed). During the first half, parents could learn about the information and how to implement it in their home while their children participate in activities supervised elsewhere by care providers or teachers in the school. In the second half, children could join their parents and participate in one of the activities introduced, such as a mindful or intuitive eating exercise with a snack or physical activity exercise. Such teacher–parent interactive programs have been found to be effective for promoting reading literacy and frequency in the home (Burningham & Dever, 2005).

Fifth, the liaison could establish a partnership with the local community youth recreational facilities (e.g., YMCAs), "farm-to-school" programs, and other interested community agencies to arrange for programs that support the ethos (as well as free or low-cost transportation to allow children to attend these programs). The liaison could work with community centers and YMCAs to host parent–child workshops on intuitive eating, mindful eating, enjoyable exercise, and media literacy as well as work to provide access to an assortment of physical activity free for children. For older children, after-school programs could be held at the YMCA, where they could participate in activities of their choice. Farm-to-school programs are an excellent way to bring healthy food to students. They connect schools with local farms to serve healthy meals in school cafeterias, improve student nutrition, provide agriculture and health and nutrition education opportunities, and support local farmers. They help students understand where their food comes from and how their food choices affect their bodies, the environment, and their communities. In addition to including farm-fresh salad bars and local foods in cafeterias, these programs engage students in experiential activities such as planting school gardens, learning how to prepare foods, and going on farm tours. The liaison could consult with an agriculturalist to develop a school garden. Tending school gardens can be a valuable learning experience. Watching the various vegetables grow and nurturing these vegetables could educate children about science and nutrition. All 50 states have at least one farm-to-school program. The website http://www.farmtoschool.org/ offers resources for educators who wish to create such programs in their school, such as tips for initiating the programs, funding opportunities (e.g., Captain Planet Foundation grants, Braitmayer Foundation grants), publications, and webinars. Regional lead agencies and national staff provide free training and technical assistance; information services; networking; and support for policy, media, and marketing activities.

Develop a School Ethos That Emphasizes Body Respect and Self-Regulation

A key feature of all three models presented in this chapter, as well as the three pillars presented in Part II, is encouraging children to respect their bodies by maintaining awareness of, and eating according to, their internal hunger and satiety cues. Because children need guidance and supervision in so many ways to stay safe and healthy, caregivers assume that they have to guide their children's food intake because children do not know how much they should eat. This is far from the case. Research demonstrates that infants and very young children naturally self-regulate—that is, they eat according to their internal cues of hunger and satiety (Birch, Johnson, Andresen, Peters,

& Schulte, 1991). Infants will turn away from their mother's breast or bottle when no longer hungry. Three-year-olds will eat half of their cheeseburger and French fries at fast food restaurants then turn their interest to playing with their meal toy or friends. At this point, caregivers, with a preconceived idea in mind of how much children should eat, try to bargain with them to eat a few more bites, not realizing that children inherently know how much fuel their bodies need. In reality, the amount of food that children eat (and require) is a small fraction of the extra-large portion sizes often presented to them. When caregivers look at the amount eaten and compare it with the amount given, it seems insignificant or not enough. Plus, children's eating style may seem chaotic to parents; however, they need to focus on the overall picture. Toddlers eat rather irregularly—even though their intake at each meal varies greatly, they eat roughly the same amount of calories each day (Birch et al., 1991). Thus, young children may consume a lot of food at breakfast but compensate by eating less at lunch.

Simply put, regularly encouraging children to eat beyond their satiety cues diminishes the salience of these cues in helping them determine when and how much to eat. Research suggests that around age 5 children who are detached from their hunger and satiety cues begin to eat for reasons outside of hunger, such as the mere presence of food, the smell of tasty foods, and emotional distress (Rolls, Engell, & Birch, 2000). Many caregivers take notice, and a new set of worries develops. In the spirit of securing healthy weight and good nutritional habits in children, they blatantly restrict children's access to calorie-dense foods (Birch, Fisher, & Davison, 2003). These feeding practices often backfire when the restriction is detectable by children (Brown, Ogden, Vogele, & Gibson, 2008); for example, "You aren't allowed to have cake anymore," and "We aren't buying potato chips because we don't want you to gain weight." When tasty foods are restricted in such a manner, young children become preoccupied with them (even when these foods were not highly desired prior to the restriction; Fisher & Birch, 1999), eat them secretly and in the absence of hunger (Carper, Fisher, & Birch, 2000; Fisher & Birch, 2000), and experience weight gain over time (Fisher & Birch, 2002). Using direct pressure to get children to eat nutrient-dense foods like vegetables and fruit backfires as well. Children often end up disliking the foods they feel forced to eat, which, as teenagers and adults, confines their diet to fewer nutrient-dense foods and more calorie-dense foods (Batsell, Brown, Ansfield, & Paschall, 2002; Galloway, Fiorito, Francis, & Birch, 2006; Lee, Mitchell, Smiciklas-Wright, & Birch, 2001).

Blatantly restricting children's access to calorie-dense foods and pressuring them to eat nutrient-dense foods diminish their natural ability to self-regulate (Fisher & Birch, 2000). These overtly controlling practices teach children to focus on external cues, such as the amount of food on their plate, rather than respond to their internal hunger and satiety cues to determine when and how much to eat. Awareness of and responsiveness to these internal cues could be used as defenses for children in this abundant tasty food environment: These cues may help children (a) resist eating when they are not physically hungry but are surrounded by palatable foods (Eneli, Crum, & Tylka, 2008) and (b) eat an appropriate amount of food to maintain a healthy weight (Satter, 2005). Fortunately, many children who are detached from their internal hunger and satiety cues can relearn how to self-regulate (Johnson, 2000). The three models presented next, which can be adapted to school settings, encourage self-regulation as well as body respect in children.

FOUNDATIONAL MODELS

The trust model, the health at every size (HAES) model, and the positive psychology paradigm can facilitate intuitive eating and mind–body connection for children and adults. In this section, we review these models.

Trust Model

Developed by Ellyn Satter (1986), a dietician and social worker with extensive experience in child–caregiver feeding dynamics, the *trust model* articulates, divides, and assigns feeding responsibility between caregivers and children (Eneli et al., 2008). The model integrates authoritative concepts wherein caregivers provide structure, guidance, warmth, and expectations for children's behavior (Baumrind, 1966). Its basic premise is that feeding takes place within a dynamic and reciprocal relationship between caregivers and children (Satter, 1995). Specifically, when caregivers perform their feeding responsibilities without infringing on their children's feeding responsibilities, then children can naturally self-regulate their food intake, trusting their body's signals to tell them whether to eat, which of the presented foods to eat, and how much to eat. This will allow their bodies to grow as they were meant to grow, and children should attain a weight that is representative of their genetic endowment—spikes in weight gain or weight loss outside of developmental growth spurts should not occur.

What are caregivers' responsibilities in the feeding relationship? First, caregivers need to provide children with structured meals and snacks. Satter (1986, 1995, 2005) recommended that children have three structured meals and one to three structured snacks a day, each spaced between 3 and 4 hr apart from one another. Having regular eating opportunities will minimize food obsession with children; they will know and trust that another feeding opportunity is just around the corner. Satter further suggested that children should not eat or drink anything besides water between meals and snacks, which will permit them to remain connected with their internal hunger cues; children will come to the table hungry, but not ravenous. Second, caregivers need to feed children within a pleasant distraction-free environment; that is, they need to direct children to eat at a table apart from computers, electronic devices, video games, and television. They need to engage in pleasant conversation with children that is not focused on the quantity of the food being consumed. Satter recommended that caregivers also eat with children, as they can model respectful mealtime behaviors and consuming foods not yet tried by children. Third, caregivers are responsible for providing well-balanced meals and snacks, offering wholesome and tasteful foods that include a protein source; carbohydrates; fruits, vegetables, or both; dairy–calcium; and fat. At times, they can integrate a single-size portion of dessert within this array of foods. Satter encouraged caregivers to include at least one known food that the child likes within this array. Caregivers should not be swayed by children to replace foods within this array with other foods and, thus, serve as short-order cooks for their children. After they perform these three responsibilities, caregivers need to sit back and let children perform their responsibilities.

So, what are children's responsibilities in the feeding relationship? According to Satter (1986, 1995, 2005), children are in charge of deciding whether they want to eat, and if so, which and how much of the presented foods to eat. If caregivers consistently offer a feeding opportunity every 3 to 4 hr, children implicitly know that if they are not hungry they can eat at the next available meal–snack time. This structure, and the freedom to eat within this structure, set the stage for children's internal hunger and satiety cues to take over and direct their eating. Ideally, with each eating opportunity, they begin eating when moderately hungry and stop eating when comfortably full. If they are not hungry, they do not eat. They trust their body's cues.

To be effective, caregivers must let children perform their responsibilities. The effectiveness of the trust model hinges on this feature, as children cannot follow their internal hunger and satiety cues in an overtly controlling environment. Therefore, caregivers should neither place pressure on children to eat or to eat a certain amount or type of food nor restrict a certain type of food (with the exception of allergies and illnesses) or place limits on the amount of food children consume. Again, these controlling practices backfire (Carper et al., 2000; Fisher & Birch, 1999; Galloway et al., 2006). Overweight parents who attended an intervention designed to teach Satter's division of feeding responsibility reduced pressuring their young daughter to eat and restricting her food intake relative to a control group (Agras et al., 2012).

Caregivers could be reassured that when this division of responsibility is followed, mechanisms are in place for children to regularly eat a well-balanced array of nutritious foods (with some dessert opportunities, of course) in a supportive environment. Although the trust model discourages overt food restriction and pressures to eat that are detectable by children, it encourages caregivers to implement covert control, or control that is undetectable by children. Specifically, caregivers can control what foods are presented at each feeding opportunity and offer a wide range of nutritious foods. They can offer sweet and fatty foods on occasion but keep the bulk of the foods wholesome and nutritious. They can prepare healthy yet simple meals at home to reduce fast food visits. If caregivers consistently provide structured meals and snacks, children are not likely to be preoccupied with food in between eating opportunities. Because children see adults eating food they have not yet tried, children are more likely to try the food (although Satter noted that multiple exposures to food may be necessary before children try—and like—a new food). If caregivers have ensured that the feeding environment is distraction free and pleasant, children do not associate stress and anxiety with eating. They can sit down with children and eat, providing a role model for appropriate mealtime behaviors and support. This "family meal" style is associated with improved dietary habits and improved perceptions of support among children (Neumark-Sztainer, Hannan, Story, Croll, & Perry, 2003).

Satter (1986, 1995, 2005) also encouraged caregivers to regularly structure physical activity opportunities in which whole systems (e.g., family, class) can partake. Again, the division of responsibility should be followed: Caregivers structure "the what, when, and where" of the activity, such as identifying what the activity should be, when it takes place, and where it takes place, being mindful to incorporate activities that children enjoy, such as kickball and activity games, rather than running for miles. It is then children's responsibility to determine whether they will participate in the activity, although the option would be to sit out. They cannot choose an alternative activity, such as watching TV or playing video games. Although the trust model was originally developed for parents, it could be easily tailored to schools. In fact, schools may be the conduit to introducing parents to this approach.

Health at Every Size

Although some professionals have used concepts from the HAES movement in their practice for decades, Bacon and her colleagues (Bacon, 2010; Bacon et al., 2002; Bacon, Stern, Van Loan, & Keim, 2005) have skillfully integrated these concepts into a comprehensive program. Bacon's HAES program emerged from careful consideration of scientific findings of what works and what does not work, rather than from media (and often medical) hype that does not hold up when tested.

Are people more likely to treat someone they like or dislike with respect, dignity, and care? Obviously, someone they like. HAES implements this fundamental question with the body: People are more likely to treat their body with respect, dignity, and care, and give it the nutrients it needs to perform well, if they like it. Therefore, we need to help children like—and hence appreciate, respect, and care for—their bodies to have them pursue the road to healthy eating and enjoyable physical movement. When children feel better about themselves, they will make better choices. When children experience body shame, however, they will be more likely to act destructively and punish their bodies by overeating, rigid dieting, EDs, ignoring their hunger cues, or engaging in militant exercise (Tribole & Resch, 2003; Tylka & Hill, 2004). If children exercise only for weight loss, how can they learn to enjoy being active? If they eat salads only to change the body they hate, how will they enjoy the taste of fresh vegetables?

The HAES program has five components (Bacon et al., 2005), which interact to promote healthful eating, enjoyable physical activity, respect and acceptance of the body, self-esteem, and psychological well-being; and to decrease food obsession, body shame, and depression. This is opposite to dieting and weight-centered approaches, which lower self-esteem and breed body shame, food obsession, and depression (Bacon et al., 2002; Birch et al., 2003; Fisher & Birch, 1999, 2000, 2002; Mann et al., 2007). Whereas HAES reflects "eating to live," the dieting–weight-centered approach promotes food preoccupation or "living to eat."

Although each component was originally tailored for adult women, ideas for how it can be adapted for children and carried out in the school setting are provided in the summary at the end of this chapter. The first component is enhancing body and self-acceptance. Specifically, individuals are encouraged to live their lives fully now, in their present body. If they wait until they lose weight, it will just delay their happiness and life satisfaction, as dieting rarely leads to long-term successful weight management (Mann et al., 2007). Therefore, in this component, individuals disentangle feelings of self-worth from their weight.

The second component of HAES is "taking care of your hungers," which supports intuitive eating, or letting go of restrictive and other forms of external eating and instead using internal cues of hunger and satiety to guide food intake. Intuitive eating is more effective at managing weight than dieting (Avalos & Tylka, 2006; Bacon et al., 2005).

How can internal cues be nurtured in children? Bacon (2010) provided evidence that children can achieve and maintain a healthy weight when they eat food they enjoy and eat mindfully. These are natural forms of portion control. Children who eat mindfully are more likely to stop eating a certain food once they notice that it loses its flavor (referred to as *sensory-specific satiety*; Hetherington, Rolls, & Burley, 1989). Children who realize they can regularly have food they enjoy will stop eating when they are content; when they enjoy the food they eat, cholecystokinin is released, helping them feel fuller sooner (Bacon, 2010). These children start to listen to messages from their body and tell themselves, "Even though cake tastes good, it just doesn't sound good right now because I'm not hungry . . . I can eat it when I'm hungry." Also, children need to learn to decipher their physical hunger from their emotional needs, as sometimes they become jumbled due to pairing food with emotional distress.

The third component of HAES is "living well." This is a challenge for children, given the enormous social pressure for them to be lean within a consumer culture that promotes fast food, extra-large portions, television, and video games. To choose a different lifestyle is hard for children, as they are somewhat dependent on adults to structure their environment with certain foods and opportunities for exercise and help them challenge unrealistic media-promoted body ideals.

The fourth component of HAES is "change your tastes." The goal is to help children appreciate a wide range of flavor sensations and tone down their cravings for certain foods that may, in excess, cause harm. Pleasure pathways exist in the brain that are designed to reinforce eating and other survival behaviors; sugary and fatty foods may trigger this response more so than other foods (Erlanson-Albertsson, 2005). Whereas some professionals suggest that this makes sugary and fatty foods "addictive," restricting these foods clearly backfires (Fisher & Birch, 1999, 2000, 2002). Instead, following the HAES approach, caregivers (including schools) could help children celebrate the fact that food makes them feel good but help them enjoy food and eating without eating beyond satiety.

People have a remarkable ability to learn to love the taste of almost anything, given enough time (Bacon, 2010). This has an implication for converting food preferences. Children who have a strong preference for processed foods and fast food can convert their tastes toward wholesome foods. Because it may take 10 to 20 exposures before a child accepts a new food (Birch, Johnson, & Fisher, 1995), caregivers need to be patient. They need to introduce the food to children, eating it themselves without negatively commenting on it, involving the children with preparing it, all while not pressuring them to eat it. This is a form of covert control (J. Ogden, Reynolds, & Smith, 2006), as discussed in the Trust Model section of this chapter.

The fifth component of HAES is "solving the weight problem." Fighting fat has not made fat go away. Becoming thinner will not make people healthier or happier (Bacon et al., 2005). Weight stigma causes damage to health and well-being, especially for children (Lemmens, Rutters, Born, & Westerterp-Plantenga, 2011). Fighting fat causes divisiveness between heavy and thin children, as heavy children measure themselves against others and outside standards. *Fat talk*, self-disparaging statements about being heavy (e.g., "I'm so fat!") that are meant to elicit contrary responses by others (e.g., "No you're not!"), adds to the divisiveness and stigma surrounding fat. Sometimes children and adults find it socially acceptable to tell thin individuals, "I hate you because you're thin." Obviously, this can be damaging to the self-esteem and social identity of thin children. Solving the weight problem entails not judging the self and others by size as well as encouraging positive health behaviors for people of all sizes. Following these paths will avoid stigmatizing people and give both heavy and thin people the attention and support they deserve.

Positive Psychology Paradigm

Positive psychology, a perspective rooted in *hygiology* (i.e., the promotion of health), is a catalyst for preventing psychological distress and promoting lifelong emotional, physical, social, and psychological well-being. This paradigm can be integrated effectively into schools, benefitting educators and students (Snyder & Lopez, 2007).

Positive psychology serves to help people identify, amplify, and nurture their strengths and use these strengths to foster pleasurable, engaging, and meaningful lives—in other words, to flourish (Seligman & Csikszentmihalyi, 2000). People who flourish appreciate and see beauty within themselves, others, and nature. They strive to continually grow within the context of accepting who they are. Their positivity breeds the desire and tendency to help others, creativity, flexible thinking, interpersonal enhancement, the ability to generate novel solutions to their problems, and proactive coping. They nourish themselves by tuning in to their needs and taking care of their body, mind, and spirit. Flourishing cannot be nurtured by focusing on negative characteristics or treating pathology. It can only be nurtured by teaching adaptive characteristics.

Positive psychology and the characteristics of flourishing have been applied to body image and eating behavior (Tylka, 2011a; Wood-Barcalow, Tylka, & Augustus-Horvath, 2010). *Body appreciation*, an important facet of positive body image, is uniquely associated with well-being, even after controlling for low levels of negative body image (Avalos, Tylka, & Wood-Barcalow, 2005). Similarly, intuitive eating contributes unique variance in well-being after the influence of low levels of disordered eating is considered (Tylka & Wilcox, 2006). Thus, moving beyond preventing body image disturbance and EDs to enhancing positive body image and intuitive eating can enhance students' well-being.

Similar to HAES, the positive psychology paradigm argues that individuals are more likely to engage in healthy behaviors if they like their body rather than dislike it. Research supports this assertion: Individuals are more likely to engage in healthy and balanced eating if they initially respect and appreciate their body rather than abuse it or feel shameful toward it (Avalos & Tylka, 2006).

Specific features of positive body image have been identified through qualitative and quantitative research on adolescent and adult females and males who hold a positive body image (Avalos & Tylka, 2006; Frisén & Holmqvist, 2010; Wood-Barcalow et al., 2010). One core feature is body appreciation—gratitude related to the function, health, and features of the body.

Another core feature is *body acceptance and love*—being comfortable with how they are packaged. A third core feature of positive body image is being able to *broadly conceptualize beauty*—not holding beauty to a narrow culturally defined Western standard, such as a thin body for women or a muscular and lean body for men (Tylka, 2011a). Broadly conceptualizing external beauty helps students feel beautiful on the inside. The core feature of *inner beauty* includes happiness and joy as well as optimistic thoughts about themselves.

The final core feature of a positive body image is being able to *filter information in a body-protective manner* (Wood-Barcalow et al., 2010). Confronted daily with many appearance-related media images and messages as well as others' comments directed at their body and self, individuals must choose whether to accept or reject each bit of information. Those with a positive body image regularly engage in protective filtering, whereby they hold a schema that helps them accept most positive information, preserving their positive body image, and reject most negative information that, if internalized, would harm their body image. Protective filtering, however, is not foolproof. Because of the preponderance of media messages and images as well as others' appearance-related comments, it is unrealistic to believe that students who have a positive body image can reject all negative information. Therefore, this information at times may bypass their protective filter and be internalized. This may manifest as a "bad body image day," whereby students may need caregivers' assistance in challenging this mentality. It is encouraging that students can move from a negative body image to a positive body image. Many of the participants in Wood-Barcalow et al.'s (2010) study at one point had a negative body image and successfully transitioned to a positive body image via developing their protective filter.

Unconditional body acceptance from important others, which could include peers and educators, helps promote positive body image (Avalos & Tylka, 2006; Frisén & Holmqvist, 2010; Tylka, 2011a). Girls and boys with positive body image tend to not be immersed in environments that prioritize thinness or muscularity; weight and body shape are not frequent topics of conversation within their social networks. They feel loved, special, and valued for their authentic inner qualities like their personality, sense of humor, creativity, and intellect.

Media literacy also promotes positive body image (Frisén & Holmqvist, 2010; Wood-Barcalow et al., 2010). Girls and boys with a positive body image are able to thoughtfully analyze and critique the images, messages, motives, and methods media use to entertain, inform, and persuade society (Frisén & Holmqvist, 2010).

Cultivating positive body image in the school system could have many personal and social benefits for students (Frisén & Holmqvist, 2010; Wood-Barcalow et al., 2010). As indicated in this research, students who hold a positive body image seek out friends who also accept their bodies, proactively shaping their social networks. They avoid or at least minimize their exposure to media that endorse a narrow definition of beauty. They encourage others to love their bodies, which in turn helps them feel even more appreciative and respectful of their own body. They do not partake in fat talk and often inform others of the destructiveness of this type of discourse. They are confident and assert themselves when needed. They take pride in listening to their body's needs and making decisions to promote their health more so than their appearance. They engage in pleasurable exercise and adaptive stress relief (e.g., meditation, writing poetry) on a regular basis. They tend to eat intuitively and healthy foods that help their body perform well. These behaviors help them maintain a stable weight, which often is in the normal range. They typically avoid behaviors that could harm their body, such as smoking.

INTEGRATING MODELS TO FORM A WORKING FRAMEWORK FOR SCHOOLS

The trust model, the HAES model, and the positive psychology paradigm can guide school personnel as they facilitate intuitive eating and mind–body connection for students, helping them arrive at the "adaptive core" of our model (see Figure 1.4). Cutting across these models are distinct themes and strategies the liaison can use to provide a framework for a healthy student approach. These themes and strategies are presented below. Chapters 4 through 6, this volume, provide empirically supported programs that help educators translate these themes into practice.

Focus on Promoting Health Rather Than Avoiding Obesity

Educators need to focus on the science of what is helpful (i.e., promoting health) and harmful (i.e., antiobesity programs, focusing on weight, dieting) to children. Antiobesity campaigns, such as BMI screening, weight-related report cards, and messages emphasizing the dangers of carrying excess weight set children up for a lifetime of hating their body (Bacon, 2010). Children who hate their body are more likely to abuse it—not treat it with respect, which could translate into inappropriate nourishment and activity. Further, antiobesity programs ignore thin children, who may have similarly unhealthy habits or may be maintaining their low weights through damaging diets or obsessive exercise, while stigmatizing heavy children, leaving them susceptible to being pathologized, bullied, and teased. Heavy children then may turn to food to cope with this stress and eat in the absence of hunger (Lemmens et al., 2011), or turn away from food and develop ED symptoms (Neumark-Sztainer et al., 2002). Thin children may be told that they are hated because of their size, straining social relationships. Fat myths that children hear in the media need to be debunked in the classroom and in the home. The liaison would need to ensure that parents receive similar messages as the students.

Applying the trust model ideas, schools could include mostly healthy options in the cafeterias, largely offering balanced meals with a lean protein source, fresh fruit or vegetables, whole-grain foods, and dairy. Science teachers could teach children the basics of healthy nutrition (what protein, fat, and carbohydrates each do for the body). A description and instructions on constructing well-balanced meals and snacks that include a protein source; carbohydrates; fruits, vegetables, or both; dairy–calcium; and fat could be posted in the cafeteria, integrated into the curriculum, and included in a handout distributed to parents. Cafeteria personnel should not pressure children to eat certain foods or to "clean their plate." Students could select the foods (and amount of each given food) from the array of options in front of them. Only water could be available in beverage machines and fountains. Vending machines could include produce and flavorful healthy options.

Home economics (also known as human ecology, family and consumer sciences) educators could have students prepare vegetables grown in school gardens or provided by farms in the local community, getting students involved in harvesting, cleaning, cooking, and eating the produce. These educators could help children understand where their food (processed vs. wholesome) comes from. To further promote health, health educators could teach (a) intuitive eating principles and review how they are a healthier alternative than dieting, (b) that many body types can be healthy, (c) that health is associated with behaviors rather than weight, and (d) that health is more important than weight. Health and science educators can help children understand more nutritious versions of their favorite foods (e.g., a high fiber and protein chocolate bar). Health educators also could have children separately list five of their favorite nutrient-dense foods and share their food lists with other children. Hearing that other children enjoy healthy foods could reinforce their consumption of these foods. Health educators can also have children practice stress management exercises (e.g., deep breathing exercises, meditation, yoga), reveal the health benefits of these exercises as children practice them, and ask children to report how they feel afterward (Serwacki & Cook-Cottone, 2012). Discussing that eating in the absence of hunger does not make stress and negative feelings go away would be helpful information for children. School nurses can reinforce these messages through presentations.

Educators need to create and maintain regular opportunities for physical activity (within the curriculum and as extracurricular options). Physical education (PE) teachers need to ensure that there are enough activities so that children of all body types can participate and enjoy. They also could encourage children to integrate short bursts of activity in their day, such as dancing to music, playing basketball if they have an outdoor hoop, chasing their pets during a game of fetch, playing jump rope, riding their bicycle, going on a walk with a friend, and swimming. Physical education teachers could direct children to reflect on what their body can do during the exercise—children can focus away from their appearance and focus in on how amazing their body feels and the various functions it can perform. They also could reveal the nonappearance-related benefits of moving, such as having time for themselves, stress relief, improved mood and energy, setting up challenges to do more, and (if done with another person) social connections. Physical education teachers could have children generate a list of five physical activities they like to do, and they can share with other children the activities they chose. Hearing the various activities other children like to do can provide ideas for new activities to try. Children can find others who like similar activities, which can spur the formation of teams or groups.

In an effort to focus on health and not weight, school personnel need to remove terminology focused on weight. First, they need to confront their own biases regarding weight and reinvest their understanding of health within an antagonistic culture. They need to avoid words like *overweight* and *obese*, which promote judgment and stigma. School administrators need to enforce an "anti–fat talk" policy. Children first need to be informed of the negative effects of this discourse. Certain school personnel, that is, PE educators, cafeteria staff, those who supervise lunch and recess, school psychologists, may be more likely to encounter fat talk, and they need to be vigilant in detecting this discourse. School personnel could encourage the students affected by fat talk conversations to engage in a deeper form of communication, reminding students of its negative effects. School personnel must enforce zero-tolerance policies regarding weight-based victimization as well as be available and approachable to students who are victims of such bullying. School personnel need to recognize that they are role models for their students, challenge their own size bias, and incorporate healthy habits and attitudes into their lifestyle.

Practice Intuitive and Mindful Eating

Home economics educators could have students practice intuitive eating and mindfulness as they eat the foods they have just prepared. Health and home economics educators could help children identify how certain foods impact their body. Beyond what a food initially tastes like, how do they feel after they eat it? an hour after they eat it? 2 hours after they eat it? If they overeat their favorite food, do they feel sluggish? Are they hungry again soon after they eat ice cream? A salad with chicken? Knowing this may help children eat less of this food—not to restrict calories but to feel better. Thus, raising children's awareness of how certain foods affect their body can direct them toward eating to honor their health. Before lunch, school personnel could encourage children to notice their hunger level and eat until they feel neutral or full but not stuffed. Instead of portraying hunger as something to be resisted, they could present physical hunger and satiety as important bodily signals to respect and honor. This could help children realize that hunger is not the enemy but rather a friendly, helpful voice within them that urges them to take care of themselves. Science teachers can discuss sensory specific satiety, reinforcing the principle that the body no longer registers pleasure after a few bites of a tasty food, as well as eating the food they desire releases cholecystokinin, which makes them feel satisfied sooner and less likely to overeat.

Health and PE educators could provide simple guidelines to children. First, they could help children generate a list of activities they love to do, making sure they think of activities that they enjoy that pass time, help them relax, and include others. When children notice the drive to eat, they could be encouraged to pause and ask themselves two questions: "What is my hunger level?" and "What am I trying to satisfy?" The hunger scale, such as the one provided in the Regulation of Cues (ROC) intervention (see Chapter 7, this volume) could be incorporated into the curriculum to encourage children to be aware of and listen to their hunger and satiety signals. If their satiety level is at a 3 or higher (e.g., on a satiety scale ranging from 1 to 5, with a 5 indicating that they are *very full*), and they notice that they are sad, frustrated, lonely, bored, or nervous, then they could choose an activity on their list that best matches their emotion. If their feeling emerges from the need to sort out a tough situation that involves others, simple assertiveness skills could be helpful.

Schools can enforce a "no electronics" policy in the cafeteria to keep children from eating mindlessly while playing with these devices. Cafeteria monitors should be instructed to not encourage children to engage in behaviors that interfere with intuitive eating (e.g., "You must eat all that," "You need to hurry up and eat"). Teachers who have lunchroom duty could eat their lunch with students (this should be the same lunch offered by the cafeteria), providing support while modeling mindful and healthful eating. These teachers also could do a mindful eating exercise during lunch: The teacher would guide children to choose a food on their plate that looks particularly appealing, take a bite, notice how the food tastes, then swallow. Pauses in between these steps could facilitate slower eating. An activity that may be useful to help children become aware that food tastes better initially, then loses its luster over time or when the child is full, is to pass out a small treat (e.g., chocolate piece, potato chip) before lunch and have children rate their hunger level and how good the food tastes on a scale ranging from 1 (*tastes so-so or worse*) to 5 (*tastes amazing*). Then the same activity is performed after lunch, and children can see how their hunger levels influence their taste of food. Given sensory-specific satiety, children could enjoy a few bites of their favorite food, eating mindfully, and stop once their pleasure subsides.

Promote Positive Body Image

Health educators, in particular, could cover the core features of positive body image (i.e., body appreciation, body acceptance and love, broadly conceptualizing beauty, focusing on inner beauty, filtering information in a body protective manner) and design several activities to promote them. For example, students could label the various functions their body does for them as well as note their body's nuances that make them unique and write something positive about these body areas. Coaches can help children focus on how their bodies function ("Wow, your body can do a lot for you; look at how it can move") rather than appear ("You need to lose weight so you have the right body for this sport").

Students could be reassured that they do not have to be completely satisfied with all aspects of their body but unconditionally accept it and love it for what it is. They could be asked to identify people, pets, and things they love and then ask whether these people and things are "perfect" according to societal attractiveness standards. Health educators could draw the connection to students' own body attitudes—they can love their body even though it is not perfect. Science educators could discuss the genetic limitations for body type and composition.

Health educators can emphasize that what makes people beautiful is carrying the self well, such as being well-groomed and confident—a variety of weights and shapes can be beautiful. Students can be encouraged to "rock what they've got" and treat their body with respect by choosing clothing and hairstyles that help them feel good about themselves and confidently express their body. Inner beauty can be fostered by having students articulate their character strengths. Social studies educators can have students explore how appearance ideals change over time and are different between cultures, to emphasize that there is not a universal ideal body type for women or men.

Health educators could direct students to recognize and acknowledge when they are having a bad body image day; this awareness could serve as a signal for them to redirect their thoughts to foster and protect their positive body image. Educators also need to teach students how to contextualize this negative information by placing the negativity back to its source (e.g., "It is not okay to talk about my body; please stop") rather than internalizing it (e.g., "I do need to lose weight, don't I?"), which helps nullify it. Health and art educators can further help students realize that most media images of women and men are digitally altered to appear flawless and acknowledge that these ideals are unattainable and contribute to negative body image if they are internalized.

It would benefit students with a negative (or even neutral) body image to know it is possible to adopt a positive body image. Health educators can encourage students to identify reasons to hold a positive body image, such as avoiding the psychological and emotional distress that accompanies a negative body image. To thrive, students need positive peer networks that focus on inner strengths, body functionality, and social support rather than appearance and body disparagement, such as fat talk. Such opportunities need to be built into the school systems and communities. They could set up programs in which older students mentor younger students by discussing the characteristics and benefits of positive body image. Eventually, the learners could become the teachers for a new group of protégés, so that they pay it forward by affecting their environment in a growth-enhancing way. This continuity from learner to teacher also may help strengthen their own commitment to holding a positive body image, which is needed given the strong and continuous Western cultural pull to be dissatisfied with the body. Because children learn to have a positive body image through observing others with a positive body image, all school personnel should consciously work on adopting the characteristics of a positive body image and model them for their students.

SUMMARY: APPLIED EXAMPLES USING THE THREE THEMES

The three themes that cut across these foundational models (i.e., promoting health rather than avoiding obesity, practicing intuitive and mindful eating, and nurturing positive body image) can be integrated into schools to enhance the physical and psychological health of their students. To summarize, we illustrate how these themes can be applied to enhance students' health within our two case examples: City Central Elementary School and Bayside High School (see Introduction, this volume, for a complete description of these schools).

City Central is an underfunded elementary school housed in an urban, high-crime, low socioeconomic status neighborhood that has little access to fresh produce. Bayside, in contrast, is a well-funded high school housed in an affluent, suburban, low-crime neighborhood that has a wealth of opportunities to purchase fresh produce and engage in community-based physical activity. Yet, each school brings forth its challenges, and the health of its students can be improved. Next, we turn the spotlight on how these schools can be enhanced through each of the three themes.

Promoting Health Rather Than Avoiding Obesity

School personnel at City Central first need to construct and implement a school wellness policy (see http://www.schoolwellnesspolicies.org/WellnessPolicies.html for model programs) that focuses on health promotion. They would need to replace their vending machines with water, whole-grain snacks, and produce (if possible). The cafeteria would need to begin serving well-balanced meals that meet the U.S. Department of Agriculture requirements. The content of their nutrition presentations should be centered on promoting health and constructing balanced meals through the trust model rather than mentioning weight or body fat (note that Jacqueline began skipping meals after she received the message that "too much food can make you fat" at a school nutrition presentation). The school could forge a collaboration with the local community garden to bring fresh produce to students. City Central can hold a school-family based program in which parents are introduced to the wellness policy and ways to promote children's health and given material to take home and practice with their child. Parents could receive information on healthy foods that are inexpensive (e.g., old-fashioned oatmeal in the tub, eggs, brown rice, potatoes, apples, bananas, garbanzo beans, frozen berries, frozen vegetables, broccoli, canned tuna, watermelon, whole-grain pasta, baby carrots, low-fat milk, canned refried beans, whole wheat bread), and schools can provide recipes and sample grocery lists that use these ingredients.

Bayside has different challenges. Although Bayside emphasizes health and nutrition through a school wellness policy that is strict on offering nutritious foods and beverages, they permit and even perhaps encourage students to focus on weight (i.e., being lean and controlling food intake). This emphasis needs to be modified and redirected to health. Myths that fat people are unhealthy need to be challenged (especially with coaches). Stress management strategies also need to be taught, as students perceive academic-related pressure that could interfere with their well-being.

Intuitive and Mindful Eating

Students at both City Central and Bayside need to learn and practice intuitive eating and mindful eating. Breakfast and lunch at City Central would be great opportunities for school personnel to teach and practice intuitive and mindful eating strategies with students to ensure that they are learning tools to prevent eating in the absence of hunger. Teachers could be directed to more effective reward and punishment strategies that are not tied to food, eating, weight, or exercise. At Bayside, school personnel could debunk myths that dieting and controlling food intake lead to weight loss and emphasize that intuitive eating and mindful eating are more effective strategies for physical and psychological health (Bacon et al., 2005).

Positive Body Image

Students at both City Central and Bayside would benefit from learning strategies to have a positive body image. Programs that enhance tolerance of and appreciation for diverse body sizes should be integrated within both schools. Additionally, personnel at both schools should enforce a zero-tolerance policy for weight-related teasing–bullying. It is imperative that negative stereotypes of weight floating around the school, such as those offered by coaches at Bayside, be replaced with messages to appreciate your body and treat it well by nourishing it and engaging in self-care behaviors. For example, coaches could focus on having students appreciate how their body functions during sport. Fat talk and other body talk should be prohibited, with students receiving an explanation on why that discourse is not permitted and detrimental. School personnel at Bayside should challenge the idea that something can be "perfect" (including media images of models and actors) and to help shift students from maladaptive perfectionism (i.e., unrealistic goals) to adaptive perfectionism (i.e., high standards that are realistic; Slaney, Rice, Mobley, Trippi, & Ashby, 2001).

A school pledge is a no-cost way schools could remind students of the basic principles that cut across these foundational models. The HAES "live well pledge" (Bacon, 2010) may be a simple yet effective way to help students absorb the themes of focusing on health, intuitive–mindful eating, and positive body image:

> Today, I will try to feed myself when I am hungry.
> Today, I will try to be attentive to how foods taste and make me feel.
> Today, I will try to choose foods that I like and that make me feel good.
> Today, I will try to find an enjoyable way to move my body.
> Today, I will try to look kindly at my body and to treat it with love and
>   respect. (p. 273)

Within City Central and Bayside, this pledge could be discussed and reinforced by health and PE educators, as well as coaches and nurses, and posted in the gym and cafeteria.

4

PILLAR I: INTUITIVE EATING AND NUTRITION

Healthy eating is important for children of all shapes and sizes (Daníelsdóttir, Burgard, & Oliver-Pyatt, 2010; Hayes, 2010). Helping students stay healthy is a fundamental part of the mission of schools, as a body of research shows that the health of students is linked to their academic success (Centers for Disease Control and Prevention [CDC], 2011b). The World Health Organization (2011) defined *health* as "a state of complete physical, mental and social well-being and not merely the absence of disease or infirmity." This chapter is divided into two parts: The first part describes the factors that influence healthy eating at school, and the second part presents examples of effective school-based programs.

DOI: 10.1037/14180-005
Healthy Eating in Schools: Evidence-Based Interventions to Help Kids Thrive, by C. P. Cook-Cottone, E. Tribole, and T. L. Tylka

FACTORS THAT INFLUENCE HEALTHY EATING AT SCHOOL

Schools can play a significant role in improving the eating behaviors of students. The school's environment, nutrition guidelines, food-related policies, characteristics of federally subsidized meals, nutrition education, and other activities that promote healthful eating and wellness are central to this mission (Briefel, Crepinsek, Cabili, Wilson, & Gleason, 2009).

Nutrition Guidelines and School Environment

The school environment and policies can have a large impact on the quality of diets eaten by students because youth consume, on average, 35% of their daily food intake at school (Briefel et al., 2009). Most children and adolescents do not meet the U.S. Dietary Guidelines for Americans, which, in brief, advise increasing recommended levels of fruits, vegetables, whole grains, and calcium as well as decreasing sodium, sugar, saturated fats, and calories from fat. Furthermore, children and adolescents tend to have diets high in added sugar, which contributes approximately 18% of their total daily calories (CDC, 2011b).

In response to growing concerns over obesity, the U.S. Congress directed the CDC with the Institute of Medicine (IOM) to evaluate and make recommendations to help create school nutrition standards for the availability, sale, content, and consumption of foods at school. This culminated into two separate reports. The first report was IOM's (2007) *Nutrition Standards for Foods in Schools: Leading the Way Toward Healthier Youth*, the guiding principles of which are summarized in Exhibit 4.1. Subsequently, the CDC (2011b) issued its *School Health Guidelines to Promote Healthy Eating and Physical Activity* report, which resulted in nine evidence-based guidelines for schools, kindergarten through 12th grade. The CDC guidelines integrated the IOM's recommendations, the Dietary Guidelines for Americans, the Physical Activity Guidelines for Americans, and the Healthy People 2020 guidelines (see Exhibit 4.2).

The following section describes three of the key recommendations from the CDC (2011b) school guidelines to encourage healthy eating. (For the details of and the rationale for the specific guidelines recommended for schools, see these reports: the IOM's *Nutrition Standards for Foods in Schools: Leading the Way Toward Healthier Youth; Nutrition Standards and Meal Requirements for National School Lunch and Breakfast Programs;* and *School Meals: Building Blocks for Healthy Children;* and the CDC's *School Health Guidelines to Promote Healthy Eating and Physical Activity* (CDC, 2011b; IOM, 2007, 2008, 2010).

The first CDC (2011b) guideline that we discuss is Guideline 3 from Exhibit 4.2, "Provide a quality school meal program and ensure that students

EXHIBIT 4.1
Institute of Medicine's 10 Guiding Principles for Eating Healthy at School

1. The present and future health and well-being of school-age children are profoundly affected by dietary intake and the maintenance of a healthy weight.
2. Schools contribute to current and life-long health and dietary patterns and are uniquely positioned to model and reinforce healthful eating behaviors in partnership with parents, teachers, and the broader community.
3. Because all foods and beverages available on the school campus represent significant caloric intake, they should be designed to meet nutritional standards.
4. Foods and beverages have health effects beyond those related to vitamins, minerals, and other known individual components.
5. Implementation of nutrition standards for foods and beverages offered in schools will likely require clear policies; technical and financial support; a monitoring, enforcement, and evaluation program; and new food and beverage products.
6. The federally reimbursable school nutrition programs should be the primary source of foods and beverages offered at school.
7. All foods and beverages offered on the school campus should contribute to an overall healthful eating environment.
8. Nutrition standards should be established for foods and beverages offered outside the federally reimbursable school nutrition programs.
9. The recommended nutrition standards should be based on the Dietary Guidelines for Americans, with consideration given to other relevant science-based resources.
10. The nutrition standards should apply to foods and beverages offered to all school-age children.

Note. From *Nutrition Standards for Foods in Schools: Leading the Way Toward Healthier Youth,* 2007, Washington, DC: National Academies Press. Copyright 2007 by the National Academy of Sciences. Reprinted with permission.

EXHIBIT 4.2
Centers for Disease Control and Prevention's 2011 School Health Guidelines to Promote Healthy Eating and Physical Activity

1. Use a coordinated approach to develop, implement, and evaluate healthy eating and physical activity policies and practices.
2. Establish school environments that support healthy eating and physical activity.
3. Provide a quality school meal program and ensure that students have only appealing, healthy food and beverage choices offered outside of the school meal program.
4. Implement a comprehensive physical activity program with quality physical education as the cornerstone.
5. Implement health education that provides students with the knowledge, attitudes, skills, and experiences needed for healthy eating and physical activity.
6. Provide students with health, mental health, and social services to address healthy eating, physical activity, and related chronic disease prevention.
7. Partner with families and community members in the development and implementation of healthy eating and physical activity policies, practices, and programs.
8. Provide a school employee wellness program that includes healthy eating and physical activity services for all school staff members.
9. Employ qualified persons, and provide professional development opportunities for physical education, health education, nutrition services, and health, mental health, and social services staff members, as well as staff members who supervise recess, cafeteria time, and out-of-school–time programs.

Note. From "School Health Guidelines to Promote Healthy Eating and Physical Activity," 2011, *Morbidity and Mortality Weekly Report, 60,* pp. 1–76. In the public domain.

have only appealing, healthy food and beverage choices offered outside of the school meal program" (p. 21). The CDC recommended that schools model and reinforce healthy eating behaviors by ensuring that only nutritious and appealing foods and beverages are provided in all venues accessible to students. This guideline addresses the often contentious issue of competitive foods (i.e., foods and beverages from vending machines, snack bars, school stores, and fundraisers).

Schools must address competitive foods. Unlike school meals, competitive foods are largely exempt from federal nutrition standards. As a consequence, competitive foods are the principal source of the low-nutrient, energy-dense foods that students eat at school. The increase in the availability of competitive foods in schools is estimated to account for one fifth of the increase in body mass index (BMI) observed in adolescents during the past 10 years (Anderson & Butcher, 2005). The *Children's Food Environment State Indicator Report* (CDC, 2011a) found that 64.4% of high schools offered sugar drinks as competitive foods, 51.4% of middle and high schools offered less healthy competitive foods, and 49.0% of middle and high schools allowed advertising of less healthy foods.

There are two controversial issues regarding banning or limiting the use of low-nutritional value foods: (a) the concern that there would be a compensatory rebound effect on student eating behavior, and (b) the impact on school revenue. There is also concern that limiting low-nutrient foods in the school could backfire and would instead trigger an increased desire for those particular "forbidden" foods, resulting in compensatory eating outside of school. This concern stems from a body of research showing that when parents rigidly restrict a child's food in the interest of health and weight, it creates the opposite effect—an increased desire and consumption of the restricted foods, resulting in an overweight child.

To address this concern, Schwartz, Novak, and Fiore (2009) evaluated whether a school-wide policy limiting competitive foods would have a similar psychological effect by conducting a 2-year intervention study involving six middle schools. Three intervention schools removed snacks that were low in nutritional value, and the other three schools served as controls. Compared with the control schools, the intervention resulted in students eating snacks of higher nutritional value, without triggering compensatory eating at home. One explanation offered for this outcome is that the students' experience of having foods removed from school may be psychologically very different from that of a parent who restricts particular foods. It is possible that when some parents restrict children's access to high-fat or high-sugar foods, the implicit or explicit message may be that this is a punishment because the child is overweight. This carries much greater potential psychological distress for the child than an impersonal decision made by a board of education to change what is available to all students in the cafeteria. Another significant finding was that although prevalence of body dissatisfaction and dieting were "disturbingly high"[1] in these schools, there was no evidence that school-wide interventions to promote healthful eating perpetuated these problems—as there were no significant differences between the intervention and comparison schools. These findings suggest that implementing a school policy limiting foods of low-nutritional value would not inadvertently perpetuate unhealthy eating practices or body dissatisfaction.

In regard to the impact of limiting competitive foods on school revenue, a recent systematic review suggested that the majority of schools have been able to improve the nutritional quality of competitive foods without impacting their overall revenue (Story, Nanney, & Schwartz, 2009). Schools can also use the contracting process to improve the nutritional quality of competitive foods and beverages. Most middle and high school students (67% and 83%, respectively) attend schools that have beverage contracts. Schools that adopt strong nutrition standards for competitive foods should revise existing food and beverage contracts so that healthier options are available for students (CDC, 2011b).

The second CDC guideline that we discuss is part of Guideline 2 in Exhibit 4.2: "Establish school environments that support healthy eating" (CDC, 2011b, p. 18). The CDC recommended the following measures to create supportive environments in the cafeteria and classroom as well as to improve the psychosocial and eating atmosphere at school.

Changes can be made within the classroom environment. The CDC (2011b) recommended that student rewards and incentives should support health. Using food as reward is problematic for several reasons. This practice establishes an emotional connection between foods and accomplishments, and it has the potential to instill a lifetime habit of rewarding or self-soothing with food. Rewarding students with food during class can also encourage eating in the absence of hunger. A growing body of evidence indicates that eating in absence of hunger increases the risk of weight gain (Shomaker et al., 2010). Using food as an incentive also provides a mixed message to students, as it is not aligned with the promotion of healthy eating or self-attunement to cues of hunger and fullness. Therefore, student achievement or positive classroom behavior should only be rewarded with nonfood items (e.g., stickers) or privileges (e.g., extra time for recess). The Center for Science in the Public Interest created a free guide describing inexpensive nonfood rewards for the classroom, which is listed in the Suggested Resources section of this book.

Kubik, Lytle, and Story (2005) evaluated the impact of seven common school-wide food practices, which included using food as a reward or incentive, allowing students to eat and drink in class or in the hallways, and selling food for fundraising purposes. For every increase in the number of negative school-wide food practices (up to a total of seven), there was an associated

---

[1]Two thirds of girls reported wishing they could weigh less; half reported they were currently dieting.

significant increase of 10% in the students' BMI. The most prevalent practice reported in this study was using food as a reward for students.

School personnel can address the psychosocial environment. The school environment should encourage a healthy body image, shape, and size among all students, and staff members and should not tolerate weight-based teasing. Furthermore, the psychological environment should support all students in making healthy eating choices. Schools can take numerous steps to help shape a health-promoting psychological environment, such as (a) establishing a climate that encourages and does not stigmatize healthy eating, (b) adopting and enforcing a universal bullying prevention program that addresses weight discrimination and teasing, (c) displaying posters or other visual materials that feature a diverse combination of students being active and eating healthy, and (d) avoiding practices that single out students on the basis of body size or shape.

The eating environment can also be addressed. The school environment should allow students to pay attention to what they are eating in an enjoyable manner. Some ideas for this guideline include (a) providing an adequate amount of time to receive and eat a meal, with at least 10 min for eating breakfast and 20 min for eating lunch, after being seated; (b) providing recess before lunch; (c) decreasing student wait time in line for food purchases; (d) ensuring that students have access to free and well-maintained drinking fountains, to replace sugar-sweetened beverages; and (e) providing adequate and safe spaces and facilities for healthy eating, including tables and chairs of appropriate size.

Addressing the cafeteria environment is critical. Healthy food choices can be promoted by using marketing strategies. Nutritious foods can be placed within easy reach and in prominent places, such as near the cafeteria line, and fruits and vegetables can be moved to the front of the school meal serving line. The lighting in the serving area could be improved, and the salad bar can be placed near the cashier. Healthy eating through point-of-purchase promotions can be promoted. Pricing strategies—such as offering nutritious items at a reduced price—can be applied. School personnel can involve students in taste testing, as this strategy provides students with an opportunity to inform staff members which healthy food and beverage products they like and dislike. Vegetables and dip and wedged versions of fruits and vegetables can be offered in a la carte lines. School personnel can solicit and collect suggestions from students for meals and snack items that might be offered.

The third CDC (2011b) guideline that we discuss is part of Guideline 5 in Exhibit 4.2: "Implement health education that provides students with the knowledge, attitudes, skills, and experiences needed for healthy eating" (p. 33). A body of research indicates that nutrition education interventions are more effective in influencing eating behaviors if they (a) target specific behaviors, (b) focus on the interests of the students, (c) devote sufficient time to the intervention, (d) deliver clearly focused curricula, (e) involve multiple components by using a culturally sensitive social ecological approach, (f) include student self-assessments and multimedia technology tools, (g) link with the community, (h) provide staff training, (i) incorporate family involvement, and (j) implement healthful changes in the school environment to support behavior changes (Briggs, 2010; Roseman, Riddell, & Haynes, 2011).

The CDC recommends implementing a curriculum that addresses a clear set of behavioral outcomes that promote healthy eating. This curriculum will help students gain the knowledge and skills to achieve the following (including but not limited to): (a) eat a variety of whole grain products, fruits and vegetables, and nonfat or low-fat milk or equivalent milk products every day; (b) eat the appropriate amounts from each food group every day; (c) drink plenty of water and limit beverages high in added sugar; (d) limit the intake of fat and sugar; (e) eat breakfast every day; (f) eat healthy snacks; and (g) support others to eat healthy. Experiences in healthy eating can be further fostered by activities such as growing school gardens and participating in farm-to-school programs, which enrich the eating and educational experience by providing quality produce for salad bars and school lunch.

HEALTHY EATING IN OBESITY PREVENTION

Food choices and opportunities to eat at school extend beyond school meals, and the rise in obesity over the past few decades has been accompanied by a rise in the number of food options available throughout the school day (IOM, 2007). As a consequence, many school-based healthy eating programs focus on obesity prevention. Yet, if precautionary measures are not taken, obesity prevention programs that are created with the intention of promoting healthy eating may unwittingly create unhealthy eating practices, both of which can increase the risk of weight gain and eating disorders (EDs; Bacon, 2010). Given the growing concern about obesity and the concomitant public health campaigns, it is important that schools and young people know that dieting and disordered eating behaviors can be not only harmful to health but also counterproductive to obesity prevention (Neumark-Sztainer, Wall, Larson, Eisenberg, & Loth, 2011). Obesity, EDs, and unhealthy dieting practices among youth are a serious public health concern due to their high prevalence and adverse effects on nutritional status, as well as psychosocial and physical health, underscored by the findings from Project EAT III, a 10-year longitudinal study.

Project EAT III tracked the dieting and disordered eating behaviors of nearly 2,300 adolescents for a decade into their young adulthood (Neumark-Sztainer et al., 2011). The prevalence of dieting and disordered eating behaviors was rampant—about 50% of girls and 25% of the boys reported dieting, and the prevalence of dieting remained constant through young adulthood. Particularly worrisome was the large escalation in extreme weight-control behaviors among youth transitioning from adolescence to young adulthood—including use of laxatives, diet pills, and self-induced vomiting. This decade-long study indicates that these behaviors in adolescence are not just a phase or rite of passage. Rather, early dieting and disordered eating appear to set the stage for more problems into adulthood. Together, the findings suggest a need for both early prevention and treatment interventions.

There is strong empirical support for integrating efforts to prevent obesity and EDs, which suggests that these weight-related disorders are not distinct from each other and have a number of shared risk factors (Darby et al., 2009; Haines & Neumark-Sztainer, 2006; Neumark-Sztainer, 2005). First, body dissatisfaction is prospectively associated with poorer nutritional and physical activity behaviors in both adolescent girls and boys (Austin, 2011). It is a shared risk factor, rather than just a consequence of weight gain and obesity. Body dissatisfaction is also an established risk factor for EDs. Second, dieting behaviors appear to be causally linked to both obesity and EDs (Haines & Neumark-Sztainer, 2006). A large 3-year population cohort study on adolescents found that dieting is the most important predictor of new EDs (Patton, Selzer, Coffey, Carlin, & Wolfe, 1999). Furthermore, Field et al. (2003) found that the odds of binge eating increased by a factor of six- to 12-fold among boys and girls who dieted compared with their nondieting peers. Therefore, it would be counterproductive and harmful to emphasize dieting within obesity prevention programs (O'Dea, 2005). Third, weight-related teasing is associated with both binge eating and other disordered eating behaviors (e.g., purging, restricting), suggesting that it may have potential relevance for the development of obesity and EDs (Aubie & Jarry, 2009; Haines & Neumark-Sztainer, 2006).

Individuals may cross over from one weight-related disorder to another. A case-control study designed to identify factors associated with the development of bulimia nervosa found that the odds of being obese as a child were 3 times higher among individuals with bulimia, compared with healthy controls (Darby et al., 2009). Also, overweight adolescents are more likely than their nonoverweight peers to engage in unhealthy weight-control behaviors, such as diet pill use, vomiting, and laxative use.

What Are the Unintended Consequences of Obesity Prevention Programs?

It is surprising that few child obesity prevention studies have been evaluated on their impact on eating disordered symptoms and behaviors or psychosocial well-being, which is important given the interrelated nature of EDs and obesity. A recent review of child obesity prevention trials revealed minimal assessment of eating-disorder behaviors and risk factors, such as body dissatisfaction and dieting (Austin, 2011).

Similarly, a review of 53 school-based obesity intervention programs revealed that only seven of them (13%) reported their impact on the psychosocial well-being of children (Van Wijnen, Wendel-Vos, Wammes, & Bemelmans, 2009). Another study revealed that just a single exposure to a prodieting message elicited greater levels of established risk factors for eating pathology (Roehrig, Thompson, & Cafri, 2008). Examples of the prodieting messages used in the study that should be avoided in schools include (a) consulting a BMI chart to determine ideal weight, (b) choosing lower fat and lower calorie foods to attain or maintain low body weight, (c) and reducing caloric intake by limiting portions and avoiding going back for seconds.

What to Do in Obesity Prevention Programs

The 2010 Academy for Eating Disorders (AED) Guidelines for Childhood Obesity Prevention Programs recommend that care be taken to minimize any harm that might result from the implementation of obesity prevention programs (Daníelsdóttir et al., 2010) and include the following:

- Focus on health, not weight—where the ultimate goal is the health and well-being of all children.
- Focus only on modifiable behaviors (e.g., physical activity, intake of sugar-sweetened beverages, teasing, time spent watching television), where there is evidence that such modification will improve children's health.
- Weight must be handled as carefully as any other individually identifiable health information. Weighing students should only be performed when there is a clear and compelling need for the information (e.g., update health record for sport participation or in collaboration with health care providers for monitoring).

Expanding the vision of obesity prevention programs to include the prevention of EDs may help ensure that they promote overall health. The fields of obesity prevention and ED prevention also share the core recommendations of promoting and sustaining healthful and balanced nutritional and physical-activity behaviors (Austin, 2011).

The types of interventions that have the potential to reduce the incidence of obesity and EDs are ones that increase intuitive eating, body appreciation, healthy movement, and media literacy while decreasing rigid dieting behaviors, body dissatisfaction, internalization of media ideals, and weight-related teasing and bullying, which are described in more depth in Chapters 7 and 8 of this volume (Austin, 2011; Darby et al., 2009; Haines & Neumark-Sztainer,

2006). Indeed, for an integrated approach, the AED recommended including positive behaviors aimed at balanced nutrition, mindful eating, and promoting positive body image (Daníelsdóttir et al., 2010).

To date, emerging evidence from school-based interventions that focus on health rather than weight is encouraging—it appears that prevention of overweight and disordered weight-control behaviors and symptoms in students can be achieved together in a single program and is cost-effective. For example, Planet Health, a 2-year whole school intervention designed by Harvard researchers to promote healthful nutrition, promote physical activity, and reduce television viewing resulted in lowered rates of disordered eating and bulimia (Austin, 2011; Austin, Field, Wiecha, Peterson, & Gortmaker, 2005).

What Works—Intervention Studies

Although there have been several systematic reviews on school interventions to promote healthy eating and prevent obesity—their effectiveness is inconsistent in part because the intervention components vary considerably (Katz, O'Connell, Njike, Yeh, & Nawaz, 2008). A Cochrane systematic review of interventions lasting more than 1 year and designed to prevent obesity in children and adolescents found little evidence to support school-based initiatives (Kropski, Keckley, & Jensen, 2008). Another systematic review on school-based interventions that focused on modifying eating behavior revealed that only six out of 25 were able to demonstrate significant changes (Sharma, 2011). It is surprising that very few interventions include a component on identifying and responding to hunger and satiety cues (i.e., intuitive eating). However, given the growing body of evidence indicating that eating in the absence of hunger increases the risks of overeating and weight gain, it would seem that hunger awareness–intuitive-eating training would be an important component of any healthy eating program (Shomaker et al., 2010). Emerging research indicates this is a significant issue for young people.

After adapting the Intuitive Eating Scale (Tylka, 2006) for an adolescent audience, Dockendorff, Petrie, Greenleaf, and Martin (2011) investigated intuitive eating with 515 middle school students. Dockendorff et al. found that intuitive eating was inversely related to body mass index, body dissatisfaction, negative affect, pressure for thinness, and internalization of media body ideals; it was also positively related to life satisfaction and experiencing greater positive affect. Four key aspects of intuitive eating emerged: (a) awareness of internal hunger–satiety cues, (b) trust in internal hunger–satiety cues, (c) unconditional permission to eat, and (d) eating for physical rather than emotional reasons.

The interventions described in the following section were selected because they are excellent examples of evidenced-based programs that promote healthy eating without focusing on weight, integrating the above characteristics of intuitive eating. In addition, they are cost-effective, novel, effective in reducing risk of both EDs and obesity, and effective with high-risk groups (such as low socioeconomic status or girls).

Planet Health

The Planet Health program was developed by researchers at Harvard University in collaboration with teachers and principals of public middle schools (Gortmaker et al., 1999). The aims of this interdisciplinary curriculum are to improve cardiovascular health and lower the prevalence of obesity among sixth- through eighth-grade students. Notably, this intervention focuses on improving the activity and eating behaviors of all students, without singling out those who are obese. Also, weight status and obesity are not explicitly addressed in the curriculum, in an effort to avoid stigmatizing overweight youth. Similarly, weight control, EDs, and dieting are not mentioned in order to prevent students from learning dangerous methods that they might try to use to lose weight (Austin et al., 2005). Extreme dieting behavior was measured both at baseline and follow-up periods to assess whether the intervention could have produced unintended side effects.

The curriculum was designed to fit easily into existing classes and to provide teaching materials that are easy to use. One Planet Health innovation is stressing the importance of spending less time watching television, based on evidence that television viewing contributes to obesity because it is a sedentary act and exposes viewers to relentless commercials highlighting the appeal of eating high-calorie, high-fat, nutrient-poor foods (A. Franks et al., 2007).

A 21-month randomized controlled study evaluating the effectiveness of Planet Health in 10 public middle schools found that the intervention reduced the odds of obesity in girls through prevention and remission during 2 school years (Gortmaker et al., 1999). Compared with the control schools, there was a reduction in television watching for both girls and boys and an increase in fruit and vegetable consumption among girls. In addition, girls who participated in Planet Health were less likely to report unhealthy weight-control behaviors.

In 2005, the Planet Health researchers published a follow-up study that evaluated the impact of the Planet Health intervention on risk of engaging in disordered weight-control behaviors after a 21-month follow-up (Austin et al., 2005). The results were encouraging. The Planet Health intervention had an unanticipated protective effect on disordered eating behaviors. Nondieting girls in the intervention schools were 12 times less likely to report the use of purging or diet pills to control their weight compared with the girls in control schools.

A larger study that used the Planet Health intervention revealed that the risk of vomiting or using laxatives or diet pills to control weight at a 2-year follow-up was reduced by two thirds in girls in the intervention schools compared with the girls in the control schools (Austin et al., 2007). There is a caveat. The Planet Health program was designed to promote healthful eating and physical activity to reduce obesity, not EDs. So the researchers were not able to test what specific aspects of the program prevented disordered weight-control behaviors. However, these findings strengthen the merits of implementing programs that promote healthful behaviors appropriate for all youth and not just those who are overweight.

New Moves

New Moves is an innovative program created to address the broad spectrum of weight-related problems among high school girls (Neumark-Sztainer, Friend, et al., 2010). It was developed after a needs assessment indicated that girls wanted an opportunity to learn about healthy eating and exercise in a supportive setting. New Moves is based on the theoretical foundation of social cognitive theory, which targets socioenvironmental factors, personal factors, and behavioral factors to bring about changes in physical activity, eating, and weight-control behaviors. Motivational interviewing is used to help advance the girls through the stages of change (precontemplation, contemplation, and preparation stages) for targeted behavior change. The development of the program was guided by extensive research and pilot testing (Neumark-Sztainer, Friend, et al., 2010). The full program is available without charge, and its details are provided in the Suggested Resources section of this book.

The core objectives of New Moves are to "Be Fit" (bring about positive change in physical activity and eating behaviors to improve weight status and overall health), "Be Fab" (help girls function in a thin-oriented society and feel good about themselves), and "Be Fueled" (help girls avoid unhealthy weight-control behaviors; Neumark-Sztainer, Friend, et al., 2010). Be Fit provides an environment in which all girls feel comfortable being physically active, aiming for moderate-to-vigorous activity levels for at least 50% of the class period. There is a focus on lifestyle activities such as dancing, yoga, walking, and strength training. Be Fab aims to improve body image and self-esteem by providing strategies on psychosocial issues such as media influences and peer pressure. The format is interactive, with small-group discussions and hands-on activities. Be Fueled component uses a nondieting approach toward healthy eating and focuses on behaviors that could be sustained, such as eating breakfast daily and increasing fruit and vegetable consumption. Taste testing healthy foods and beverages are also incorporated.

The effectiveness of the New Moves program was evaluated by using a school-based group randomized controlled design with 356 girls in six intervention and six control high schools (Neumark-Sztainer, Friend, et al., 2010). More than 75% of the girls were racial–ethnic minorities, and nearly half were overweight or obese. Girls in both the intervention and control groups participated in an all-girls physical education class. During the first semester, girls in the intervention group participated in Be Fit 4 days a week and once a week alternated between an interactive lesson on Be Fueled or Be Fab. They received a workbook, designed like a teen magazine, with eight chapters corresponding with the lessons on Be Fit, Be Fueled, and Be Fab. (Note that the workbook is also included in the downloadable program materials). Eight specific behavioral goals are targeted in classroom lessons, as well as in individual coaching sessions: (a) aim to be physically active at least 1 hr per day, (b) reduce screen time to no more than 1 hr per day, (c) eat at least five servings of fruits and vegetables each day, (d) limit pop and soda and other sweetened beverages and instead drink noncaloric beverages, (e) eat breakfast every day, (f) pay attention to portion size and to your body's signs of hunger and fullness, (g) avoid unhealthy weight-control practices, and (h) focus on your positive traits.

The maintenance phase was implemented during the second semester, using a weekly "lunch bunch" get together held during lunch period but outside of the regular lunchroom to provide a comfortable and safe environment for talking. During this time, there was group discussion around New Moves topics, and a healthy lunch was provided.

The results of this intervention are encouraging (Neumark-Sztainer, Friend, et al., 2010). At follow-up, the percentage of girls in the intervention group engaging in unhealthy weight-control behaviors decreased by nearly 14% compared with girls in the control group. In addition, girls in the intervention group showed significant improvement in body satisfaction, eating patterns, perceived athletic competence and self-worth as compared with girls in the control group. There was also a reduction in sedentary behaviors by one 30-min block per day.

Healthy Buddies

Healthy Buddies is a promising evidence-based health promotion program developed by doctors and educators (Stock et al., 2007). Healthy Buddies has two unique features: It addresses prevention of both obesity and EDs, and it is a teacher-guided, student-led program. The program focuses on promoting healthy attitudes and behaviors toward body image, nutrition, and activity combined with education about healthy growth and development. It is divided into 21 healthy-living lessons, based on the premise that health depends on three equally important themes: (a) moving your body, or Go Move!; (b) eating healthy foods, or Go Fuel!; and (c) feeling good about yourself and having a healthy body image, or Go Feel Good!

The pilot study involved two Canadian elementary schools, with 232 children in the intervention school and 151 children in the control school.

At the beginning of the school year, students in fourth through seventh grades were paired with younger "buddies" in kindergarten through third grade. The older buddies (fourth through seventh grades) first received a healthy-living lesson from their teachers. These older buddies then acted as peer teachers to deliver that lesson to their younger buddies. Teachers did not conduct separate lessons with the younger buddies. The intervention students showed an increase in healthy-living knowledge, behavior, and attitude scores and a smaller increase in systolic blood pressure, compared with the control students. There was also a significant decline in weight trajectory in the older students.

Learning Gardens: The LA Sprouts Gardening, Nutrition, and Cooking Intervention

Gardening intervention studies in combination with nutrition education are encouraging. A randomized controlled trial showed that fourth and fifth graders most exposed to a school-based nutrition and gardening intervention increased their preference and intake of fruits and vegetables by half a cup a day. Another randomized controlled trial found that a 6-month nutrition and gardening program in fourth-grade classrooms resulted in increased preference and willingness to eat a variety of vegetables compared with nutrition only and control groups (J. N. Davis, Ventura, Cook, Gylenhammer, & Gatto, 2011). The benefit of a garden-based nutrition intervention for changing nutrition-related behavior was also demonstrated on sixth-grade students, which resulted in significant increase in fruit and vegetable consumption (McAleese & Rankin, 2007).

Over the past 2 decades, school gardens have contributed to improved dietary intake and eating behaviors among children, but until recently their effectiveness on health and obesity had not been evaluated. A promising study known as the LA Sprouts (J. N. Davis et al. 2011) evaluated the impact of a culturally tailored intervention consisting of gardening, nutrition, and cooking, on Latino fourth and fifth graders living in an impoverished area.

The LA Sprouts intervention consisted of a 12-week curriculum with three parts: (a) nutrition education, (b) cooking and gardening, and a (c) parent component. The intervention classes were delivered in 90-min sessions once a week for 12 weeks during an after-school care program. Sessions began with participants receiving a 45-min interactive cooking and nutrition education lesson. Following the cooking and nutrition component, students participated in a 45-min interactive gardening lesson. The gardening curriculum used a hands-on approach where children learned and participated in planting, growing, maintaining, and harvesting organic fruits and vegetables. Examples of three lessons are in Exhibit 4.3.

EXHIBIT 4.3
LA Sprouts Sample Lessons

Session	Nutrition topic	Recipe	Gardening topic
4	Real Food versus Packaged Food	Vegetable quesadillas with salsa	Transplanting
6	Health Benefits of Fiber	Whole-grain pasta with veggies	Composting
10	Selecting a Healthy School Lunch	Ultimate sandwich	Watering

Note. From "LA Sprouts: A Gardening, Nutrition, and Cooking Intervention for Latino Youth Improves Diet and Reduces Obesity," by J. N. Davis, E. E. Ventura, L. T. Cook, L. E. Gyllenhammer, and N. M. Gatto, 2011, *Journal of the American Dietetic Association, 111,* p. 1226. Copyright 2011 by the American Dietetic Association. Adapted with permission.

The parents of the participants received three separate 60-min nutrition and gardening classes, which were conveniently timed for when parents typically picked up their children, during the 12-week intervention. The LA Sprouts intervention was effective in reducing blood pressure, BMI, and rate of weight gain (J. N. Davis et al., 2011). Growing food in home, school, or community gardens is a promising means by which low-income families can increase access to nutritionally rich foods that may otherwise be unavailable to them.

There are several resources to help schools implement schoolyard gardening programs. For example, KidsGardening.org is a website provided by the National Gardening Association that provides detailed instructions for garden-related activities in the classroom.

CONCLUSION

Health and healthy eating are important for all students regardless of their body weight or size. Obesity and EDs are weight-related disorders that are not distinct from each other and that share several risk factors, including body dissatisfaction, dieting, and teasing. Obesity prevention programs that are created with the intention of promoting healthy eating by dieting and restricting unhealthy foods may unwittingly create unhealthy eating practices, both of which can increase the risk for weight gain and EDs. Modifying obesity prevention programs to include the prevention of EDs may help to ensure that they promote overall health without collateral damage. This chapter includes several free resources to help assess and implement a healthy school environment, including food-related policies and nutrition guidelines. The school environment should foster a safe atmosphere that encourages diversity and healthy eating without stigma.

5

PILLAR II: HEALTHY PHYSICAL ACTIVITY

Schools provide a unique venue for promoting physical activity for children, as they reach 98% of youth, serving nearly 56 million students (Centers for Disease Control and Prevention [CDC], 2010a). With the average student spending 1,300 hr at school each year, schools can be a valuable physical environment and social resource in efforts to promote physical activity (Anthamatten et al., 2011). Unfortunately, schools can also be a barrier for physical activity because students are required to sit in class for the majority of the day, which averages 6 hr (Donnelly et al., 2009). According to the CDC, only 15% of school-age children used active travel (such as walking or riding a bike) to get to and from school. Yet in 1969, 87% of these children who lived within 1 mile of school got there by walking. Children in the United States spend an estimated 75% of the day being inactive (Norman, Schmid, Sallis, Calfas, & Patrick, 2005).

DOI: 10.1037/14180-006
Healthy Eating in Schools: Evidence-Based Interventions to Help Kids Thrive, by C. P. Cook-Cottone, E. Tribole, and T. L. Tylka

Public health agencies recommend that children and adolescents get 60 min of physical activity every day (U.S. Department of Health and Human Services [DHHS], 2008). Yet, there has been a staggering decline in physical activity among U.S. children. The 2005 Youth Risk Behavior Surveillance System showed that only 44% of boys and 28% of girls were physically active for the recommended level (LaFontaine, 2008). Yet, schools are increasingly challenged to allocate time and resources for physical education (PE) and physical activity during the school day. Demand for schools to improve academic achievement has led to decreased amounts of time allotted for recess, lunch, and PE (Beets, Beighle, Erwin, & Huberty, 2009). This chapter reviews effective school-based programs for healthy physical activity, with an emphasis on empirical support and practical applications. First, we review the benefits, recommendations, and factors influencing physical activity.

BENEFITS OF PHYSICAL ACTIVITY

Physical activity has a myriad of health benefits, including building strong bones and muscles and decreasing the risk for chronic conditions such as diabetes and heart disease. Youth who engage in regular physical activity have a better chance of a healthy adulthood (U.S. DHHS, 2008). Physical activity also promotes positive mental health, promotes social development, and improves academic performance. The CDC (2010a) evaluated 50 studies on the effect of physical activity on academic performance and found substantial evidence that physical activity helps improve grades and standardized test scores. Physical activity at school (from a combination of recess, PE, classroom, and extracurricular activities) was found to have a positive impact on cognitive skills, attitudes, and academic behavior, which includes enhanced concentration and attention as well as improved classroom behavior.

In the field of obesity research, exercise has been traditionally viewed as a strategy to burn calories, but that viewpoint is changing. Research shows that exercise can decrease total and abdominal body fat without corresponding changes in body weight or body mass index (BMI; Chaput et al., 2011). In adults, cardiovascular fitness is a more powerful predictor of heart disease and mortality risk than body weight (Chaput et al., 2011). Accordingly, physical activity should be encouraged for its own sake, without the emphasis on weight loss. Otherwise, it minimizes the myriad of significant health benefits, and because not all individuals who exercise will lose a significant amount of weight, they could become discouraged. Physical activities should be selected that support a wide spectrum of physical and mental functioning, bring pleasure, and enhance feelings of strength and self-efficacy (Calogero & Pedrotty, 2007).

WHAT KIND OF PHYSICAL ACTIVITY DO YOUTH NEED?

Physical activities should be age appropriate, enjoyable, and offer variety. These activities should include aerobic activity as well as muscle- and bone-strengthening activities (see Table 5.1 for examples of age-appropriate activities). A body of research suggests that children's total amount of physical activity is more important for achieving health benefits than is any one component (frequency, intensity, or duration) or type (aerobic, muscle strengthening, bone strengthening) of activity (U.S. DHHS, 2008).

FACTORS INFLUENCING PHYSICAL ACTIVITY

Several factors influence the pursuit of physical activity. In this section, we review body dissatisfaction, obesity bias, enjoyment, school environment, gender, and age.

Body Dissatisfaction

Research indicates that body dissatisfaction appears to be a significant obstacle for participation in physical activities, which is contrary to popular consumer perception that disliking your body would be a motivating factor to exercise (Haines & Neumark-Sztainer, 2006). Thus, interventions to promote positive body image, regardless of weight, are necessary for children (Avalos & Tylka, 2006). (See Chapters 3 and 8, this volume, for such interventions.)

Obesity Bias

Reported examples of obesity bias include making sounds while students move, criticizing skill performance, and name calling. The bias also exists among PE teachers and coaches. Obesity bias is prevalent and potentially the most harmful in physical activity settings (Rukavina & Li, 2008). Not only are students' bodies on public display but their movement skills and abilities are, too. Obesity bias during physical activity is an overlooked barrier to adopting or maintaining an active lifestyle. A growing body of research shows that negative treatment toward overweight students is associated with lower physical activity and has both short- and long-term psychological consequences (Rukavina & Li, 2008). For example, weight-related teasing can perpetuate a cycle of inactivity as well as prompt maladaptive coping mechanisms, such as self-isolating and watching more television or eating to self-soothe. As the stigmatism grows, a psychological barrier is created, where students internalize others' beliefs that their body is a physical and social

TABLE 5.1
Types of Physical Activity

Type	Children	Adolescents
Aerobic moderate–intensity	Active recreation, such as hiking, skateboarding, and rollerblading Bicycle riding Brisk walking	Active recreation, such as canoeing, hiking, skate-boarding, and rollerblading Brisk walking Bicycle riding (stationary or road bike) Housework and yard work, such as sweeping or pushing a lawn mower Games that require catching and throwing, such as baseball and softball
Aerobic vigorous–intensity	Active games involving running and chasing, such as tag Bicycle riding Jumping rope Martial arts, such as karate Running Sports such as soccer, ice or field hockey, basketball, swimming, and tennis Cross-country skiing	Active games involving running and chasing, such as flag football Bicycle riding Jumping rope Martial arts, such as karate Running Sports such as soccer, ice or field hockey, basketball, swimming, and tennis Vigorous dancing Cross-country skiing
Muscle-strengthening	Games such as tug-of-war Modified push-ups (with knees on the floor) Resistance exercises using body weight or resistance bands Rope or tree climbing Sit-ups (curl-ups or crunches) Swinging on playground equipment/bars	Games such as tug-of-war Push-ups and pull-ups Resistance exercises with exercise bands, weight machines and hand-held weights Climbing wall Sit-ups (curl-ups or crunches)
Bone strengthening	Games such as hopscotch Hopping, skipping, jumping Jumping rope Running Sports such as gymnastics, basketball, volleyball, and tennis	Hopping, skipping, jumping Jumping rope Running Sports such as gymnastics, basketball, volleyball, and tennis

Note. From *Physical Activity Guidelines Advisory Committee Report, 2008* (pp. 3–4), by Physical Activity Guidelines Advisory Committee, 2008, Washington, DC: U.S. Department of Health and Human Services. In the public domain.

limitation and think of their body in this manner. Ultimately, this internalization leads overweight students to feel that physical activity barriers are too great to overcome and avoid physical activity because they do not enjoy it.

Enjoyment

Hedonic theory suggests that people are motivated to engage in behaviors that bring them pleasure while avoiding activities that are not enjoyable. Consistent with this theory, students who reported enjoying PE engage in more activity outside of school than do students who do not enjoy PE (Schneider & Cooper, 2011). Also, positive affective response to exercise is associated with activity in adolescents and adults. Studies show that regular exercise cultivates enjoyment of physical activity (Schneider & Cooper, 2011).

Ironically, interventions designed to encourage students who do not enjoy exercising to be more active may only serve to confirm their dislike of activity. Physical activity interventions are more effective when they include strategies to enhance enjoyment that are targeted to low-active adolescents. For example, Schneider and Cooper (2011) found that enjoyment of exercise mediated the impact of a school-based intervention to promote physical activity among adolescent girls. Moreover, the improvement in physical activity among the girls who did not enjoy exercise at baseline was linear over time. Consequently, schools should provide physical and social environments that encourage and enable enjoyable and safe physical activity (Huberty et al., 2011).

School Environment

There is evidence that schools with adequate space, facilities, equipment, and supervision promote greater physical activity in students, before and after school. Sallis et al. (2001) evaluated 24 middle schools and found that physical amenities, such as area type, area size, and permanent improvements (e.g., basketball courts), were associated with increased physical activity among boys and girls. However, an absence of environmental support and adult supervision was associated with near-zero levels of physical activity. Sallis et al. concluded that "if we build it, they will come" because school design and renovation efforts may improve physical activity among children. Small, inexpensive schoolyard interventions can help to promote activity levels. These interventions include painting the schoolyards, providing game equipment, and even increasing the quantity of balls available to youth. Higher physical activity levels have been observed in schoolyards that have multicolored painting compared with those without it (Anthamatten et al., 2011).

A sense of safety in the neighborhood is an important determinant affecting physical activity. Parents rank safety as the most important factor in deciding whether to let their young children play in a given location (Sallis, McKenzie, Elder, Broyles, & Nader, 1997). A pilot intervention study provided a safe play space in a low-income, inner city neighborhood by opening a schoolyard and providing supervision to ensure children's safety (Farley et al., 2007). As a consequence, there was a substantial (84%) increase in the total number of children outdoors and physically active in the intervention area, relative to the comparison area, as well as evidence that the intervention may have reduced the time spent in sedentary activities.

Gender

Physical activity and fitness decline sharply during puberty, especially among girls, and continue to decline through high school, widening the gender gap (Davison, Cutting, & Birch, 2003). By the time they reach 12th grade, the decline in girls' physical activity level is nearly twofold (Neumark-Sztainer, Story, Hannan, Tharp, & Rex, 2003). A cohort study of 200 high school girls revealed that time constraints were a barrier to physical activity; support for physical activity from parents, peers, and teachers was positively associated with physical activity; and self-perception (e.g., feeling better about themselves and possessing confidence in physical activity ability) led to greater activity (Neumark-Sztainer, Story, et al., 2003). The authors conclude that interventions aimed at getting girls more physically activity should include social support, address time barriers, and help girls feel better about themselves, in general, and in their physical activity skills.

Self-efficacy theory proposes that girls who have confidence in their capability to be physically active will (a) perceive fewer barriers to physical activity and be less influenced by them, (b) be more likely to pursue perceived benefits of being physically active, and (c) be more likely to enjoy physical activity (Dishman et al., 2005). Barr-Anderson et al. (2008) evaluated 1,500 sixth-grade girls and found that self-efficacy and teacher support were two of the strongest correlates of enjoying PE classes. Their findings also suggest the need to recognize that a girl's size may impact her enjoyment of PE. Barr-Anderson et al. recommended that PE specialists should strive to ensure that PE class is comfortable, enjoyable and a supportive environment for all students, regardless of size, physical fitness, or competence level. Girls may particularly benefit from a girls-only class in a noncompetitive environment, with skill-enhancing programs to increase self-efficacy.

Age

Physical activity decreases with age. As adolescents move into their teenage years, they likely increase the time that they spend engaging in multiple sedentary behaviors that compete with physical activities (Norman et al., 2005). In 2009, only 18% of American high school students reported having been moderately or vigorously active for 60 min or more on all days of the week (Wall, Carlson, Stein, Lee, & Fulton, 2011).

WHAT WORKS—INTERVENTIONS TO INCREASE PHYSICAL ACTIVITY

An extensive review of 76 physical activity intervention studies by Salmon, Booth, Phongsavan, Murphy, and Timperio (2007) concluded that interventions delivered in the school setting that included some focus on PE, activity breaks, or family strategies appeared to be the most effective among children. Salmon et al. (2007) also found interventions that used activity breaks with simple environmental changes in the school setting to be promising because they are sustainable, require little training, and promote unstructured physical activities with little equipment.

However, several of the interventions that were evaluated were not effective at improving physical activity (Salmon et al., 2007). For example, only two out of 12 curriculum-only interventions were found to increase physical activity. This finding underscores the importance of using evidence-based interventions. Expert panels have identified intervention development for increasing the physical activity of children as a major public health priority (Beets et al., 2009; National Association for Sport and Physical Education, 2008). The following section highlights effective interventions, but it is by no means complete.

Classroom Curriculum-Based Physical Activity Intervention

Donnelly and colleagues (Donnelly et al., 2009; Donnelly & Lambourne, 2011; Gibson et al., 2008) designed an innovative and effective approach to increase physical activity in the classroom. They linked physical activity with academic learning objectives, without decreasing class teaching time and with minimal teacher preparation time. This 3-year, school-based intervention involved nearly 5,000 children in 24 public elementary schools (14 intervention and 10 control) located in the Midwest region of the United States. Regular classroom teachers were taught how to integrate 10 min of physical activity into existing academic lessons, building on a classroom-based program called TAKE 10!, which was developed by the International Life Sciences Institute Center for Health Promotion. The combination of TAKE 10! activities plus existing lessons from teachers and refinement of the lesson plans by the researchers were collectively called the Physical Activity

Across the Curriculum (PAAC). The PAAC not only promotes brief physical activity segments but also reinforces academic learning objectives for language arts, science, mathematics, and social studies among kindergarten to fifth-grade students. All lesson plans were designed to be consistent with the cognitive and motor development of students at each grade level. These plans also offer different activities based on the skill levels of beginner, intermediate, and advanced.

For example, the "invisible jump rope" activity teaches math skills. The students pretend to have an invisible jump rope and start to jump while counting aloud by increments of five up to 100 (five jumps, 10 jumps, 15 jumps, etc.). The lesson plan provides other examples, such as counting backward from 100. An advanced activity suggestion is to select a leader to call out different math problems while everyone jumps rope at a steady pace. These math problems can be addition, subtraction, and multiplication problems to make it more difficult. Once someone says the correct answer, everyone jumps that number of jumps while counting all together.

In a language arts lesson plan, the teacher reads aloud a story called "First Kid on the Moon." Any time a word or phrase appears in the color *red*, the class dramatizes the actions. For example, when the kids land on the moon and experience weightlessness, jumping is described in the story as follows: " . . . it was so much more fun. Everything seemed like it was in slow motion, so when they jumped, they really jumped!" For an advanced activity option, the teacher calls on a student to add a creative sentence to the story, which leads to more adventures—and more physical activity, such as the space crew chases a falling star or discovers a new planet.

The findings from this intervention are encouraging. The amount of daily physical activity significantly increased in children in the PAAC compared with children in the control group. Weekend physical activity was also significantly greater for the PAAC children. Notably, academic achievement was significantly improved for children in the PAAC group, which also affirms that it was not disruptive for learning. Moreover, both teachers and students enjoyed the active lessons more than the traditional ones, which is important because enjoyment is an important factor associated with participation in physical activity (Schneider & Cooper, 2011). Notably, when the intervention study was completed, the teachers continued to use the PAAC, even though there was no further contact by the investigators. (The teachers were surveyed 9 months after the completion of the study.)

The PAAC offers many advantages. It can be easily disseminated, it does not require a change to the current school curriculum, few (if any) additional supplies are needed, it is not time consuming, and the cost is minimal. The PAAC reduces long periods of sedentary behavior in the classroom and reinforces academic learning objectives. It complements rather than replaces other activity programs such as PE and after-school activities. The PAAC also supports previous research that classroom physical activity helps to mediate common barriers to learning such as inattentiveness and misbehavior (National Association for Sport and Physical Education, 2008).

Recess Intervention Studies

Recess is an integral part of school-based physical activity. Indeed, the Robert Wood Johnson Foundation reported that recess provides nearly half (42%) of the available opportunity for physical activity among students, followed by PE class (32%) and after-school programs (26%; Huberty et al., 2011). PE alone does not provide sufficient activity for children because of the infrequency of PE and the need to teach PE content during lessons.

Given the opportunity, most children will engage in meaningful amounts of physical activity during recess, especially when they are in a conducive environment. Huberty et al. (2011) designed Ready for Recess, a promising intervention for elementary schools. Ready for Recess shows that a combination of staff training, adequate recreational equipment, and modifying the playground markings are simple and effective ways to maximize physical activity during recess with minimal expense.

The Ready for Recess program was adapted from the Active and Healthy Schools Program (AHSP), which was designed to change the school environment to encourage healthy lifestyles (see the Suggested Resources section in this book). Huberty et al. (2011) focused on one specific environment component from AHSP—"activity zones." The concept of dividing the schoolyard environment into activity zones was based on several observations by Gopher Sport (2006). First, the schoolyard did not create a safe haven for all students, as students could opt to play anywhere, regardless of whether it bothered others or was unsafe. Second, the number of activities was limited, and little or no equipment was available to increase the opportunity for play. Third, dominant students or athletically gifted students may control the play space and equipment, whereas less assertive students acquiesce and move aside, standing around with nothing to do.

Activity zones were created and mapped to optimize activities during recess (Huberty et al., 2011). Each map was drawn specific to the playground at each school. For example, a school with a smaller playground had five activity zones, whereas a school with more space had seven activity zones. Each activity zone had the necessary equipment or space to play a game or activity safely. For example, three-ball soccer was an activity played on the soccer field with goals, modified kickball was played in the black top area, and tag games took place in a large open space. If a particular zone did not attract students, the activities were changed.

Prior to recess, student helpers placed materials required for activities in the zones. Materials included zone marker cones, dry erase zone signs (to inform the children of the activity occurring in each particular zone), and playground equipment. Ten to 15 pieces of equipment were available within each zone so that multiple games of each activity could be played. Children were allowed to switch zones as they wished throughout recess.

The intervention resulted in nearly a twofold increase in both moderate and vigorous physical activity, compared with baseline activity levels during recess. Although there was no control group, Huberty et al. (2011) concluded that the schoolyard recess environment should be designed to encourage physical activity and should be part of a school's wellness policy. Recess-friendly games can be integrated into the PE curriculum, which could help optimize recess time by teaching games that children can participate in during recess. Also, they recommended that a portion of the beginning of the year's professional development meetings could be used to train teachers and staff to maximize physical activity during recess (when teachers serve as recess monitors and a school does not have funding to train recess staff separately).

School-Based Physical Education Intervention Studies

Although PE is mandated in almost every state, requirements for the amount of PE instruction are generally low. Few middle and high schools require daily PE, and schools face increasing pressure to eliminate PE to make more time available for academics (CDC, 2009). PE is frequently marginalized and suffers from low subject status and inadequate financial and personnel resources (McKenzie, Sallis, & Rosengard, 2009).

High School Physical Education

Traditional PE classes often provide little physical activity and fail to teach behavioral skills that help students to be active in other settings (Pate et al., 2005). However, a new standard has been set for high schools, thanks to one of the few controlled intervention trials that demonstrated significant increase of overall physical activity—the Lifestyle Education for Activity Program (LEAP). LEAP increased overall physical activity in high school girls (a high risk group for low physical activity), and the effect of the intervention was sustained for 4 years, even though the intervention took place for only 1 year (i.e., during the ninth grade; Pate et al., 2005, 2007; Ward et al., 2006). LEAP focuses on changing personal, social, and environmental factors related to physical activity, which involves core changes to the school environment and instructional programs (Ward et al., 2006).

To be specific, LEAP was a large-scale study that initially involved 31 middle schools, 24 high schools, and more than 4,000 adolescent girls who were diverse in terms of socioeconomic status, location (urban, suburban, and rural), and BMI. There were approximately equal numbers of White and African American girls. Schools were not required to implement a specific LEAP curriculum; rather, the study used a flexible facilitative approach to implement the intervention. To be specific, teachers in all intervention schools received standardized training in seven core components or essential elements of LEAP and were able to modify their program as needed to fit their particular school environment. The first component is to provide *gender-separated classes* to create a supportive environment for girls. The second component includes *cooperative activities* (i.e., games, activities, and team building) along with the traditional competitive sport activities. The third component emphasizes a variety of *lifelong physical activities* girls enjoy, such as dance, aerobics, and strength training. The fourth component suggests that classes should be *fun and enjoyable*, including positive interactions with their PE teacher and other girls as well as enhancements such as music and a variety of activities. The fifth component requires that classes promote *physical activity*, with students engaged in moderate-to-vigorous physical activity for at least 50% of the class time. The sixth component emphasizes *small-group activities*, as they promote enjoyment and fun. Last, *behavioral skills* to adopt and maintain an active lifestyle are taught in physical or health education; these skills include decision making, goal setting, overcoming barriers to physical activity, time management, and communication (support seeking).

The LEAP School Environment was modified to create an environment that supports physical activity for girls. To enable this, the principal must provide tangible support for physical activity promotion, such as providing time and resources for PE classes and physical activity programs. The school should also have a *physical activity team* (LEAP Team) that regularly plans, implements, and evaluates student and faculty physical activity programs. Last, schools should prominently display messages promoting physical activity in newsletters, school announcements, television, videos, stall talkers, and bulletin boards.

LEAP was the first study to show that an intervention that focuses on mastery of individual skills and fosters a supportive activity friendly environment influenced the prevalence of regular participation in vigorous physical activity among high school girls. Furthermore, girls at the intervention schools who did not take a PE class during ninth grade also had a higher level of regular vigorous physical activity compared with the control group. The researchers attribute this significant finding to the creation of an activity friendly environment that provided active adult role models and helped girls identify fun opportunities to be active outside of PE classes. This finding is particularly significant because previous large-scale studies have shown that interventions can increase physical activity within PE but not outside of classes. An important advantage of the LEAP model is that it emphasizes reallocation of existing resources while providing flexibility for schools to adapt the intervention to their local conditions.

The findings of the LEAP intervention studies show that sustained modification of the school environment and instructional practices can exert a positive influence on girls' physical activity across their entire high school career. Although the LEAP study was conducted in high schools and targeted girls, the researchers suggest that the benefits of LEAP should apply to both boys and girls at all school levels because it is highly generalizable and could be disseminated readily to most schools in the United States (Pate et al., 2007).

Elementary and Middle School Physical Education

The Sports, Play, and Active Recreation for Kids (SPARK) program is one of the most researched PE programs. SPARK was initiated in 1989 with a large 7-year grant to San Diego State University from the National Institutes of Health to create, implement, and evaluate innovative approaches to PE content and instruction in "real world" settings. SPARK PE was designed to be more inclusive, active, and fun than traditional classes. The PE curriculum was designed to be a practical resource for both classroom teachers and PE specialists. The SPARK programs for elementary and middle schools have been subjected to numerous scientific tests, and they are among only a few programs to have been disseminated nationally (McKenzie et al., 2009).

Initial SPARK studies involved nine schools, consisting of seven control schools (standard PE programs) and two SPARK PE classes, which were designed to promote high levels of physical activity, teach movement skills, and be enjoyable. This 2-year intervention focused on increasing children's physical activity in PE lessons in Grades 4 and 5. It included a curriculum-based program, homework, and monthly newsletters to parents to stimulate parent–child interaction.

A typical SPARK lesson was conducted 3 days a week by either a PE specialist or by regular classroom teachers, who received PE training. The lesson lasted 30 min and had two parts: 15 min of health-fitness activities and 15 min of skill-fitness activities (Sallis, McKenzie, Alcaraz, et al., 1997). There were nine sport lessons to help develop skill-related fitness, such as basketball and soccer. These sports and games were chosen because they had the potential for promoting cardiovascular fitness. Traditionally low-activity games, such as softball, were modified to make them more active.

During a 36-week school year, SPARK students spent approximately 13 more hours in moderate-to-vigorous physical activity compared with students in the control schools. Also noteworthy was that elementary classroom teachers who received adequate training and support were able to improve the effectiveness of their PE teaching. Compared with teachers in control schools who did not receive training, teachers in the SPARK program taught more PE and provided students with more activity. Following SPARK's success in elementary schools, the investigators expanded their work into middle school, which was called Middle School Physical Activity and Nutrition (MSPAN). MSPAN used a combination of environmental, policy, and social marketing interventions to increase physical activity and was tested in 24 middle school campuses in five school districts in Southern California.

This program had similar goals as SPARK, but it differed in its type of curricula. MSPAN provided only sample curricular materials and emphasized providing assistance to the middle school physical educators to help them revise their existing programs and instructional strategies to increase student moderate-to-vigorous physical activity. This contrasts with SPARK elementary program, which had a structured curriculum. MSPAN resulted in an 18% increase in activity during PE without hiring new teachers or taking more time away from other academic coursework (McKenzie et al., 2009).

In 1993, San Diego State University Research Foundation established a program to disseminate SPARK on a nonprofit basis. However, over time those efforts far exceeded the capacity of the program designers and the academic institution. Therefore, in October 2002, the university licensed the rights to disseminate SPARK programs to SPORTIME (http://www.sportime.com/), an equipment distributor and a long-time corporate sponsor of SPARK. (See the Suggested Resources section in this volume for more information).

Environmentally Based Program

In Denver, the Learning Landscapes (LL) program has constructed over 98 culturally tailored schoolyard play spaces at elementary schools with the goal of encouraging use of play spaces and physical activity. LL is a novel type of schoolyard that offers a diversity of elements that traditional schoolyards lack, including schoolyard gateways, shade structures, banners, gardens, public art, student art, and art tile projects. LL was designed and built by a nonprofit partnership between the University of Colorado Denver's College of Architecture and Planning and a local school district. The first LL schoolyard was completed in 1998 after 6 years of collaboration between parents, elementary school students, staff, faculty, neighbors, local businesses, and landscape architecture graduate students.

Anthamatten et al. (2011) investigated the effect of these schoolyard renovations in low-income urban areas on physical activity among children by comparing use of LL schoolyards with unrenovated schoolyards. The LL schoolyards were used significantly more during all observation periods. During "optional" periods (e.g., after school, on weekends), there was also greater use and activity for boys and girls. Anthamatten et al. provided evidence that renovation of schoolyards results in an increase in physical activity and active use by schoolchildren during both mandatory and optional play periods, but it is not clear for how long this effect is sustained. LL, then, offers a promising method to encourage physical activity.

PRACTICAL APPLICATIONS AND RECOMMENDED ACTIVITIES

This section highlights practical resources and recommended activities for a variety of school settings. One of the first steps is to assess the strengths and weaknesses of your school.

School Health Index

The School Health Index (SHI) is a free self-assessment and planning guide created by the CDC (2005) that enables schools to identify the strengths and weaknesses of their health promotion policies and programs, and it ultimately enables schools to develop an action plan for improvement. There is one version for elementary schools and another for middle and high schools. The SHI includes eight assessment modules and five health modules, one of which is for PE and physical activity.

Here are sample questions from the SHI self-assessment guide. (See the Suggested Resources section for where to obtain a complete copy.)

1. Are students provided at least 20 minutes of recess (unstructured physical activity) during each school day, and do teachers or recess monitors encourage students to be active?
2. Does the school prohibit using physical activity and withholding physical education class as punishment?
3. Do teachers avoid using practices that result in some students spending considerable time being inactive in physical education classes? Such practices could include using games that eliminate students, having many students stand in line waiting for a turn, organizing activities in which fewer than half of the students have a piece of equipment and/or a physically active role, and allowing highly skilled students to dominate activities and games.

How Can Schools Help Youth Be More Physically Active?

According to the CDC (2009), a large percentage of physical activity can be provided through a comprehensive school-based physical activity program that includes six components. The first component is quality PE, which (a) gives students the knowledge and skills to participate in a lifetime of physical activity, (b) teaches movement skills and how to assess physical activity, (c) uses materials that are appropriate for the age and skill level of the students, (d) uses activities that keep students active for most of class time (more than 50% of class time), (e) meets the needs of all students, and (f) is an enjoyable experience for all students. A policy recommendation is that schools should require daily PE for students in kindergarten through Grade 12 (150 min per week for elementary schools and 225 min per week for secondary schools). The second component is recess, which gives students the chance to have unstructured physical activity and to practice what they learn in PE class. Recess also benefits students by helping them learn how to play together and handle conflict as well as improving their attention and concentration in the classroom. Its corresponding policy recommendation is that schools should incorporate at least 20 min of recess per day in addition to PE classes. The third component is regular physical activity breaks that are built into classroom lessons and enhance on-task classroom behavior of students. Ideas for physical activity breaks are to take a walk outside as part of a science class or ask students to name and act out action words from a story through physical activity. The fourth component includes intramural sports. Schools should offer physical activity opportunities before, during, and/or after school hours. They need to provide students with a choice of activities like walking, running, hiking, swimming, tennis, dancing, and bicycling. They must offer students of all skill levels an equal chance to participate. The fifth component includes interscholastic sports. Schools need to help students work together, engage in friendly competition, and learn sport-specific and general motor skills. This component may improve psychological well-being and reduce some risky health behaviors, such as cigarette smoking, illegal drug use, and having sexual intercourse. The sixth component involves walk- and bike-to-school programs, which can increase student levels of physical activity and promote partnerships among students, parents, and community organizations and members. Further, these programs can improve the safety of those walking and biking around schools and decrease traffic near schools. Schools could participate in International Walk to School Week, create safer routes to school, and provide access to secure bike racks. Many examples of physical activities for children and adolescents are included in Table 5.1, which is divided into types of activities (aerobic, muscle strengthening, and bone strengthening).

The CDC further collaborated with Partnership for Prevention to create an action guide to help schools increase physical activity. This action guide (see Partnership for Prevention, 2008) is available at no charge and is a very helpful tool that translates evidence-based recommendations into the necessary "how to" guidance for implementation of effective strategies (see Suggested Resources, this volume, for more details). Effective evidence-based strategies for creating more active PE classes include (a) implementing an evidence-based PE curriculum that increases students' physical activity levels, (b) incorporating cardiovascular physical fitness activities into current lessons (e.g., step aerobics), (c) adopting new techniques for teaching current lessons to increase students' physical activity levels (such as small-sided games of three-on-three), (d) extending the length of PE classes (e.g., 45 min instead of 30 min), and (e) adding extra PE classes to the school week (e.g., daily PE instead of three times per week).

CONCLUSION

Children need 60 min of physical activity each day, but they fall dramatically short of meeting this recommendation. This chapter highlighted several programs that (a) illustrate how to remove barriers to physical activity and (b) provide concrete and effective ideas for promoting physical activity. Schools should provide physical and social environments that encourage and enable safe, inclusive, and enjoyable physical activity. Specifically, schools need to structure PE classes to be comfortable, enjoyable, and supportive for all students, regardless of their size, physical fitness, gender, or competence level. Recess and classroom curriculum-based activities also need to be tailored to increase activity. Schools can also make the schoolyard a more conducive facilitator for physical activity by making sure there is adequate equipment, structured opportunities for moderate-to-vigorous activity, and supervision.

6

PILLAR III: MINDFULNESS, SELF-CARE, AND EMOTIONAL REGULATION

Mindfulness, self-care, and emotional-regulation approaches can be beneficial in the prevention and treatment of poor body image and maladaptive eating behaviors (Albers, 2003; C. Cook-Cottone, 2006b; Greco & Hayes, 2008; Linehan, 1993; Scime & Cook-Cottone, 2008). *Mindfulness* involves cultivation of awareness of the present moment and acceptance of our experiences, both internal (e.g., thoughts, reactions) and external (e.g., interpersonal and environmental events; Burke, 2010; Schonert-Reichl & Lawlor, 2010; Siegel, 2010). Among its many benefits, mindfulness practice improves attention and concentration as well as social and emotional competence (Schonert-Reichl & Lawlor, 2010; Shapiro, Oman, Thoresen, Plante, & Flinders, 2008; Siegel, 2010). *Self-care* practices include nutrition, hydration, exercise, self-soothing, and rest (Linehan, 1993). *Emotional regulation* involves awareness, identification, monitoring, and negotiating of emotional experience (Macklem, 2008). Research indicates that integrating mindfulness, self-care,

DOI: 10.1037/14180-007
Healthy Eating in Schools: Evidence-Based Interventions to Help Kids Thrive, by C. P. Cook-Cottone, E. Tribole, and T. L. Tylka

and emotional-regulation techniques into current school practice is acceptable and feasible (Burke, 2010; Macklem, 2008; Schonert-Reichl & Lawlor, 2010). Furthermore, based on studies done primarily with adults and a growing body of evidence specific to children and adolescents, mindfulness, self-care, and emotional-regulation techniques also show benefits across a range of affective and behavioral outcomes (e.g., school attendance, decision making, healthy eating, safe sex; Burke, 2010; Greco & Hayes, 2008; Macklem, 2008; T. Mendelson et al., 2010; Schonert-Reichl & Lawlor, 2010; Shapiro et al., 2008). In this chapter, we describe the mechanisms of action, effects, and typical protocols, and we offer practical suggestions for school personnel.

As Figure 6.1 shows, self-care, mindfulness, and emotional regulation can be viewed as interactive layers that create a supportive base for healthy intuitive eating. It is from a base of mindfulness and a practice of consistent self-care (Layer 1) that emotional regulation (Layer 2) is most accessible (Macklem, 2008; Schonert-Reichl & Lawlor, 2010). Mindfulness and self-care practices are interdependent and often cultivated in tandem: (a) Mindfulness is most easily accessed when an individual's physiological needs are met, and (b) a routine practice of self-care requires a mindful focus (Linehan, 1993). This is why, for thousands of years, the fields of yoga and mindfulness have included instruction on daily health practices. Specifically, daily self-care practices (e.g., hydration, rest, nutrition, exercise) provide a physiological stability on which emotional experiences are supported (Macklem, 2008). Simply put, a stable body allows for a stable mind. Thus, the second layer in this framework is emotional regulation (Linehan, 1993). A growing body of evidence suggests that it is within the context of emotional regulation that mindful and intuitive eating (Layer 3) is possible (Baer, Fischer, & Huss, 2005). That is, an individual can be present with food and eat based on internal, physiological hunger cues rather than emotional or external cues (Baer et al., 2005). Using this framework, we can guide students toward mindful eating and deter emotional eating.

UNDERSTANDING EMOTIONAL EATING AND EMOTIONAL RESTRICTION OF FOOD

Researchers and practitioners have conceptualized emotional vulnerability, lack of emotional attention and clarity (emotional unawareness), difficulty negotiating emotions, and emotional distress as triggers for emotional eating and the restriction of food intake (Corstorphine, 2006; Kemp, Bui, & Grier, 2011; Kristeller & Wolever, 2010; Safer, Couturier, & Lock, 2007). In the pathway to emotional eating, the triggering event or thought leads to a negative emotional reaction and negative interpretation of the event, which

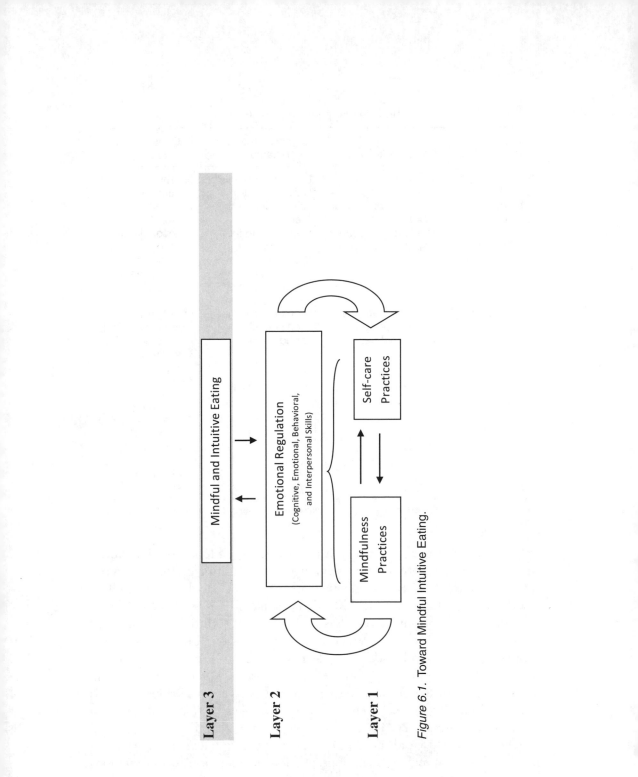

Figure 6.1. Toward Mindful Intuitive Eating.

Layer 3

Mindful and Intuitive Eating

Layer 2

Emotional Regulation
(Cognitive, Emotional, Behavioral, and Interpersonal Skills)

Layer 1

Self-care Practices

Mindfulness Practices

TABLE 6.1
The Pathway to Emotional Eating

Trigger (example)	Reaction (example)	Interpretation (example)	Consequences (example)
Event Unrealistic standard Thought Memory Invalidating environment	Negative affect Distress Unwanted emotional experience "I feel bad/mad/sad" "I want . . ."	"I can't handle this" "I am not okay" "I can't tolerate this feeling" "I am weak to feel this way" "Something is wrong with me for feeling this way" "I must have . . ."	Narrowing of attention Reduction of inhibition Emotional eating or restriction (to numb or block out, distract, or soothe)
Homework is difficult	Feelings of anxiety and of being overwhelmed	"I can't handle this" "I can't do this" "I need a break"	Intention— to avoid homework and uncomfortable feeling associated with it Attention— narrowed, little problem solving Behavior—leaving homework and going to kitchen to eat (to numb, distract, or soothe)

Note. Data from Baer, Fischer, and Huss, 2005; Corstorphine, 2006; Kemp, Bui, and Grier, 2011.

in turn lead to emotional eating or the restriction of food (see Table 6.1). *Emotional eating* involves episodes of binge eating, grazing on food when not hungry, and eating when not hungry to numb or block out, distract oneself, or soothe feelings (Corstorphine, 2006; Kemp et al., 2011; Kristeller & Wolever, 2010). For some, this involves a loss of control over eating that is associated with uncomfortable emotions, such as anxiety (Goossens, Braet, Vlierberghe, & Meis, 2009). For others, the less clear and attentive they are to emotions, the more likely they are to eat in the face of emotions (Moon & Berenbaum, 2009). The *restriction of food* in response to emotions involves skipping meals and snacks during the experience of uncomfortable situations and emotions (Haynos & Fruzzetti, 2011). In these ways, emotional and disordered eating can be attempts to avoid or escape uncomfortable internal or external experiences, which may include cognitions, physiological sensations, and emotions (Baer et al., 2005; Haynos & Fruzzetti, 2011).

According to Kemp et al. (2011), emotional-regulation theory posits that individuals engage in behaviors, or take action, to either maintain or change the experience of feeling states. Most of us work to extend positive feeling states (e.g., comfort, satisfaction, happiness, excitement) and shorten, end, or down-regulate (i.e., minimize) negative feeling states (e.g., anxiety, depression, anger, loneliness, helplessness). Using this conceptualization of emotions and behaviors, emotional eating is viewed as a pattern of self-reward (i.e., an attempt to increase the chances of having a positive feeling state) and avoidance (i.e., an attempt to decrease, shorten, or avoid a negative feeling state).

There is also evidence that some individuals may be more susceptible to pleasure and aversion responses to food and affect as well as to social norms and triggering food advertisements (Kemp et al., 2011). Further, so called emotional eaters may be more likely to indulge in the consumption of indulgent–hedonic foods (i.e., foods which are high in fat and calories and most often eaten for pleasure). These foods include fried foods, chocolate, pizza, ice cream, chips, and desserts of all kinds. In addition, researchers have suggested that emotional eaters may be more susceptible to food advertisements (Kemp et al., 2011). Together, the increased likelihood to ruminate on negative emotional states, to judge or react to initial and adaptive primary emotional states with maladaptive secondary emotional states (e.g., guilt, anger or shame about feeling angry, anxious, or even happy), and the increased susceptibility to food advertisements may create a risk for emotional eating in an effort to down-regulate negative mood (Corstorphine, 2006; Kemp et al., 2011). Notably, there is debate as to the contributing role of each of these factors, and there is much more to understand about emotional eating (Corstorphine, 2006). For example, other variables, such as social norms and hedonic rationalizations (i.e., thoughts people use to justify yielding to an eating temptation), have been identified as important in this process (Kemp et al., 2011).

MINDFULNESS

The field of mindfulness spans disciplines and practices, is thousands of years old, and has only very recently been applied to disorders of eating. Mindfulness techniques fall under the broad conceptual umbrella that encompasses formal protocols that emphasize unique aspects of practice and bring in varied techniques from the field of psychology (e.g., mindfulness-based cognitive behavioral therapy). Mindfulness is considered a relevant component of the third generation of behavioral therapies, including acceptance and commitment therapy (ACT), dialectical behavioral therapy (DBT), mindfulness-based stress reduction (MBSR), and mindfulness-based cognitive therapy (MBCT; Shapiro et al., 2008; Wanden-Berghe, Sanz-Valero, & Wanden-Berghe, 2010). These protocols differ from more traditional interventions (e.g., cognitive behavioral therapy) in the manner in which they address private events (i.e., thoughts, feelings, and bodily sensations; Greco & Hayes, 2008). Greco and Hayes (2008) indicated that rather than identify and change the content, frequency, and form of thoughts and feelings, these third-generation therapies serve to address and alter the function of private events and, in turn, diminish their behavioral impact. Recently, these programs have been adapted for and applied to children and adolescents (Greco & Hayes, 2008; Huppert & Johnson, 2010). The interested reader is directed to the book *Acceptance and Mindfulness Treatments for Children and Adolescents: A Practitioner's Guide* (Greco & Hayes, 2008).

Mindful Awareness and Mindful Practice

Mindfulness refers to both mindful awareness and mindful practice (Shapiro & Carlson, 2009; Siegel, 2010). Specifically, *mindful awareness* is the state of being present and attentive (to body sensations, perceptions, cognitions, and/or emotions) and free from reaction, judgment, or attachment in one's moment-to-moment experiences (Dorjee, 2010; Grabovac, Lau, & Willett, 2011; Kemp et al., 2011; Shapiro & Carlson, 2009). The experience of mindfulness has been described as *bare attention*, which involves nonelaborate attention to sensory-level aspects of the moment, such as sounds, tastes, and visual input (Dorjee, 2010; Shapiro et al., 2008). Mindful bare attention involves a shift away from the linguistic storying or thought-filled processing of our experiences (Dorjee, 2010; Shapiro et al., 2008; Siegel, 2010). *Mindful practice* is the pathway to mindful awareness (Shapiro & Carlson, 2009; Siegel, 2010). It is the systematic practice and conscious development of skills such as intentional attention, increased discernment and compassion, and reduced reactivity and identification (Kemp et al., 2011; Shapiro & Carlson, 2009; Siegel, 2010). Mindfulness practices serve to address the source of suffering, which is conceptualized as the uncontrolled mind that can be easily guided by anger, attachment, and ignorance (Dorjee, 2010). Unique to mindfulness work is the experiential knowing of mindfulness teachers (Burke, 2010). Unlike practitioners of other therapies or interventions, mindfulness practitioners are expected to engage in daily practice of techniques such as meditation and in ongoing professional development (Burke, 2010; Greco & Hayes, 2008; Siegel, 2010). Burke (2010) wrote, "Just as swimming teachers need to be able to swim, so do mindfulness teachers need the experiential knowing that comes from riding the waves, the ebb and flow, of their internal experiences" (p. 2).

Grabovac et al. (2011) distilled the practice into exploration of the three characteristics of mindfulness: (a) impermanence, (b) suffering, and (c) not-self. *Impermanence* refers to the acceptance that all feelings, thoughts, and sensory experiences are impermanent. That is, they arise and then pass away. *Suffering* is the result of our habitual reactions (i.e., attachment or

TABLE 6.2
The Pathway to Mindful–Intuitive Eating

Trigger (example)	Reaction (example)	Interpretation (example)	Consequences (example)
Physiological cue for hunger Meal time	Notice cue Sense aspects of meal–food	None—just observe No judgment or interpretation Realization that thoughts and feelings are not facts or "I am not my thoughts" "These are just thoughts/feelings"	Mindful eating Response to satiety cues
Unrealistic standard Thought Memory	Notice and observe Emotional experience "I am feeling bad/ mad/sad"	None—just observe No judgment or interpretation Realization that thoughts and feelings are not facts or "I am not my thoughts" "These are just thoughts/feelings"	Decreased reactivity Increased ability to make adaptive choices
Homework is difficult	Notice and observe "I feel anxious" "My stomach feels tense, and my thoughts are fast and negative"	"I am not my thoughts or my feelings"	"I am going to work through one problem and call a friend for help if I get stuck."

Note. Data from Baer, Fischer, and Huss, 2005; Kemp, Bui, and Grier, 2011; Shapiro and Carlson, 2009; Siegel, 2010.

aversion) to feelings, thoughts, and sensory experiences. Finally, *not-self* is the understanding that feelings, thoughts, and sensory experiences do not contain anything lasting and are not aspects of the self. Mindfulness practice involves the exploration of the aspects of mindfulness in formal and informal practices (Grabovac et al., 2011; Shapiro & Carlson, 2009). Formal practices include activities such as meditation, relaxation techniques, and yoga. Informal practice involves the awareness of the aspects of mindfulness in everyday activities such as doing the dishes, mowing the lawn, and, yes, eating. In the pathway to intuitive eating, the triggering event or thought leads to an emotion or a physical feeling, which the individual notices and observes without judgment. The individual is less reactive and responds more mindfully to the experience (see Table 6.2). More recent conceptualizations of mindfulness applications have integrated a focus on what are referred to as *wholesome emotions*. This focus is intended to help people shift intentions and behaviors toward loving kindness, compassion, joy, and equanimity or serenity (e.g., variations of DBT; Dorjee, 2010).

Mindfulness is believed to contribute to a decentered approach to internal events (i.e., thoughts, feelings, and memories; Baer et al., 2005). These events are considered to be the same as external sensory impressions. For example, Mathilde (a seventh grader) feels overwhelmed and anxious as she looks at her math homework. She can observe these feelings, and they do not need to be any more meaningful than looking at a tree through the window. She might say, "Oh, look, there is a tree outside my window." Just as she might say, "I am feeling anxious as I look at this math problem." She need not attach, judge, or react to either experience (the tree or the anxiety). She can learn to recognize internal states just as she has learned to recognize external experiences (Baer et al., 2005). Such an approach may be effective for a few reasons. First, mindfulness is believed to result in increased self-observation and improved recognition of internal states and, therefore, lead to better choice of coping strategies. Because she is able to key into her anxiety associated with math homework, Mathilde can make effective behavioral choices such as anticipation (getting help after school), self-soothing (making chamomile tea for study time), or active coping (using deep breathing to address the anxiety as she works). Second, by recognizing internal experiences, the mindfulness strategies may serve as an exposure procedure resulting in less aversion and avoidance. That is, being that she is directly acknowledging, experiencing, and effectively coping with the anxiety that accompanies math, Mathilde no longer reacts to math as a trigger for anxiety. Last, she may also experience an overall decrease in the believability of negative thoughts.

Currently there are several mindfulness-based protocols. These include MBSR, MBCT, DBT, and ACT (Burke, 2010), adaptations specific to schools (e.g., mindfulness education [ME]) and emerging work in the field of yoga (Greco & Hayes, 2008; T. Mendelson et al., 2010; Scime & Cook-Cottone, 2008). Recent innovations have used these techniques to address the role of thoughts and dysregulated emotions in eating and body image disturbance (Greco & Hayes, 2008; Safer et al., 2007).

According to Burke (2010), mindfulness-based approaches share a fundamental focus on developing mindfulness skills. However, they differ in their approach to developing these skills. Both MBSR and MBCT use mindfulness meditation as a pathway to mindfulness, and DBT and ACT include more nonmeditative skills and behaviors (Burke, 2010; Heffner, Sperry, Eifert, & Detweiler, 2002). Furthermore, MBSR and MBCT are programs anchored in experiential learning that integrate weekly group sessions and home practice (Burke, 2010). The core curriculum of formal mindfulness practices include body scan, sitting, and various meditation techniques (e.g., movement, walking meditations; Burke, 2010). The curriculum also provides instruction in informal mindfulness practices, such as learning how to bring mindfulness into daily living activities like doing chores and eating. During a group session, members are guided through formal practices, discuss experiences, and are given information (i.e., psychoeducation) about topics such as the role of perception, mind–body association, stress, and how to develop internal resources for coping and developing health (Burke, 2010). These programs have been successfully adapted to meet the needs of those with eating difficulties (see Table 6.3; e.g., Proulx, 2007).

According to Burke (2010), MBCT also includes additional psychoeducational components and activities designed to address depressive symptomatology. MBCT has been successfully applied to a variety of populations (Baer et al., 2005). Interestingly, MBCT does not instruct individuals to change thought content, as does CBT. In the same way, the technique does not train individuals to modify emotional states, to engage in problem solving, or improve other (e.g., interpersonal) skills. An example of an MBCT strategy would be to encourage participants to engage in more activities that induce feelings of mastery and to reduce engagement in activities associated with low mood.

Mindfulness-based techniques have been found to be effective for prevention and treatment (Heffner et al., 2002; Safer et al., 2007; Shapiro et al., 2008; Wanden-Berghe et al., 2010). In an extensive review of the literature, Wanden-Berghe et al. (2010) concluded that mindfulness-based therapies may be effective in the treatment of eating disorders (EDs). They noted caution in regard to trial qualities and small sample sizes, yet they found it noteworthy that all of the articles reviewed (that met criterion) found statistically positive outcomes. Positive outcomes were observed for bulimia nervosa, anorexia nervosa, and binge-eating disorder (BED; Safer et al., 2007; Wanden-Berghe et al., 2010). Some studies have shown efficacy in combining mindfulness and emotional-regulation skills (Wanden-Berghe et al., 2010). Treatment components in the studies reviewed include psychoeducation, controlling external and diet triggers, change in problematic thought processes, mindfulness skills, coping skills, emotional-regulation strategies, experiential meditation practices, distress tolerance skills, interpersonal effectiveness skills, practice identifying and responding to primary emotions adaptively, body scan, mindful stretching and walking, generalizing mindfulness to daily life, and behavioral change commitment (Wanden-Berghe et al., 2010).

Kristeller and Wolever (2010) created the mindfulness-based eating awareness training (MB-EAT) program for individuals who are struggling with binge eating. This program integrates training in mindfulness meditation and guided mindfulness practices that are designed to address the core issues of BED. Program components help participants control responses to emotional states, make conscious food choices, develop awareness of hunger and satiety cues, and cultivate self-acceptance. Preliminary evidence suggests

TABLE 6.3

Components of Mindfulness and Emotional-Regulation Interventions

Technique	Emphasis	Sample practices
Acceptance and commitment therapy (ACT)	Commitment to goals and values Behavioral change commitment Addressing experiential avoidance Creative hopelessness Control is the problem Self as context Choosing a valued direction Letting go of struggle Embracing symptoms Cognitive fusion (cognitive, emotional, and behavioral aspects of a person have become fused) Negative self-evaluations concerning the beauty ideal[a] Empower students to live with fidelity to oneself in a culture that promotes gender-role stereotypes, body objectification, and a thin ideal[a]	Psychoeducation Values assessment (create a value compass) Cognitive defusion Use of metaphor for understanding (Mule in the well; Leaves on a stream) Experiential exercises (LIFE exercises) Cognitive behavioral change (Activities such as Milk, Milk, Milk) Health promotion (practice health and self-care)[a] Weaken attachment to sociocultural expectations through media critical-thinking skills[a]
Cognitive-emotional-behavioral therapy (CEBT)	Understanding the experience and expression of emotions Attend and respond to feelings adaptively	Psychoeducation Monitor emotions and function of emotions (diary) Identify, challenge, and restructure beliefs Behavioral experiments
Dialectic behavioral therapy (DBT)	Three states of mind (i.e., reasonable mind, emotional mind, and wise mind) What-mindfulness skills (observing, describing, and participating) How-mindfulness skills (nonjudgmentally, one-mindfully, and effectively) Distress tolerance Mindfulness Emotional regulation (awareness and nonreaction, wise mind) Nonjudgmental Reality acceptance Interpersonal effectiveness	Psychoeducation Self-soothing and distraction Observing breath Functional analysis of emotions Scheduling–engaging in pleasant events Rehearsing interpersonal skills Homework Symptom tracking (diary cards)[a] Behavioral chain analysis of eating struggles[a] Appropriate self-disclosure[a] Role playing[a] Family meetings[a]

TABLE 6.3
Components of Mindfulness and Emotional-Regulation
Interventions *(Continued)*

Technique	Emphasis	Sample practices
Mindfulness-based cognitive therapy (MBCT)	Formal integration of MBSR and CBT Emphasis on understanding moods–emotions and stress Relapse prevention Changing the awareness of and relationship to thoughts Breaking the automatic, dysfunctional thought processes associated with mood–anxiety disorder Accepting, nonjudging, and decentering Mindfulness	Weekly sessions Group discussions Self-help book with guided meditation CD Psychoeducation Mindfulness practice (thoughts, feelings, and body sensations) Thoughts observed, not changed 3-min breathing space Body scan Sitting mediation Walking meditation Informal daily mindfulness Mindful eating[a] Mindful eating of challenging foods[a] Mindful eating buffet[a] Limited yoga for body work[a]
Mindfulness-based eating awareness training (MB-EAT)	Cultivating mindfulness Cultivating mindful eating Cultivating emotional balance Cultivating self-acceptance	Breath awareness Body scan Healing self-touch Chair yoga Mindful walking Loving-kindness and forgiveness meditations Seated meditation Wisdom meditation Mindful eating activity[a] Hunger meditation[a] 500 calorie challenge[a] Identifying black-and-white thinking[a] Surfing the urge[a] Exploring the chain reaction model[a]
Mindfulness education (ME)	Quieting the mind Mindful attention Managing negative emotions and negative thinking Acknowledgment of self and others Team work-goal setting as a group Interpersonal relationship skills Healthy self-care	Psychoeducation Mindful attention training Affirmations Visualizations

(continues)

TABLE 6.3
Components of Mindfulness and Emotional-Regulation
Interventions *(Continued)*

Technique	Emphasis	Sample practices
Mindfulness-based stress reduction (MBSR)	Formal and informal mindfulness practice Self-regulation of attention Self-compassion Nonjudgment Loving-kindness Orientation of curiosity, openness, and acceptance Mindful eating Mindfulness in relationships Mindfulness at work and school Mindful approaches to pain, suffering, and stress	Weekly sessions and silent weekend retreat Leader feedback Group discussions Psychoeducation Body scan Mindfulness meditation Loving-kindness meditation Walking meditation Cognitive labeling Mindful eating Mindful movement Yoga Breath work Pleasant and Unpleasant events calendars[a] Media awareness and journal response[a] Eating exercises addressing awareness of hunger, fullness, taste, and satiety[a] Self-portraits[a]

Note. Data from Corstorphine, 2006; Dorjee, 2010; Greco and Hayes, 2008; Heffner, Sperry, Eifert, and Detweiler, 2002; Kristeller and Wolever, 2010; Proulx, 2007; Schonert-Reichl and Lawlor, 2010; Safer, Couturier, and Lock, 2007; Shapiro and Carlson, 2009; Shapiro, Oman, Thoresen, Plante, and Flinders, 2008; Wanden-Berghe, Sanz-Valero, and Wanden-Berghe, 2010.
[a]Indicates that this is a modification of the technique used with individuals with eating issues.

that the program decreases binge episodes, improves self-control, and reduces depressive symptoms.

Despite the rapidly developing body of knowledge, there is still a need for research on the efficacy of mindfulness-based techniques with children (Burke, 2010; Flook et al., 2010; Schonert-Reichl & Lawlor, 2010). In her extensive review, Burke (2010) indicated that the application of mindfulness-based techniques with children is well-accepted and tolerated by the populations studied. Effects ranged from nonsignificant to significant, and effect sizes ranged from small ($d = -0.2$) to very large ($d = 1.4$). Burke (2010) and Wanden-Berghe et al. (2010) noted that many studies contained methodological issues, including small sample sizes, few controls or lack of randomization, few objective measures, recruitment biases, a reliance on self or nonblind parent–teacher reports, and insufficient follow-up data.

The current body of evidence suggests positive results in application of mindfulness-based techniques among children and adolescents in decreasing anxiety, internalizing and externalizing behaviors, depression, substance use, worry, aggression and noncompliant incidents, and relevant to eating behaviors, body weight. Improvements were found in attention, concentration, accomplishment of goals, behavioral regulation, metacognition, executive functioning, happiness, mental health, compliance, self-esteem, social skills, social and emotional competence, and mindfulness (Burke, 2010; Flook et al., 2010; Schonert-Reichl & Lawlor, 2010). It is important to note that some studies conducted with children and adolescents have found trends toward improvement in functioning but no significant benefit over children in control groups (Huppert & Johnson, 2010). Overall, Burke (2010) concluded that these techniques are a judicious approach and there is a reasonable base of support for the feasibility and acceptability among older children and adolescents and a need for more data for use with younger children.

To provide an example of how mindfulness techniques might be integrated into classrooms, we briefly describe the ME program. The ME program is a theoretically derived, teacher-taught universal prevention intervention that integrates daily mindful attention training (three times a day) and focuses on the development of social emotional development and positive emotions. The program includes a 10-lesson manualized curriculum that involves all children in the classroom and applies the lesson content to other aspects of curriculum and aspects of the children's lives (Schonert-Reichl & Lawlor, 2010).

The program has four key components (Schonert-Reichl & Lawlor, 2010). The first two components are quieting the mind and mindful attention. To address these components, students begin to quiet the mind by sitting in a comfortable position and attentively listening to a single sound (e.g., a bell or chime). Next, they engage in mindful attention by using their breath as the focal point of their concentration and presence in the moment. Students were also asked to bring their attention to bodily sensations thoughts and feelings, an exercise similar to the body scan conducted in other mindfulness interventions. For the study, these daily core mindfulness attention exercises were completed three times a day for 3 min. The 3-min duration was gradually extended throughout the course of the intervention as the students were ready. The interested reader is referred to Stahl and Goldstein's (2010) A *Mindfulness-Based Stress Reduction Workbook* for detailed instruction on mindfulness-based techniques.

The third key component addresses managing negative emotions and negative thinking. This was done in two ways. First, daily affirmations and visualizations were practiced in conjunction with the mindful practices to foster positive affect and optimism. Second, the 10-lesson manualized curriculum addressed topics such as learning how to eliminate negative thinking, goal setting, and turning problems into opportunities. The last component addressed acknowledgement of self and others. This content was also delivered through lessons that included topics such as making friends and team work. The ME program lessons were taught approximately once per week for a duration of 40 to 50 min (Schonert-Reichl & Lawlor, 2010).

Program outcomes indicated that early adolescents who participated in the ME program showed significant increases, compared with controls, in optimism, positive affect, general self-concept (preadolescents only), and teacher-rated attention, emotional regulation, and social–emotional competence (Schonert-Reichl & Lawlor, 2010). Significant decreases in teacher-rated aggression and oppositional–dysregulated behavior also were noted among students who received the intervention. There was no change in negative affect. Finally, there was an interesting finding that general self-concept (early adolescents only) decreased for the treatment group and increased for controls. Schonert-Reichl and Lawlor (2010) theorized that there may be a developmentally sensitive period at early adolescence during which increased attention and reflection on the self may result in the adolescents developing a more critical or realist view of the self that translated to less positive ratings of self-concept. As the ME program is one of the first school-based research studies on a universal application of mindfulness techniques, much more is to be understood as the research in this area develops.

Yoga as a Mind and Body Intervention

Yoga is a mind and body practice that has evolved over thousands of years (Galantino, Galbavy, & Quinn, 2008). It is a comprehensive practice that entails many facets, including the practice of postures (*asanas*), relaxation, meditation, breath work, and service to others (T. Mendelson et al., 2010; Serwacki & Cook-Cottone, 2012). As yoga has become Westernized, much of the focus has centered on the practice of the postures, relaxation, and breath work (for a brief history of yoga in America, see Douglass, 2007). The *asanas* serve to stretch, strengthen, and relax the muscles of the body, whereas the breathing and relaxation exercises serve to calm the mind and the nervous system (Galantino et al., 2008; Scime & Cook-Cottone, 2008).

Although much more research is needed, the body of empirical evidence documenting the benefit of yoga practice is growing (Galantino et al., 2008; T. Mendelson et al., 2010). First, studies have shown that using yoga as an intervention in schools is feasible and acceptable (e.g., T. Mendelson et al., 2010). Second, positive effects have been found for children and adolescents in neuromuscular, musculoskeletal, and cardiopulmonary functioning; mood regulation; self-regulatory capacity; reduction in persistent worrying; and stress management (Galantino et al., 2008; T. Mendelson et al., 2010; Scime & Cook-Cottone, 2008). Third, as first demonstrated by the Satsanga Research Project, led by Cook-Cottone, there is preliminary evidence that yoga may be helpful in the prevention and treatment of disordered eating, overweight, and obesity (Boudette, 2006; Carei, Fyfe-Johnson, Breuner, & Brown, 2009; C. Cook-Cottone, Beck, & Kane, 2008; Douglass, 2009; Galantino et al., 2008; Guarracino, Savino, & Edelstein, 2006; Scime & Cook-Cottone, 2008; Scime, Cook-Cottone, Kane, & Watson, 2006).

Yoga can be easily integrated into the school setting in several ways. As illustrated in the work of Schonert-Reichl and Lawlor (2010), breath and mindful attention can be incorporated into the school days in short 3- to 5-min sessions to quiet the mind, increase mindful awareness, and center students' attention. The asanas can be taught in physical education and health classes, as part of sports-team preparation, or part of after-school offerings for interested students and families before or after school hours (see Scime & Cook-Cottone, 2008). For a review of yoga and the treatment of disordered, see Douglass (2009) and Boudette (2006). For a comprehensive review of yoga in the schools, see Serwacki and Cook-Cottone (2012).

SELF-CARE AND EMOTIONAL REGULATION

Emotional regulation involves awareness, identification, monitoring, and negotiating of emotional experience (Macklem, 2008). Adaptive functional emotional-regulation skills are present when a student is able to recognize and regulate emotions and then use that information to problem solve (Corstorphine, 2006). Emotional-regulation instruction should integrate the following components: self-care (Linehan, 1993), psychoeducation (C. Cook-Cottone, 2006a), and active practice (Corstorphine, 2006).

Self-Care Practices as the Foundation of Emotional Regulation

Emotional regulation is inextricably connected to physiological stability and homeostasis. An individual's physiological status must be steady in order for the limbic system (the emotional part of the brain) to function in a regulated and consistent manner. Daily self-care practices can ensure physiological stability, thereby supporting emotional regulation (Linehan, 1993). Such practices include nutrition, hydration, exercise, self-soothing behaviors (e.g., breath work, relaxation), sleep and rest, and when appropriate, taking prescribed medication (e.g., antibiotics when sick, or stimulant medication for attention deficits; see Figure 6.2). By stabilizing these basic self-care domains, emotional regulation becomes much more accessible to children and adolescents. To illustrate, studies exploring malnutrition and undernutrition (which can occur concomitant with overweight and obesity) in children and adolescents have suggested that effects can be emotionally destabilizing (Hay & Sachdev, 2011). Effects of malnutrition and

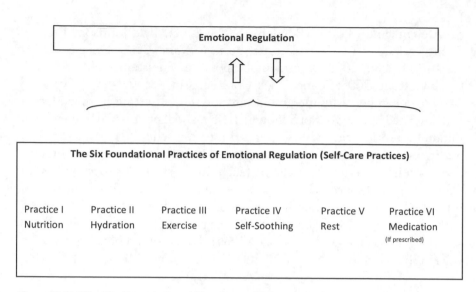

Figure 6.2. The Six Foundational Practices of Emotional Regulation.

undernutrition include impaired concentration, stress, difficulty making decisions, reduced judgment, poor intellectual functioning, and depression (Hay & Sachdev, 2011; Martins, Toledo Florêncio, Grillo, & do Carmo, 2011). Underscoring the importance of basic self-care behaviors (i.e., physiological stabilization) for successful school functioning, both federal and state legislation have addressed nutrition, hydration, and exercise in the school setting (see Chapter 9, this volume).

Basic Emotional-Regulation Training for Children

Cognitive emotional behavioral therapy (CEBT) is viewed as a psychological intervention designed to reduce pathology rather than to simply help individuals tolerate affect as seen in DBT (Corstorphine, 2006). To make the concepts inherent in CEBT and dialectical behavioral approaches (e.g., DBT) accessible to children, adaptations of the protocol used with adults have been made (Callahan, 2008; C. Cook-Cottone, 2006b; Macklem, 2008). For example, in a very simple adaption of CEBT, the basic areas of the brain are described and diagramed (see Figure 6.3) to support the understanding of emotions. Young children often struggle to understand abstract concepts, making work with feelings difficult. As shown to be effective in a primary prevention program for EDs, the illustration of the thinking and the feeling parts of the brain provides a concrete view of emotional experience for children (C. Cook-Cottone, 2006b; Macklem, 2008; Scime & Cook-Cottone, 2008; Scime et al., 2006). Using the illustration, an instructor explains the

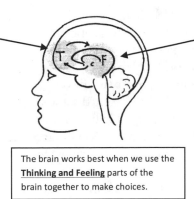

The **Thinking** part of our brain helps us understand and make sense of things, put things in order, connect ideas, and make plans. Breathing helps us pay attention to this part (even when we are upset).

The **Feeling** part of our brain is the emotional part of our brain. It allows us to feel our feelings and is strongly connected to our bodies. Breathing helps this part calm down.

The brain works best when we use the **Thinking and Feeling** parts of the brain together to make choices.

Figure 6.3. The Thinking (T) and Feeling (F) Brain.

importance of integrating both thoughts and feelings when responding to others and making decisions (C. Cook-Cottone, 2006b; Macklem, 2008).

Using this method, the students can go through a series of scenarios in which either the thinking or the feeling aspects of the situation were over-emphasized and then restructure the situation by using both aspects of the self (i.e., thinking and feeling) to make a choice (C. Cook-Cottone, 2006b; Scime et al., 2006). To do this, decision making is broken down into five steps, and the child's hand is used as a memory tool. Step one (first finger) is to label the feeling: "I feel _____." Step two (second finger) is to label the thought: "I think _____." Steps three and four (third and fourth fingers, respectively) are to choose what to say, do, or both. Students are encouraged to breathe slowly (i.e., inhale for a four count, hold for a four count, and exhale for a four count) to encourage the feeling part of the brain to relax and to allow the thinking part of the brain to help with the problem (C. Cook-Cottone, 2006b; Scime & Cook-Cottone, 2008; Scime et al., 2006). Once they carefully consider their options, they can indicate with a thumbs up or down if they are going to act (thumbs up, say or do something) or give the issues some time (thumbs down). In a current study, Raby and Cook-Cottone (2012) are exploring the ability of enhancing the effects of basic emotional-regulation techniques with children and training parents so that the process can be reinforced at home.

Other classroom-based practices and interventions that address emotional regulation include adhering to routine and schedules, scheduling down time, setting goals, keeping the classroom emotional climate at a low even level, modeling positive thinking and problem solving, using stories to illustrate positive emotional regulation and problem solving, separating feelings from behaviors (e.g., "It is okay to be angry at Joey, but it is not okay to hit him"), integrating mood management into daily report cards, and teaching skills for calming down (Macklem, 2008). For a review of emotional-regulation practices for the classroom, how to adapt intervention strategies for school-age children, and strategies for parents and teachers, see *Practitioners' Guide to Emotional Regulation in School-Aged Children* (Macklem, 2008).

Although more research is needed to establish reliable efficacy, CEBT has been successfully applied to eating disordered populations (Corstorphine, 2006). Using this technique, the facilitator focuses on emotions and encourages both the experience and expression of emotions. Emotional experience is explored by identifying (a) a triggering event (i.e., external–environmental [e.g., comment by a friend] or internal [e.g., thoughts, physical sensation, emotion]), (b) thoughts (i.e., the interpretation of the triggering event), (c) emotions (i.e., brain and body changes and the sensing of the emotional experience), and (d) behavior as the communication of emotions (i.e., body language, language–words, and actions). Techniques also include keeping a diary of emotions and the functions of emotions, listing pros and cons of emotional suppression and change in emotional inhibition, engaging in experiential experiences–behavioral experiments, and learning strategies for restructuring beliefs about experience and expression of emotions (Corstorphine, 2006).

GENERAL TIPS FOR ADAPTING TECHNIQUES FOR SCHOOL-BASED APPLICATION

School personnel should attend to several areas when applying mindfulness, self-care, and emotional-regulation techniques to children. First, mindfulness, self-care, and emotional-regulation skills are *practices*. That is, they must be practiced to be integrated in order for the skills to be developed. Although psychoeducation is helpful in terms of explaining techniques and benefits, the true outcomes manifest when the children, adolescents, and those around them actually practice the techniques over a period of time, throughout each day. It is analogous to learning how to ride a bike. You must learn to ride by trying to ride it rather than knowing how it works and how fun it would be if you could ride. It is important to remember that children live within the context of their schools and families and are reliant on adults to provide support and structure for daily practice (Burke, 2010). Parents and teachers can help by structuring time for children to practice as well as by practicing these techniques with their children or students (Burke, 2010).

It is important that practitioners and school personnel adapt activities for developmental limitations and needs. Consider attention span, cognitive capacities, language, physicality, and relevant content (Burke, 2010). More physical applications (e.g., yoga) may benefit younger populations, with mindfulness attention training showing more positive effects in older populations

(Schonert-Reichl & Lawlor, 2010; Scime & Cook-Cottone, 2008). As with other areas of the curriculum, sessions should be shorter and more frequent and material more concrete for younger children (Greco & Hayes, 2008; Macklem, 2008; Scime & Cook-Cottone, 2008). Adolescents are more capable of longer sessions and can negotiate abstract and logical content (Greco & Hayes, 2008; Macklem, 2008). School administrators can support the integration of mindfulness-based tendencies through workshops and training opportunities that address developmental issues and application challenges and that can be directed to both parents and teachers. See Burke (2010), Macklem (2008), Greco and Hayes (2008) for further adaptations for children.

FUTURE DIRECTIONS

The field of mindfulness, self-care, and emotional-regulation applications in the schools is growing rapidly. As a school-based standard of practice emerges, researchers will help to detail the most effective components, delivery methodology, and school personnel training programs. Future research will also explore critical issues such as compliance and integrity of school-based applications (i.e., how well school personnel stick to protocol), dosage (i.e., how many sessions and for how long), and benefits of at-home practice (Huppert & Johnson, 2010). Future research will likely also include personality measures, as aspects of personality and developmental interact with program components, activities, and outcomes (e.g., agreeableness, emotional stability; Huppert & Johnson, 2010). School personnel can move this field forward by participating in research, which often involves benefits such as free training, help in bolstering the school's wellness plan, and incentives for students and families. Check with colleges and universities located near your school district for opportunities; most research programs are searchable on their web pages.

CONCLUSION

This chapter covered the importance of mindfulness, self-care, and emotional regulation in promoting health and well-being in children. These skills are absolutely necessary to achieve the adaptive core of our model (see Figure 1.4) that is characterized by intuitive eating (i.e., awareness of hunger and satiety cues) and mind–body attunement (i.e., sensing, honoring, and respecting the body by being aware of and engaging in behaviors to take care of its needs). Skills and Suggested Resources that educators can use to foster mindfulness and emotional regulation in students are presented later in this volume.

III

SCHOOL-BASED INTERVENTIONS AND POLICIES

7

PREVENTATIVE INTERVENTION: MEDIA LITERACY, BODY IMAGE, BODY TOLERANCE, AND SELF-REGULATED EATING

Part III of this volume shines light on how school personnel can direct students away from the maladaptive endpoints of the body image (i.e., body obsessed and body ignored) and eating behavior (i.e., compulsive restriction, compulsive bingeing–eating in the absence of hunger) continua, as depicted in Figure 1.4. Part III serves as the "roof"—held in place by the three pillars of intuitive eating and nutrition (Chapter 4); healthy physical activity (Chapter 5); and mindfulness, self-care, and emotional regulation (Chapter 6), which are grounded in the foundation; that is, the models for a positive, healthy school community (Chapter 3). This metaphorical roof serves to shield students from influences that prompt them to feel badly about their bodies and develop disordered eating attitudes and behaviors and aid in their recovery within the structure of the school system. Specifically, Part III begins with describing and analyzing empirically supported preventative intervention

DOI: 10.1037/14180-008
Healthy Eating in Schools: Evidence-Based Interventions to Help Kids Thrive, by C. P. Cook-Cottone, E. Tribole, and T. L. Tylka

programs for negative body image, nascent eating disorders (EDs), eating in the absence of hunger, and maladaptive attitudinal change (i.e., toward media literacy and appreciating body diversity) within a transcontextual perspective (Chapter 7); it continues with identifying screening, assessment, and treatment supports for body image and eating behavior (Chapter 8); and it ends with a discussion of federal policy and professional guidelines (Chapter 9).

WHY SCHOOLS FOR PREVENTION EFFORTS?

Children need to be armed with the appropriate tools to avoid body dissatisfaction and EDs. These tools will help them decipher and contextualize (rather than internalize) media messages and marketing strategies that, to sell products, encourage them to be dissatisfied with their appearance. Contextualizing media messages helps children appropriately identify their distress as stemming from an external rather than a personal issue (e.g., "I feel bad because this magazine only presents one narrow image of beauty"), whereas internalizing media messages harms children in that they identify their distress as a personal flaw (e.g., "I should look like these models"; Tylka & Augustus-Horvath, 2011). The educational system is an ideal place to deliver these tools. In fact, the most successful method for preventing and reducing body dissatisfaction is through school-based curricula (Paxton, 2011).

What makes the school setting ideal for the delivery of these tools? First, primary prevention programs can be implemented when students are young, before serious problems have developed in most children, and can be used to help detect students who may already show symptoms. For these students, more rigorous (i.e., secondary and tertiary) preventative intervention programs can be implemented within schools as well. Second, attendance is likely to be strong and stable, as students are required to attend school. Third, educators are trained to be effective disseminators of information to children. Fourth, educators interact with the same children over an extended period, making it feasible to administer a manualized program in its entirety. Fifth, educators could reinforce the concepts learned in the program with parents and the community to have a positive impact on students' home environment. Sixth, educators can initiate empowerment programs within schools whereby students interact with their peers to challenge media and marketing ploys. Seventh, grade tiers inherent in the school system allow older students already involved in the program to mentor younger students.

WHAT TO AVOID

It is important to first consider what does not work. Some programs and styles of communicating information on body image and EDs can do more harm than good and even be iatrogenic (Mann et al., 1997; O'Dea & Yager, 2011). Good intentions are not enough; school personnel must commit to "do no harm" by using established methods shown to be effective.

Programs should not be introduced to students as ED prevention programs. ED prevention programs that directly refer to case studies or ED behaviors (e.g., vomiting, starvation, laxative abuse, diet pills, bingeing, excessive exercise as a form of purging, cigarette smoking for weight control) are likely to introduce these issues to children and adolescents in a suggestive manner—even if these techniques are discussed in a highly negative manner (O'Dea, 2005). Indeed, teenage girls and young women started smoking after receiving messages about the potentially slimming effects of nicotine (Tomeo, Field, Berkey, Colditz, & Frazier, 1999).

Schools should also avoid informational programs that portray body image concerns and EDs as normal and common among children. These programs are thought to prevent new cases from arising and encourage students who already have problems to seek help. This is not the case. These programs make disordered eating habits seem like common behaviors and negative body image seem like a ubiquitous attitude, inadvertently encouraging healthy students to try these behaviors and adopt this attitude (Mann et al., 1997). A quote offered by a student illustrates this idea: "Actually, I felt pretty good about my body until about 6th grade. But then everyone else hated theirs, so I thought I should, too" (Kater, 2005, p. xxi).

Using recovered peers as guest speakers in school-based prevention also is a bad idea (O'Dea, 2007). These speakers, who often look normal and attractive, may talk about dangerous methods they used to lose weight. Again, this could unintentionally normalize and glamorize EDs, leading to the adoption of dangerous techniques by students looking for ways to lose weight. They may identify with the speakers and aspire to be like them, which may include going through a similar "ED journey."

Any approach that promotes "dieting" and "weight loss" should be avoided. This point has particular relevance to obesity prevention programs. Dieting and weight-loss approaches are not effective in the long term for reducing obesity or obesity risk. For example, Field et al. (2003) followed 14,972 dieting and nondieting children ages 9 to 14 for 3 years. At the end of this period, children who were on diets gained significantly more weight and were more 8 to 12 times more likely to report binge or compulsive overeating than those who were not on diets. These approaches also encourage weight-based stigma among children—which could promote teasing, bullying, and internalized weightism (Bacon, 2010; Mann et al., 2007; O'Dea, 2007) and may inadvertently heighten weight concerns and attitudes and behaviors consistent with EDs among children and adolescents (O'Dea, 2005). Simply stated, the focus should be on fostering health, not lowering weight.

It is also important for school personnel to be aware that some media disguised as positive are hurtful. An example is a Victoria's Secret advertisement that reads, "I love my body" under a picture of a supermodel personifying the narrow beauty ideal. Girls and women could interpret this as "In order to love my body, I need to look like that." For schools, this ad campaign serves as a caution against presenting messages such as "Love your body" alongside thin, Caucasian children rather than children of diverse sizes and races. The content of media presented to students should be well thought out and monitored by the schools.

WHAT TO DO

Fortunately, clear recommendations have been provided that can be used as a guide for school personnel to prevent negative body image and eating disturbances. Programs based on these recommendations can be divided into primary prevention and secondary prevention, which are covered in this section.

Primary Prevention

The best strategies to prevent symptoms of negative body image, EDs, and eating in the absence of hunger before they emerge are to foster students' healthy self-esteem, empower them to be agents of social change, and teach them how to assert themselves, critically evaluate media messages and images, and honor their hunger and satiety cues (Levine, Piran, & Stoddard, 1999; Steiner-Adair & Sjostrom, 2006). In Table 7.1, we review four such programs.

Secondary Prevention

This approach is geared toward identifying students at risk for body image and eating concerns and intervening so that their concerns do not develop and manifest further. According to Mann et al. (1997), many secondary prevention programs, although helpful for students who show some symptoms of body image disturbance and disordered eating, actually instigate maladaptive symptoms in healthy students. Yet, one secondary prevention program, the Body Project, has been shown to not promote negative body

TABLE 7.1
Guide for School Personnel in Deciding Which Preventative Intervention Programs to Implement

Program	Media Smart	Full of Ourselves	Healthy Body Image	Everybody's Different	Body Project	ROC
Cost	$495[a]	$47.95	$65	$59.95	$35 + $5/student	No Cost[b]
Prevention type	Primary	Primary	Primary	Primary	Secondary	Secondary
Audience gender	Girls, boys	Girls	Girls, boys	Girls, boys	Girls[c]	Girls, boys
Grade level	7th–9th	6th–8th	4th–6th	7th–8th	9th–12th	4th–6th
No. of sessions	8	8	10	9	4	14
Session length	~50 min	50–60 min	~60 min	50–80 min	60 min	75 min
Empirical support	Strong	Moderate	Some	Moderate	Strong	Moderate
Hire an outside health provider or psychologist?	No	No	No	No	No	Yes
Facilitator guide—scripts	Yes	Yes	Yes	Yes	Yes	No[b]
Guide for parents	No	Yes	Yes	No	No	Yes
Handouts—Worksheets	Yes	Yes	Yes	Yes	Yes	No
Teacher training program	No	No	No	Yes	No	No
Primary risk factors targeted						
Internalizing media ideals	Yes	Yes	Yes	Yes	Yes	No
Body dissatisfaction	Yes	Yes	Yes	Yes	Yes	No
Peer relationships	Yes	Yes	Yes	Yes	Yes	No
Eating problems	No	Yes	Yes	Yes	Yes	Yes
Self-esteem	No	Yes	Yes	Yes	No	No
Other content						
Media literacy	Yes	Yes	Yes	Yes	Yes	Yes
Body diversity	Yes	Yes	Yes	Yes	Yes	No
Cultural diversity	Yes	Yes	Yes	Yes	No	No
Cognitive dissonance	No	No	No	No	Yes	No
Intuitive—Mindful Eating	No	Yes	Yes	Yes	No	Yes
Coping with pressure and stress	Yes	Yes	Yes	Yes	Yes	Yes

Note. ROC = Regulation of Cues.
[a]One-time cost, used to fund further ED research. [b]No curriculum guide for schools has been developed to date; this is a recent program. Ideas for how schools can implement the ROC program are available in this chapter. Contact Kerri Boutelle (kboutelle@ucsd.edu) for more information. [c]Ideas for how to tailor this program for boys are presented in the chapter.

image and disordered eating in healthy students and to reduce these variables in at-risk students. Thus, educators can implement this program in the school system without fear that it may harm some students. Another secondary prevention program, the Regulation of Cues (ROC) intervention, aims to help individuals cope with their food cravings and thus not eat in the absence of hunger. We present these two programs in Table 7.1.

RISK FACTORS TARGETED AND EMPIRICAL SUPPORT FOR PREVENTATIVE INTERVENTIONS

According to a review of preventative intervention programs, Stice and Shaw (2004) indicated that the most promising effects resulted from programs that target empirically supported risk factors and include cognitive interventions that alter maladaptive attitudes related to these risk factors. The central risk factors for eating- and weight-related problems are internalization of media ideals, body dissatisfaction, low self-esteem, eating in the absence of hunger–inability to self-regulate, commentary about appearance (e.g., pressure to lose weight, teasing–bullying) from important others such as parents and peers, and tension within relationships (Birch, Fisher, & Davison, 2003; Stice, 2001; Stice & Agras, 1998; Stice, Presnell, & Spangler, 2002; van den Berg, Mond, Eisenberg, Ackard, & Neumark-Sztainer, 2010; Ventura & Birch, 2008; Wilksch & Wade, 2010). The programs discussed in this chapter cover many (if not all) of these risk factors.

Determinations of the effectiveness of programs have been largely based on whether (a) they improve scores (e.g., on body dissatisfaction, ED symptoms) from baseline to posttest and follow-up and (b) the prevention group demonstrates an improvement over the control group. Each program we review has yielded at least some empirical evidence.

Exploring the true effectiveness of primary prevention programs is tricky. Typically, enrolled students are psychologically healthy at pretest and may experience ceiling and floor effects on measures of self-esteem and body–eating concerns, respectively (Stice & Shaw, 2004). Hence, there is little or no room for them to improve at posttest or follow-up, and the low levels of risk factors at pretest attenuate statistical power to detect intervention effects. Indeed, in their review of preventative intervention programs for eating concerns, Stice and Shaw (2004) noted that higher risk individuals often benefit more from programming because they have more room to grow toward psychological health from pretest to posttest. Instead, the programs' benefits may lie in building children's (a) resistance to fend off drops in self-esteem and heightened body distress and eating problems well into the future; and (b) respect for body diversity, thereby reducing bullying–teasing their peers based on weight. Because research has not yet thoroughly evaluated this extended trajectory, we encourage school personnel to use these programs and psychologists to study their long-term effectiveness.

Stice and Shaw (2004) further revealed that prevention programs that were interactive (i.e., actively engage students) rather than purely didactic (i.e., simply present the material to them), multisession rather than single session, and avoided psychoeducational content (e.g., describing ED symptoms) were the most effective. These authors stressed the need to use assessment tools with established reliability and validity for students (see Chapter 8, this volume) to appropriately evaluate these programs.

The programs presented in this chapter aim to prevent the development and progression of body image, eating, nutrition, and weight–fitness concerns and proactively teach students a model for long-term health that is realistic and nondiscriminatory. Thus, healthy body image and lifestyle choices, although not in the direct spotlight, are directed toward all students in the program, regardless of size, shape, cultural and socioeconomic background, genetic weight predisposition, and gender. All programs are interactive, as recommended by Stice and Shaw (2004), and they contain manuals to ease administration, ensure the integrity of program content, and avoid presenting contradictory information to students. When delivering these programs, it is imperative to incorporate both whole-school and transcontextual approaches, described in detail in Chapter 3. The school ethos and policy must follow the framework of the healthy student to maximize the effectiveness of the program. Thus, school personnel, parents, and even communities need to be on board with the concepts presented (Piran, 1999). This whole-school approach changes the overall climate—it helps students feel safe, respected, nurtured, and encouraged to grow and develop with appreciation and respect for their body, whatever its size.

PRIMARY PREVENTATIVE INTERVENTION PROGRAMS

Four prevention programs, as well as media literacy tools (e.g., documentary and educational DVDs and books) and interactive activities, are covered in this section. These programs, tools, and activities can be used by school personnel to prevent symptoms of negative body image and eating problems from emerging in elementary and middle school students.

Media Smart

Media Smart (see Table 7.1), a program by Simon Wilksch and Tracey Wade (Wilksch & Wade, 2010; Wilksch & Wade, 2009b) offers educators detailed lesson plans and activities, a workbook for students, background information on body image and EDs, ideas for how to analyze and challenge media messages, and tips for students to handle pressure and navigate through adolescence and adulthood as a skillful and confident person (descriptive website with link to purchase: http://sparky.socsci.flinders.edu.au/research online/projects/5).[1] Media Smart contains eight lessons that can be incorporated into English, social studies, home economics, health education, and physical education classes. Media Smart is ideal for students in eighth grade; however, Wilksch and Wade (2009b) believe that it would be beneficial for students as young as sixth grade. Although it is a bit costly up front, it is a one-time license purchase for schools (e.g., schools do not have to purchase additional student workbooks). Wilksch and Wade (2009b) used the money received to fund additional ED research.

Wilksch and Wade (2009b) emphasize the importance of the Media Smart presenter being a role model for positive, healthy body image as well as dynamic, able to engage all students, and respectful. Schools could hire a health educator (e.g., a clinical, health, or counseling psychology graduate student or professor at a local university) to be the program presenter—much of the research support accrued on Media Smart has used a health educator; however, Wilksch and Wade are now empirically evaluating how well the program works when delivered by teachers. As of September 2012, they have completed a pilot study with favorable findings that teachers (in lieu of health educators) can effectively deliver the program and have applied for a grant for a more substantial evaluation. If used, the health educator and teachers should meet to discuss program content and to determine whether the learning activities are appropriate. It is imperative that the teachers understand and respect the prevention program and how it is delivered, as they are viewed as critical to the success of the program. During the administration of the program, teachers should monitor groups during interactive activities and assist with ensuring appropriate student conduct. Teachers also should continue to integrate relevant aspects of Media Smart into their lesson plans after the program has ended.

The program is divided into three phases. Phase 1 promotes student engagement by designing the learning activities to be inclusive—for girls and boys, different races and ethnicities, diverse socioeconomic statuses represented at the school, and so forth. For instance, advertisements, stereotypes (e.g., messages that media reveal about how we should structure our life), and idealized images are presented for women and men (and of different races) in the media. Phase 2 encourages and praises students for expressing their

---

[1] This is *not* the same program as Media-Smart Youth offered by Eunice Kennedy Shriver and the National Institute of Child Health and Human Development.

opinions on the topics covered. Several activities are designed to generate a diversity of opinions. Phase 3 consolidates previously reviewed content and focuses on the future, that is, how students will translate what they have learned into their daily lives. At the end of each session, time should be allotted to (a) relate the lesson to previous lessons and (b) provide students with a chance to express their views of multiple aspects of the program.

Lesson 1 begins with the presenter providing information about the program and establishing ground rules (e.g., respecting diverse opinions). This lesson examines stereotypes. In small groups, students are handed magazines and asked to investigate how the media presents girls–women, boys–men, and lifestyles. They cut out magazine pictures, glue them on a poster board, and generate a list of words that describe typical aspects of the stereotype (e.g., women = passive, men = strong). They draw speech bubbles from the magazine character's mouth to contradict the stereotype (e.g., a woman in a skin-tight dress remarking, "I can't wait to get home and put on sweats"). Each group shows their collage/poster to the class and describes their perception of the stereotype. The class examines whether these stereotypes are fair and if there are well-known, admirable people who do not fit these stereotypes. Girls are asked whether they think stereotypes of boys and men are fair, and boys are asked whether they think stereotypes of girls and women are fair, which typically generates interesting discussions (Wilksch & Wade, 2009b).

The focus of Lesson 2 is media advertising and the tactics companies use to sell their products. Students watch a video (a link that is embedded in the lesson plan) that discusses that only four out of 40,000 women are selected to be fashion models and that they are still not "good enough" because they undergo modification to be in the ad (e.g., padded bras, extensive makeup, hairstyling) and their images undergo computer modification (e.g., airbrushing). Before and after pictures of airbrushing are provided. Presenters then help students focus on media motives for why advertisers want viewers to be unhappy with their appearance—so they "buy" their promises that their product will work and then purchase their product. Presenters ask students whether it is worth their effort to attempt to look like false computer-enhanced media images.

Lesson 3 examines pressures students receive from media, family, and friends to look and act certain ways. Presenters (a) encourage students to discuss what they can do to handle pressure placed on them, (b) help students generate ways to handle the pressure, and (c) guide students in identifying what they can do to make sure they do not place too much pressure on others. A video on handling peer pressure is shown. Students participate in activities that identify the qualities they admire in themselves. Lesson 4 continues the discussion of pressure and being assertive. Students engage in role plays where they (a) practice responding to negative comments and teasing as well as (b) how they would help someone younger than them from getting drawn into the media's pressure to worry about their appearance. The presenter leads students into a discussion on what are the "secrets" to feeling good about themselves.

In Lesson 5, presenters differentiate healthy and unhealthy media messages. The presenter shows a selection of advertisements, and students comment on whether each sends a healthy or unhealthy message. Students learn about consumer activism and brainstorm ways that they can engage in activism. Presenters review effective activism strategies and provide evidence that consumers can make a difference in shaping media. In pairs, students select an advertisement and write an e-mail of praise (for healthy messages) or protest (for unhealthy messages) either to the advertising company or to the editor of the magazine.

In Lessons 6 and 7, students discuss whether or how advertising is harmful. They break into small groups and work on a project, such as a poster, play, debate, or PowerPoint presentation. In Lesson 6, students prepare their presentation and then deliver it in Lesson 7. The presenter reveals how to give constructive feedback, and students then give constructive feedback to each group. The presenter and students discuss the content of each presentation.

Last, in Lesson 8, the presenter and students discuss feedback (if any) they received from their e-mails to advertising companies or editors. The class processes the appropriateness of the replies and generates hypotheses–opinions about the companies who did not reply. They reflect about the processes of trying to bring about change and standing up for their beliefs. Students (if they wish) share strategies that they use to maintain the positive feelings about themselves when they see media images. During the last half of the session, students share their views on the program and its usefulness. The presenter emphasizes the importance of valuing their beliefs and feeling comfortable expressing them and encourages students to generalize this philosophy to other aspects of their life. Students (and teachers) are thanked and praised for their involvement.

Media Smart has been thoroughly investigated and has been shown to be effective for a mixed-gender sample of eighth-grade (approximately 13 years old) girls and boys (Wilksch & Wade, 2009a). This large-scale research study involved 24 classes (540 students; half received Media Smart, and the other half constituted the control group). Students completed standardized and psychometrically sound measures of nine ED risk factors at four separate times: before the program started, after the program finished, 6 months after the program finished, and 2.5 years after the program finished. Those students who received the program reported, on average, (a) significantly lower scores on six of the nine ED risk factors at posttest and during the two follow-up periods when compared with their pretest scores and (b) stayed well below students in the control group throughout the duration of the study. In addition, in their discursive comments, 98% of girls and boys rated the program as valuable and enjoyable.

Healthy Body Image: Teaching Kids to Eat and Love Their Bodies, Too

Kathy Kater's (2005) Healthy Body Image curriculum (see Table 7.1) offers valuable background information as well as detailed lesson plans, preparations, activities, handouts, and materials for educators to bolster students' healthy body image and prevent unhealthy eating (for the website, see http://www.bodyimagehealth.org/index.html; a facilitator guide is available for purchase at http://www.bulimia.com/productdetails.cfm?PC=1276). Its 10 lessons fit into health, science, social studies, and history educational segments. Although the program is geared for students in fourth through sixth grades, booster lessons are recommended for teens.

Before the first lesson is administered, all school personnel are directed to read the Background for Educators section of the facilitator guide to become acquainted with the curriculum to ensure consistency in message content and delivery. Educators are informed that they must avoid culturally "toxic" fallacies, such as valuing appearance over personality and intellect, denying biological diversity in weight, promoting eating according to external cues (e.g., rigid dieting plans) rather than internal hunger and satiety cues (i.e., intuitive eating), and placing weight at the forefront and health in the background (e.g., avoiding healthy choices if they do not result in the desired size). Instead, the mission is to help students embrace their health and appreciate their body. Educators are encouraged to teach all curriculum concepts, challenge their own prejudices about weight, and incorporate the concepts in many courses.

The 10 lessons reflect three broad themes. In the first theme, students learn to recognize and respect their basic biology and what is not in their control—their size, shape, weight, and hunger. They discover that restricting their hunger (or dieting) is counterproductive to weight loss and interferes with their ability to naturally regulate food intake. The desired outcomes are body acceptance and body tolerance. The second theme helps students recognize what they do have control over. They are encouraged to consistently satisfy their hunger with enough varied wholesome food in a stable predictable manner, limit their sedentary choices to promote physical activity, and choose role models who reflect a realistic standard. The desired outcomes include enjoying eating for health, energy, and hunger satisfaction while creating a physically active lifestyle for fitness, endurance, fun, relaxation, and stress relief. In the third theme, students develop media literacy and social and cultural resiliency. Autonomy, self-esteem, confidence, and the ability for critical thinking are the desired outcomes.

An introductory lesson is given to acquaint students with the program. Educators emphasize the importance of the lessons while reassuring students that the discussions will be safe and respectful. Lesson 1 emphasizes that people become unhappy trying to control something that is not in their power to control. In terms of their looks, it is best to make the most of who they were born to be. Structured activities help students (a) gain historical and cultural perspective on body image, eating, nutrition, fitness, and weight norms; and (b) see that it is possible to resist unhealthy societal pressures.

Lesson 2 emphasizes that the way people look is only one part of who they are, and they need to pay attention to all of who they are—focusing on many different aspects of their identity makes them stronger than focusing solely on one aspect (e.g., their looks). In one activity, students each create a "balanced identity mobile," expressing diverse aspects of their own identities. Leaders show that in order for the mobile to function well, all parts of the mobile (i.e., with each part = one aspect of their identity) need to be in balance. This lesson helps students appreciate and recognize their diverse attributes, which places their appearance in context.

Lesson 3 highlights that there are many different "normal" ways for looks to change in puberty. Being able to recognize that looks are only one aspect of their identity from Lesson 2 helps students acknowledge that physical changes in puberty occur, but not to become overwhelmed by these changes. Students learn about common physical changes; talking about these changes can be reassuring and supportive. They realize that words describing body sizes are not judgments; that is, no matter what people say or think, a naturally thin predisposition is not better than a fit and healthy fatter one, but is just different, and the important thing is to be fit at any size.

Lesson 4 reveals that genetics is the greatest determinant of body size and shape. Students identify characteristics of their own personal genetic heritages and therefore learn the biological limits to what they can and cannot control in these domains. Students match each of their appearance and attribute characteristics (e.g., hair color, hair type, eye color, skin color, artistic skills, mathematic skills) with the people in their family who have that particular characteristic.

Students learn in Lesson 5 that each person's body works to grow and maintain a weight that is natural for him or her, recognizing that the body has an internal weight-regulatory system that defends its natural weight. They participate in an activity (the "Metabolism Game") in which they discover that if everyone ate exactly the same food and was active in exactly the same ways, people would still have different bodies, from fat to thin. They learn that it is not safe to assume how much a person eats or how active they are from appearance alone, as this creates a myth that fatness cannot be normal and results only from unhealthy activity and eating patterns.

Media literacy is covered in Lesson 6. Students document the pervasiveness of media images in Western culture and learn about the strong role visual media have had in determining present cultural values about looks. Students, in small groups, receive sample ads and interpret "stories" told by each image, for example, "Our product is for YOU. You are a person who could be happy, loved, cool, gorgeous, and successful if you buy it." Students recognize the ways in which unrealistic media images create false and destructive expectations. Learning to interpret media messages reduces their vulnerability to internalizing (being "sold") unhealthy messages.

Lesson 7 informs students that weight loss diets do not work—people can hold back hunger for a while but will eat more later to make up for it. They discover that food fulfills a basic need, and if their internal hunger cues are ignored, then they are likely to become obsessed with food because they are fighting against their nature. They learn that diets usually end up with individuals regaining the lost weight, if not even more weight. Students participate in the "Air Diet" in which those without asthma or other breathing problems are handed a drinking straw and told to plug their nose and breathe entirely through the straw. They see that willpower cannot control the innate urge to get more air, and educators make the connection to the body's quest for food when deprived of it. Lesson 8 piggybacks on Lesson 7, directing students that eating well (for nutrition, energy, hunger satisfaction, and enjoyment) is the first part of the equation to achieve a healthy weight that is right for them. This lesson informs students on the importance of trusting their hunger cues to regulate how much to eat. Students engage in an activity to determine whether they are eating enough nutritious food. They use a chart to record what they eat during 5 days and then graph their results. Teachers emphasize that if they eat a balanced variety of food from the five main food groups (i.e., grains, vegetables, fruits, milk, meat–beans) on most days, they can be confident they are eating for health.

Lesson 9 introduces the second part of this equation—physical activity must be paired with eating well to achieve a healthy weight that is right for them. Educators reveal the history of active and nonactive lifestyles to help students see that sedentary lifestyles can easily occur in modern times. They discuss cultural myths, for example, "No pain, no gain" and "Fatter people cannot be physically active." Students are exposed to the value of fitness and examine their own daily activity levels. They record their daily activity levels and evaluate whether they are getting enough daily physical activity and how they can fit more activity in their life.

In the final lesson, students learn how fads and fashions could influence their choice of role models and discover how to select positive and realistic role models. Educators encourage students to "dare" to stay true to their authentic self, even when under peer and cultural pressures. Students reflect on their current and future role models. Activities include students articulating two people who they view as role models in which at least one is someone they know personally. To select someone, they must know at least five nonappearance qualities that they admire about this person and would like to develop within themselves.

The curriculum has been shown to positively influence students' body image and lifestyle behaviors as well as increase their knowledge of unrealistic media images, the biology of size and shape, body size prejudice, and the hazards of dieting (Kater et al., 2000, 2002). However, there was no difference between the intervention and control groups from pre- to posttest (Kater et al., 2002). Kater recently updated her curriculum, and it is now called *Teaching Kids to Care for Their Bodies: A Comprehensive Curriculum for Addressing Concerns with Body Image, Eating, Fitness, and Weight in Today's Challenging Environment*.

Full of Ourselves

Although the phrase "full of yourself" is usually used pejoratively, Steiner-Adair and Sjostrom (2006) chose it to represent a prevention program based on girls claiming their strengths. Girls "full of themselves" know who they are, know that they matter and what matters to them, pay attention to how they feel and what they need, make choices and decisions that are good for them, take good care of their body, stand up for their beliefs, reveal their thoughts to others, are valuable friends, and know that they can make a positive difference in the world. This interactive and upbeat program (see Table 7.1) helps girls combat the ubiquitous social and cultural pressures to focus on their appearance and instead become effective leaders and agents of social change. Because girls are socialized to think of their body size and shape as the ultimate measure of their worth (literally weighing their self-esteem), they often do not identify or claim their intellect and skill-based activities as their strengths. Boys, however, seem to be more likely to articulate such strengths within themselves. For this reason, Full of Ourselves is tailored for girls only, as the presence of boys may dilute its impact on girls.

To purchase the facilitator's guide (which contains detailed and scripted lesson plans, supplemental activities, and many handouts that can be copied), go to http://www.catherinesteineradair.com/full-of-ourselves.php. It includes an 11-page guide for parents (http://www.teacherscollegepress.com/pdfs/FOOparentsguide.pdf) and an eight-page guide for schools (http://www.catherinesteineradair.com/full-of-ourselves.php) for how to incorporate the program principles; these parent and school guides are free of charge.

The program can be administered by one or two adults (preferably women). Two distinct phases, geared toward different age groups of girls, are implemented. In the first phase, eight 50- to 60-min units are delivered 1 to

2 weeks apart to a group of sixth- through eighth-grade girls. Steiner-Adair and Sjostrom (2006) recommended that the ideal group size is eight to 12 girls. During Phase 2, these same girls become peer leaders and lead several activity sessions with a group of fourth- and fifth-grade girls.

Each unit calls for girls to put their ideas into action within their relationships and encounters outside of the program (e.g., the "call to action" assignments). In Unit 1, introductions are made, ground rules are set, and leaders describe the program as a group about power, health, and leadership. They inform girls that the group is also about making a difference and that the girls are training to be mentors for younger girls. Leaders explain the positive meaning of "full of yourself": living powerfully, healthfully, and responsibly. Girls write in response to cues such as "A time I felt really confident and powerful was . . ." and are asked how they felt about their body during that time. They engage in a "body scan" guided meditation that helps them appreciate their body as a source of power and life. For the call to action assignment, each girl (a) reads a list of positive attributes, (b) checks in with her body every day, (c) interviews an adult woman about a time when she felt confident and powerful, and (d) asks two adults to tell her about a time they felt really proud of her. Unit 1 ends with girls standing in a circle and stating, "We're in this together, differences included," which is repeated at the end of all units.

In Unit 2, titled "Claiming Our Strengths," girls engage in activities that illustrate the importance of positive thinking and demonstrate how inward critical self-talk hinders growth. They identify a goal they would like to accomplish in the next few days or week and practice and give themselves encouragement for pursuing their goal. They look to other women for inspiration by engaging in the Tree of Strength exercise in which each girl lists five women she admires that have had an impact on her life (no movie stars, singers, or TV characters). On a cut-out leaf, she places the name of one woman and her admirable qualities. Each girl then takes turns introducing her woman to the group and taping her leaf to a tree branch (which can be drawn on posterboard). Girls then reflect on what they like about themselves and what they would like others to appreciate about them. They then write their name and quality on a leaf and add it to the Tree of Strength. For the call to action assignment, girls practice positive self-talk, work on attaining their stated goal, articulate 10 things they are grateful for, interview two women about a woman she admires (to be placed on the Tree of Strength in Unit 3), and tell one of the five powerful women on their list what she means to them (in person or through a letter).

In Unit 3, "Body Politics," girls reflect on how their body has changed since fourth grade and identify a nonappearance aspect of their body that they feel good about. Leaders emphasize that it is typical that girls gain 40 lb (most of which is fat) from ages 8 to 14, which is needed to be strong and healthy, and that girls' and women's bodies continue to change throughout their lives.

Girls write five sentences of appreciation to their body and contemplate what their body would say if it could speak to them. Leaders point out that societal messages teach everyone to make snap judgments of others based on their appearance, discussing weightism in the context of fat myths and other "isms," like racism and sexism. The group then takes a pledge to understand, respect, and include others regardless of what they look like. Over the week, girls are instructed to ask their mom (or another adult woman) three things she really likes and appreciates about her body and its physical capabilities. Girls also are instructed to be a "social scientist" and search for "body messages and behaviors" in their environment and media.

Unit 4, "Standing Our Ground," begins with girls participating in assertiveness training. The example of Rosa Parks is provided: She "took a stand," which is described as making eye contact and speaking in an assertive, confident voice that comes from "the gut" and is grounded in the body. In several role plays, each girl practices taking a stand against another girl in the group who has harassed her (e.g., by taking her shoe). Girls then practice being the bystander; they take a stand on behalf of the target to avoid passive inaction. Girls realize that when the bystander takes a stand on their behalf, it helps them feel confident and strong. For the call to action assignment, girls interview two adults about times when they stood up for themselves or for someone else (or wished that they had).

In Unit 5, "Countering the Media Culture," girls list 10 things they find really beautiful. They each receive a handout with 33 values (e.g., personality, self-respect, pretty face, nature, and animals), one on each square, and cut out and arrange the 10 most important qualities they value. Leaders engage girls in discussion, such as "In what ways have your values changed since elementary school?" Girls then work in pairs of "investigation teams" in which they imagine that they have just landed on Earth and are curious about the lives, values, and habits of females; they look to actual magazines to discover this information. Girls note which of the 33 values are reflected on the cover of the magazine, what the cover headlines say and how they are positioned, the nature of the photos, and the body language and facial expressions of the models. They then compare the degree to which the magazine reflects their list of personal values. Leaders reinforce that body acceptance is empowering and remind girls that bodies come in all sizes—there is nothing wrong with wanting to look their best, but there is something wrong with not caring for the body they have inherited. Over the week, girls make their 10 beautiful things part of their everyday life and record how they feel after viewing magazines in their home. They are encouraged to write letters to magazines that make them feel badly about their bodies (a template letter is provided).

In Unit 6, "Nourishing Our Bodies," girls and leaders discuss normal eating (e.g., eating until satisfied, choosing enjoyable food, giving some thought to food selection, keeping the balance tipped in favor of nutritious food), with leaders debunking common cultural myths (e.g., that fat is bad). Leaders connect food quality to energy: Power foods make people feel powerful, whereas nonnutritious foods make people tired. Girls engage in mindful eating in which they examine the appearance, smell, texture, weight, and finally taste a raisin. For the call-to-action assignment, girls practice eating mindfully in a pleasant setting at least twice a day, examine their home cupboards for power foods, talk with the family meal planner about new power foods to try, and bring in a power food to share at the next unit.

In Unit 7, "Feeding Our Many Appetites," leaders discuss emotional hunger and how eating to deal with painful feelings (or stress) does not remove the source of the pain (or stress) but leads to being disconnected from the self, feeling powerless and depressed, and having an unhealthy relationship with food. Girls consider times they felt various emotions and articulate bodily cues that accompanied those emotions. Leaders help girls pair emotions or needs with the "types" of hunger—for example, bored is paired with intellectual hunger, the need to move is paired with physical hunger, loneliness is paired with friendship hunger, the need to connect with a sense of purpose is paired with spiritual hunger, the need for inspiration is paired with creative hunger, and so forth. Ideas for activities to fulfill each of these hungers are generated. During the week, girls ask themselves what they are really hungry for and what will, in turn, satisfy them. They also ask two adults what they do to make themselves feel better when they are stressed.

The focus of Unit 8 is the "Power of Healthy Relationships." Girls participate in activities that help them connect with each other. Each girl then receives a handout in which a center circle is surrounded by eight outer circles. Girls put their name in the center circle and place the names of eight important people in the other circles. Then, they draw a double line to represent a strong connection to that person, a dashed line to represent a connection they would like to be stronger, and a wavy line to represent a connection that is characterized by stress and tension. Leaders discuss ways in which girls can foster deeper connections with others. Girls are then provided with conflict scenarios, which they work on resolving. Each group shares their conflict resolution, and others provide feedback. Leaders reinforce that girls should remain true to their values in their friendships, even if it compromises their popularity. Girls reflect back on their experience in the group, articulating two to three things they want to remember. They sign a "call to action contract" wherein they promise to combat weightism, honor and accept themselves and others, eat healthfully, nourish their diverse appetites, and anything they decide to add. They are reminded of the powerful qualities within themselves and others.

During the second program phase ("Throw Your Weight Around"), older girls (seventh–eighth grades) who have completed the first phase design and teach activities to younger girls in at least two sessions. It benefits the older girls by reinforcing the concepts learned and honing their leadership skills, while it benefits the younger girls as they are less likely to discredit information when it comes from an older girl. A guide for girl leaders is provided. Adult leaders coach and train the older girls in leading two sessions, where they rehearse considerably. Many possible 15-min activities for girl leaders are provided in the guide.

Full of Ourselves has been successfully implemented in schools and after-school programs, as well as in summer camps, churches, synagogues, and Girl Scouts meetings (Sjostrom & Steiner-Adair, 2005). When compared with a control group, girls who participated in Full of Ourselves had increased their weight-related body esteem and knowledge about health–nutrition, body–appearance, weightism, and media literacy at the end of the program (Steiner-Adair et al., 2002). These gains were maintained at a 6-month follow-up.

Everybody's Different

In Everybody's Different (O'Dea, 2007), girls and boys learn about self-esteem, body acceptance, health, and nutrition, and expand their understanding of themselves and their identity, which decreases the importance they place on physical appearance (see Table 7.1). These characteristics then act as protective factors, contributing to positive social behaviors and physical activity while buffering against weight-related teasing–bullying and eating problems. The activities promote self-acceptance, respect, tolerance, and reduce self-expectations of perfectionism. The major theme is that uniqueness is to be expected, valued, and accepted—everybody is different, and nobody is perfect. The lessons can be tailored for students in fifth grade and beyond, even though seventh and eighth grades are the targeted range (facilitator guide is available for purchase at https://shop.acer.edu.au/acer-shop/product/A1060BK).

Everybody's Different is designed to be delivered by educators. O'Dea (2007) structured her program to allow them flexibility in delivery. As a result, the handbook is not divided cleanly into lessons, and scripts are not provided for educators to follow in leading groups with students. Educators should, however, incorporate student-centered interactive approaches in a safe and respectful classroom environment with discussion, teamwork, and games that promote self-efficacy, a positive sense of self, vicarious learning, and an exchange of feedback and opinions. Many handouts and sample activities are provided that nourish these qualities in students.

The handbook also contains a wealth of information regarding children's body image and health that is grounded in research. Characteristics of body disturbance, eating problems, and obsessive exercise (relevant to both girls and boys) are described. Yet, O'Dea (2007) stresses that educators must focus on promoting self-esteem and not discussing EDs, body dissatisfaction, and dangers of excess weight with students. The importance of media literacy is emphasized. Self-esteem is defined, and its components (inner sense of self-worth and self-acceptance), how it develops, and how it can be nurtured are articulated.

Everybody's Different has two primary objectives with corresponding content–activities. The first objective is to provide students with positive strategies to deal with stress. The class dialogues about the physical effects of stress with several handouts to facilitate the discussion. Students are asked what makes them feel stressed, how they feel when they are stressed, and to articulate healthy ways that help them relax. Educators then introduce relaxation activities as healthy methods of reducing stress and ways students can feel better physically and mentally. O'Dea (2007) provides several options: one that uses progressive muscle relaxation and two that use imagery that help students feel healthy, strong, and connected so that they are able and confident that they can deal with their stress. These activities further encourage students to identify and express different emotions and communicate with others to solve problems.

The second objective helps students develop a positive sense of self and to respect individual differences. Students begin to identify the many different factors that make them and others unique. This helps broaden their self-image, which in turn diminishes the importance of physical appearance. It reinforces that individuality and diversity are normal, valued, and accepted. It also promotes self-acceptance, other-acceptance, and awareness about the destructiveness of prejudice and teasing. Activities encourage positive self-talk and other-talk, reduce obsessive and all-or-nothing thinking, and dismantle the futile pursuit of perfection. Students practice giving and receiving positive feedback.

In one suggested activity, the class brainstorms what qualities make up a person, such as physical features, personality traits, abilities, hobbies, interests, cultural background, beliefs, attitudes, values, past experiences, and character traits (e.g., honesty, trustworthiness). Educators then emphasize that humans are complex, diverse, and unique. Another hands-on activity is one in which students are provided with a bingo-type card that has one way people differ (e.g., has freckles, has a pet fish, is left-handed) instead of a number in each box, and students have to find someone in the class who has that characteristic. It is stressed that life would be boring if everyone was the same. In another activity, students trace their hands and write three positive features about themselves in the drawing. Students pair up and then swap hands and write three positive characteristics about their partners in their hand drawing. Educators do the same for each student. The class convenes and students are asked to read the comments they received and whether they agreed with the comments. Educators then summarize that everyone has positive points and is liked just the way he or she is. Students are reminded to relax and be themselves.

Students can work together (or in small groups) to answer the question, "What do I admire in others?" and then present their answers to the class, with the teacher expanding on this list (suggestions of "admirable" qualities are offered in a handout). Students then complete a handout titled, "Who Do You Admire?" They should be directed toward people from history, from their local community, and from their cultural background and directed away from choosing celebrities. They present the person they admire to the class.

Some activities help students understand their social support network. For instance, students are given a handout with concentric circles and write their name in the innermost circle. In the next layer outward, students write down the names of people they have the strongest and closest bonds with. Moving outward, in the next layer, they write the names of people they like and are friendly with and those they would like to get to know better. In the next layer outward, they write down the names of people they know and are not particularly close with but want to become friends with. When finished, students observe the people they have in their life. Educators guide students to reflect that they are lucky to have people care about them and help them understand that they can always get to know new people and bring them closer into their circle. Children learn about communication skills (verbal and nonverbal) and communication styles (assertive, aggressive, and passive), and they practice how to be assertive and effectively resolve conflicts. Children also learn about bullying and teasing. O'Dea (2007) provides tips for educators on how to discuss bullying with students and how to foster a classroom and school environment that does not tolerate bullying.

Many media literacy activities are included in which educators guide students to reject unrealistic media appearance images. Computer enhancement–modification techniques that are used to manipulate media images are reviewed. The class visits a retouching website (http://demo.fb.se/e/girlpower/retouch/) and report their opinions. Teachers reveal how easy it is to modify photographs. They take a digital picture of each student and give students the jpeg image of their photo. Students then use Photoshop to change their picture and react to the ease at which they can alter their appearance. In another activity, students write down their exposure to all different types of media within a 24-hr period and analyze the main messages from each source. Students present an example of a media source to which they were exposed, and the class tallies the media messages to illustrate how much everyone is affected by the media each day. Students are instructed to bring in a media image and message and fill out a handout asking, "Who created this image?" "Why was this image created?" "What is the main message?" "What techniques are being used to send the message?" and "Do you like the message?" In another activity, students generate lists of media stereotypes of women and men, cut out one such image from a magazine, write a contradictory comment that makes fun of the stereotype, and present their image to the class. Educators reinforce that stereotypes are exaggerated and often wrong and emphasize that students can challenge media stereotypes instead of buying into them.

Students also participate in activities that educate them about growth, development, puberty, and nutrition. O'Dea (2007) argues that the most effective strategy in teaching about these topics is to engage students with personal relevance and personal interest so that they learn to apply nutrition and integrate activity within their everyday lives. She encourages educators to help students focus on how their bodies feel after they eat certain foods, as some foods make them feel refreshed and revived, whereas other foods slow down their minds and bodies, drain their energy, and "clog" up their system. She warns educators to avoid categorizing foods as "bad," "good," and "junk" as these categories create blame and guilt. Instead of focusing on what students should not eat, educators should motivate them towards choosing healthier options. O'Dea (2007) suggests that teachers have children cook and taste food within the classroom.

Instead of using weight to gauge health, O'Dea (2007) encourages educators to engage students in monitoring their heart rate. Students can work to improve on their heart rate, and sedentary children who begin to participate in physical activity will improve the most. O'Dea (2003) noted that the most effective way to stimulate children to engage in physical activity is to focus on the benefits articulated by children who engage in physical activity: They have fun, develop friendships, enjoy being a part of a team, develop a sense of achievement and pride, feel better and are more confident, feel refreshed and "cleansed," enjoy the sensation of movement, are less tired, develop and hone their skills, improve their coordination and fitness, and enjoy the outdoors. Further, activity enhances their concentration, helps relieve their stress and other negative emotions, improves their health, and provides a "natural high."

Everybody's Different was found to significantly improve the body image of both girls and boys (O'Dea & Abraham, 2000). Those at high risk for eating problems particularly benefitted from the program, improving their body satisfaction, lowering their drive for thinness and their appearance concerns, and reducing their dieting and unhealthy weight-control behaviors. Social acceptance, including peer pressure and popularity, and physical appearance were less important, whereas close friendships were more important to both male and female students after the intervention. Improvements were still evidenced 12 months after the intervention.

Other Valuable Media Literacy Resources for the Classroom

Cover Girl Culture (Clark, 2009)

This powerful, eye-opening documentary illustrates the marketing motives, messages, and strategies embedded in fashion magazines (which can generalize to other media). It reveals how students (girls in particular) are affected by these magazines. It can be delivered to Grades 4 through 12. Although the original version is 82 min, there is a 60-min classroom version (Clark, 2011). Both are available via http://www.covergirlculture.com ($105 for 82-min version and $89 for 60-min version).

The director, Nicole Clark, is a rogue Elite international fashion model and an advocate for using media literacy to preserve children's self-esteem and mental health. In this film, Clark (2009) interviews many individuals, juxtaposing girls who internalize (or adopt) the thin ideal with girls from a media literacy group who contextualize (or refute) this ideal. She also juxtaposes fashion magazine editors, modeling agents, and models with body image experts (e.g., psychologists, body image coaches, media literacy activists–authors). The oscillation between interviews is skillfully arranged to inform students of the methods media use to sell them products at the expense of their physical and psychological health.

Educators and students can watch the film together and discuss the various points and themes. Girls in the film who contextualize media messages and images can be very powerful role models for girls in elementary and secondary schools, inspiring them to form a media literacy group within their schools (educators could initiate and facilitate the coordination of such a group). Body image experts articulate ways that students can "take back their power" from the media, encouraging them that they do have control over media influence. Although the film is tailored to girls and women, educators can bring boys into the discussion by processing similar and different pressures they feel when viewing media and helping them understand their role in perpetuating media messages in their interpersonal interactions with girls.

When viewing *Cover Girl Culture*, students witness the mixed messages and intentional positioning of advertisements–articles contained within fashion magazines, such as articles that say "love your body" next to advertisements that feature weight loss methods and cosmetic surgery procedures. They listen to fashion editors argue that their magazine's images provide a fantasy that is inspirational, joyful, fulfilling, and rewarding. Students then observe body image experts passionately challenging these statements by arguing that this fantasy cannot be achieved, precluding any positive outcome and instead promoting constant consumerism, distress, anxiety, and body image issues. This dialogue may help develop students' voices so they can refute and contextualize media content.

The classroom version contains 10 chapters, each between 3 and 10 min long. After viewing each segment, educators could pause and discuss the content with their students, helping them "make the personal political"—understand how their lives are influenced by media and how they can take back their power. It also would be helpful for educators to show this video to parents, as their behaviors can encourage or discourage children from internalizing (and even contextualizing) media images and messages. For instance, if mothers talk badly about their bodies, then this discourse will negatively impact daughters' body image.

Clark (2011) also offers a "companion guide" to *Cover Girl Culture* that serves as a valuable tool for media literacy. This guide, *Seeing Through the Media Matrix*, is also available through http://www.covergirlculture.com for only $41 if bought together with *Cover Girl Culture*. It contains brief segments designed specifically for teens and educators, which are informative, deeply engaging, and empowering—ideal for classroom viewing and discussions. Four body image experts—a psychologist, a body image coach and athlete, a psychotherapist, and the executive director of a body image group—provide compelling and poignant viewpoints (that students can observe and model) and are very passionate speakers. Intermittently, Clark (2011) presents cues to stimulate discussion, for example, "List ways that honor your body" and "List things that dishonor your body." Points made include the following:

1. People feel bad about themselves after reading fashion magazines.
2. Media cleverly manipulate consumers by creating unrealistic images and associating these images with good fortune, wealth, health, and happiness.
3. Media prey on people's insecurities by indirectly telling them that they are not good enough—but they can buy a product that will make them better.
4. People can make a conscious choice to neither hate nor talk badly about their bodies. "Fat talk" (seeking reassurance by statements such as "I'm so fat" and expecting others to respond "no, you're not") is reviewed and challenged.
5. People can resist media influence and accept their body as it is now. When people love themselves, they eat right and feel good. It is a myth that attaining "the look" reflected in media images leads to happiness.
6. Media can be changed by "critical mass"—if enough people demand that realistic messages and real images are shown.

7. Celebrities often are miserable by the façade that they have to present to people. They feel trapped within a cage of inauthenticity that is constructed by the stereotypes media portray of beautiful people.
8. It is false that thin people are the healthiest. Health and thinness are two different things. The goal should not be thinness but finding a healthy weight for each person rather than what is "average" on a chart. People should move their body to be healthy, not thin.

Seeing Through the Media Matrix also includes a guide that educators could incorporate into an evening workshop for parents. Topics presented and discussed include the following:

1. Parents need to be careful about what they say about their body, their child's body, and their partner's body, as body-related messages are absorbed by and impact children.
2. Parents can buffer media's impact on their child's body image by modeling "what a healthy self-esteem looks like" for their child. Self-esteem rules body image.
3. The importance of taking care of their body for health (rather than appearance) reasons.
4. Parents can teach children about inner wisdom: happiness does not originate from having "the look" but from being authentic. False confidence is based on appearance and attaining things, whereas true confidence is based on inner qualities.

All Made Up

This media literacy book would be an excellent resource for young children in elementary school to learn about media secrets related to appearance in consumer culture ($10; available for purchase at http://www.amazon.com/All-Made-Up-Celebrity-Celebrate/dp/0802777449). The author, Audrey Brashich (2006), begins by admitting that she formerly bought into the definitions of beauty and success hyped by the media—she was even a model and an editor for several teen magazines. Yet, she realized how much work it took to achieve "the look" and became angry that girls and women were not getting recognized for accomplishments that are based on their inner skills and abilities. She no longer accepts the symbols of beauty and success hyped by the media, and she looks for more diverse and inspiring role models.

Brashich (2006) makes media literacy understandable for elementary students. She reviews their tricks. For example, she points out that media study people's insecurities to be able to sell them products that offer a cure for these insecurities, and they cannot send the message "you look great as you are" for this reason. She reviews how images are edited by computer to appear "flawless." Brashich argues that monitoring what is wrong with the body and agonizing over "flaws" is exhausting, time consuming, expensive, and boring. She reveals that there are drawbacks to being famous for looks (e.g., no privacy, dishonest friends, knowing that rising younger stars will replace them, missing out on a normal life) that media do not show.

Brashich (2006) encourages students to become activists and realize they have a voice. She shows educators how they could help students achieve this role. They could read this book to their class, stimulating discussion and nurturing ideas. They could create assignments in which students are in charge of a media literacy project. For instance, they could leave positive Post-it notes with messages such as "Beauty comes in all shapes and colors" in their home and in schools and monitor how doing so changes viewers' self- and body attitudes. They could do a class presentation on magazine content by going through a magazine and placing the articles and images that emphasize one narrow body ideal in one pile and the articles that show alternative ideas of female (or male) success and beauty in another pile. As a class, they could jot down names of famous women in important professions in one list and female celebrities in another list and analyze why the second list is easier to generate. Students could make a list of qualities that should define success and beauty, such as caring and creative. Then they could go through a fashion magazine and look for images and articles that support the characteristics on their list. If they find something offensive (or supportive), then they could write letters of complaint (or praise) to corporations, fashion editors, and advertisers. Brashich directs them to a PBS website that provides funding to young people who create their own media. She encourages girls to use their creativity and have fun while they raise awareness about what is good media versus hype.

School personnel could request that this book be available at their school library and book clubs. It is appropriate for those at a fourth-grade reading level. Although this book is designed for girls, its content is also applicable to boys, given that media are now objectifying them. Also, hearing the book's content may help boys understand and empathize with the media pressures on their female peers.

Make Your Own Media

Following media literacy and empowerment interventions, school personnel can reinforce the knowledge learned by providing opportunities to create healthy media (C. Cook-Cottone, Jones, & Haugli, 2010; Scime & Cook-Cottone, 2008). These opportunities can include the students' version of a healthy magazine that integrates content from the activities and didactic sessions presented to them during the intervention. Students may also integrate information from lessons into their own video commercials for empowerment and body acceptance. By constructing their own meaning and creating media, the students practice using their voices to send healthy messages into today's media culture. In this way, media becomes a tool for them rather than something external that they cannot control. In a series of studies, a constructivistic approach to media literacy was a key component in an effective prevention intervention (C. Cook-Cottone et al., 2010; Scime & Cook-Cottone, 2008).

Teaching Tolerance

Teaching Tolerance is a nonprofit organization dedicated to reducing prejudice in schools. The website (http://www.tolerance.org) provides free educational materials and resources to teachers, including activities to promote size acceptance for elementary, middle, and high school students (http://www.tolerance.org/activity/accepting-size-differences), positive body image (http://www.tolerance.org/activity/reshaping-body-image), and media literacy (http://www.tolerance.org/activity/beauty-skin-deep).

SECONDARY PREVENTATIVE INTERVENTION PROGRAMS

Two prevention programs are covered in this section. School personnel can use these programs to prevent additional symptoms of negative body image and eating problems among high school students and prevent eating in the absence of hunger among elementary school students. These programs can also help school personnel treat the initial negative symptoms that have already emerged.

The Body Project

Designed by Eric Stice and Katherine Presnell (2007), the Body Project (see Table 7.1) has extensive evidence upholding its ability to help early-to-late adolescent girls accept their bodies, resist pressures to conform to societal appearance ideals, reduce their pursuit of these ideals, improve their mood, decrease their ED symptoms (e.g., binge eating, use of unhealthy weight-control behaviors), and lower their risk for developing future symptoms. Stice's earlier work focused on identifying the strongest risk factors that predict eating pathology (Stice, 2001; Stice & Agras, 1998; Stice, Presnell, & Spangler, 2002). Stice and Presnell then systematically developed and evaluated interventions to reduce the central risk factor—internalization of the thin ideal—which culminated in the Body Project. This program remains effective when delivered by school personnel, such as teachers and counselors

(Stice & Shaw, 2004; Stice, Shaw, & Marti, 2006). It has been shown to be effective students regardless of their risk level for EDs.

Although the program was designed for (and evaluated with) females, its delivery could be tailored for males by emphasizing muscularity and low body fat as the dimensions that males often evaluate their body against (Ridgeway & Tylka, 2005; Yager & O'Dea, 2008). Indeed, internalization of the meso-morphic (e.g., ultramuscular and lean) ideal has been identified as the central risk factor in male body image and disordered eating (Tylka, 2011b). As we discuss this program, we offer ideas (within parentheses) on how it can be presented and delivered to boys. The exercises would need to be carefully and appropriately modified using examples that are rooted in men's body image concerns (see Barlett, Vowels, & Saucier, 2008; McCreary, Hildebrandt, Heinberg, Boroughs, & Thompson, 2007; Tylka, 2011b). Unfortunately, no studies to date present findings for the effectiveness of modifying this program for boys and men. However, researchers at the University of West England have modified the wording of the Body Project to be unisex and are in the process of examining it with high school boys (contact Emma.Halliwell@ uwe.ac.uk or Phillippa.Diedrichs@uwe.ac.uk for more information).

The conceptual basis for this program is that if students voluntarily argue against the thin (or mesomorphic) ideal, they will reduce their pursuit of this ideal, which will then improve their body image and decrease their maladaptive eating attitudes and behaviors. Therefore, students participate in a series of verbal, written, and behavioral exercises in which they actively critique this ideal. These exercises result in cognitive dissonance—their atti-tudes (e.g., "I want to be thin," "Only if I am thin will I be beautiful") conflict with their behavior (e.g., convincing other girls that many body types are beautiful). Students will be motivated to reduce this uncomfortable disso-nance and will likely change their attitudes to fit their behaviors. It is para-mount that the students themselves, rather than the program administrators, critique this ideal—students will not experience dissonance if they are not the ones doing the critiquing. Also, students must perceive that they change their attitudes voluntarily. Leaders must not allow students to argue for the thin (or mesomorphic) ideal, nor should they attempt to persuade students to not pursue this ideal, as these behaviors will further solidify students' adherence to this ideal. (Leaders could try instead to get other group members to speak out against this ideal.) Leaders should also differentiate the thin (or meso-morphic) ideal from the "healthy ideal." The thin ideal involves "appearing ultraslender (or ultramuscular), whatever the cost," whereas the healthy ideal involves striving for a healthy body without using dangerous methods (Stice & Presnell, 2007). Leaders should ensure that each student participates in each main activity and feels that he or she has been heard and understood.

The Body Project also promotes adaptive behavior by having participants model such behavior in a group setting and allows students to disconfirm maladaptive cognitions (e.g., to be attractive, one must be thin or muscular) and replace them with adaptive cognitions (e.g., attractiveness comes in a variety of shapes). Between-sessions homework exercises assist the transfer of the learned skills to students' after-school and home environments.

Students should not be directly pressured or forced to attend the program, as defending their destructive attitudes and behaviors can intensify their adherence to these attitudes and behaviors (Stice, Mazotti, Weibel, & Agras, 2000; Stice, Trost, & Chase, 2003). Students can be recruited through a combination of the following methods: flyers; e-mails, mailings, or both (sent to all female or male students [depending on target group]); school newspapers; school web pages; and homeroom or class announcements. The program should be described as an interesting and fun opportunity for students who need help with body-related concerns. Stice and Presnell (2007) recommend that educators who wish to run this program use flyers with pictures of students from a wide variety of ethnic groups to obtain a diverse group of students.

It is recommended that this program be held at school, immediately following the school day, in a comfortable space where students can sit face to face (Stice & Presnell, 2007). Two leaders, if possible, should run the group: One should be an educator, and the other could be an educator or an older student who had previously participated in the program. Educators should be familiar with cognitive dissonance theory, understand the sociocultural pressures students face to be thin (or mesomorphic) in Western culture, and possess basic empathy skills. Successful leaders are enthusiastic, engaging, professional, and capable of facilitating lively discussions of the material. The optimal group size is six to eight students, which will encourage the participation of all group members and allow for individualized leader attention during the in-session exercises.

The handbook outlines each of the four sessions and contains scripts (and plenty of examples) that leaders can use to facilitate the various activities and discussion topics. Tips for leaders to avoid potential problems are also provided. Students have workbooks that assist them in doing each activity and at-home assignment (it should be noted that these workbooks are tailored to adolescent girls; gender-specific workbooks need to be designed for adolescent boys).

Session 1 overviews the program and introduces students to the rules and expectations of the group. Specifically, students are informed that this intervention is based on the idea that they can feel better about their body by (a) understanding that cultural pressures to be thin (or mesomorphic) influence their body image and (b) learning how to respond to and challenge these pressures. After introductions, leaders ask students if they are willing to voluntarily commit to participating—that is, to attend all meetings, verbally participate, and complete all between-meeting exercises. A program outline is given to students. Confidentiality is emphasized.

In the first exercise of Lesson 1, leaders and students discuss the definition and origins of the thin (or mesomorphic) ideal. Leaders spread out magazine images of female models for girls (or male models for boys), and students each choose one picture that appeals to them. Then, leaders ask group members to tell the group what they notice about the picture and what it says about society's view of women (or men). The handbook contains a facilitator fact sheet that contains statistics and findings that help them facilitate discussion. In the second exercise, leaders prompt students to identify the costs involved with the thin (or mesomorphic) ideal—including costs to the individual person and society as well as who benefits from promoting this ideal, and then ask, "Given all these costs, does it make sense to try to look like the ideal?" Students are encouraged to make a public statement against the thin (or mesomorphic) ideal. For the home exercises, students are asked to (a) write a letter to a teenage girl (or boy) who is struggling with her (or his) body image and focus on the costs associated with trying to look like the thin (or mesomorphic) ideal; and (b) stand in front of a mirror and write down all their positive qualities, including physical, emotional, intellectual, and social qualities.

Session 2 begins with students verbalizing several of the costs of pursing the ideal that they identified in her letter, which helps increase cognitive dissonance regarding their adherence to this ideal. Leaders help students personalize the identified costs to their life. Leaders then ask students to share two qualities they like about themselves, with one being a physical feature, and they encourage students to remember their positive qualities especially when appearance pressures surround them. Students engage in a role play: One leader assumes the role of either a severe dieter or an eating disordered individual. Each student takes turns dissuading this leader from pursuing the thin (or mesomorphic) ideal. If students had previously articulated a *pro-thin* (mesomorphic) ideal statement, then the leader repeats this statement back to the students, forcing them to develop a counterargument against their own statement, in turn amplifying their cognitive dissonance. After the role play, students reflect on how it felt to argue against someone who is fixated on pursuing this ideal. For the home exercises, students generate three examples from their lives in regard to pressures to be thin (or mesomorphic) as well as verbal challenges to these examples. Second, students write a "Top 10" list of things that they can do, avoid, or say to resist the thin (or mesomorphic) ideal.

In Session 3, leaders continue to help students discuss how to resist the thin (or mesomorphic) ideal, challenge personal body-related concerns, and respond to pressures to be thin (or mesomorphic) that they will encounter.

A role play is implemented to facilitate these goals: Students generate two counter thin (or mesomorphic) ideal statements in response to leader-spoken statements, such as "I would never be friends with someone that heavy" and "I am thinking of going on a diet (or trying steroids), do you want to?" Leaders then encourage students to recognize their self-defeating behaviors and to expose themselves to one of their feared situations in the next week—to do something they would otherwise do if they did not have body image concerns. Leaders make sure that each student leaves with a reasonable plan. Students also are asked to choose one of the body activism behaviors on their Top 10 list they generated the previous session and follow through with it.

In Session 4, the final session, leaders ask students how the first take-home exercise influenced their thoughts and feelings toward their body. Students are (a) reminded that overcoming their negative body image takes time and ongoing efforts to challenge their body-related thoughts and feelings and (b) encouraged to engage in similar activities in the future. When reviewing the body activism home exercise, leaders guide students to talk themselves into doing more of these types of body activism and how these activities can be beneficial to themselves and others. Session 4 then focuses on what students say about their body and others' bodies and how these statements can promote and maintain the thin (or mesomorphic) ideal. Some examples should be acknowledged by leaders, such as complimenting others on weight loss (or muscle gain), joining in on *body talk* (i.e., making disparaging statements about their body and joining in when they hear others complain about their own bodies). Students read (but do not say out loud) examples of body talk statements that they see in their workbook and then discuss how these statements maintain the thin (or mesomorphic) ideal, what they can say to stop this body talk, and how changing the way they talk about their body might impact how they feel about it and how others respond to them. Students anticipate triggers and discuss how they will deal with potential pressures to be thin (or mesomorphic) that they will face in the future. Leaders encourage students to visualize applying the strategies that they have learned to these anticipated pressures and practice responding to them as well as challenge their body-related concerns and talk about their body in a positive rather than a negative fashion. Leaders and students both provide examples. Leaders request that students perform one of these activities over the week and write a letter to a teenage girl (or boy) detailing how to avoid developing a negative body image. Students and leaders then process how the program has helped them reduce their body concerns and how they now feel about their body.

We have a warning about the follow-up healthy weight intervention. We do not condone many aspects of Stice and Presnell's (2007) 4-week "Healthy Weight" intervention in their handbook, which is designed to segue from the Body Project intervention. The goal is achieving and maintaining a healthy body weight, which could enhance body acceptance and help participants avoid unhealthy weight-control (or muscle enhancement) behaviors. Although the program offers many useful strategies for how to eat healthfully and incorporate exercise into daily life, we have concerns with its focus. We are troubled that it prioritizes weight, which runs counter to the recommendations to focus on health rather than weight (Bacon, 2010; O'Dea, 2007). The program also encourages students to follow portion sizes, an external indicator that detaches students from their internal hunger and satiety cues (Tribole & Resch, 2003). Being detached from these cues disturbs self-regulation in the long term and promotes guilt and disinhibited eating when the portion-size rule is broken (Bacon, 2010; Tribole & Resch, 2003). Stress and social eating (i.e., eating with others), which are commonplace among students, often prompt individuals to break the portion-size rule (Hays & Roberts, 2008; Rutters, Nieuwenhuizen, Lemmens, Born, & Westerterp-Plantenga, 2009).

If educators wish to implement this follow-up program within the schools, then we emphasize that its title and focus should be altered from "The Healthy Weight Intervention" to "The Healthy Ideal Intervention." Also, portion sizes should be replaced with a hunger meter, such as the one covered in the Regulation of Cues (ROC) intervention, discussed next, or intuitive eating (Tribole & Resch, 2003), with group leaders helping students recognize and respond to their satiety cues that naturally tell them to stop eating. Because it can take 20 min from the onset of eating for satiety cues to be triggered, group leaders could facilitate mindful eating strategies with students. For instance, leaders could teach students strategies to be able to detect that they have eaten enough (e.g., subtle cues such as food stops tasting as good, awareness of how much food it typically takes to raise them from a 2 to a 4 on a 5-point satiety scale, where higher levels reflect greater satiety) and review strategies to savor their food and eat slowly so that they are more likely to enjoy the eating experience and appreciate the tastes of a variety of foods. These relatively minor changes largely retain the integrity of the program while still following the recommendations set forth by O'Dea (2007) and O'Dea and Yager (2011) for prevention programs for body-related and eating concerns.

Regulation of Cues Intervention

The ROC intervention (see Table 7.1), developed by Boutelle, Zucker, Peterson, and Rydell (2011), helps children who have lost touch with their internal hunger and satiety cues become reacquainted with these cues by providing practical and engaging tools for managing food cravings. For program information, contact Kerri Boutelle (kboutelle@ucsd.edu). There are two components to the ROC program: (a) increase children's awareness and responsiveness to internal hunger and satiety cues and (b) decrease children's reactivity to external food cues. Parents participate in the intervention, recognizing that children's eating problems are likely rooted in the family.

The ROC intervention draws from Schachter's externality theory (Schachter, 1971; Schachter & Rodin, 1974), which suggests that individuals weigh more than their natural set point because they (a) are less sensitive to their internal hunger and satiety cues and (b) are more reactive to external cues to eat—they are more likely to eat when they see or smell tasty food. Fortunately, children who are detached from their hunger and satiety cues respond favorably to interventions designed to improve their connection to these cues and decrease their eating in the absence of hunger (Bloom, Sharpe, Heriot, Zucker, & Craighead, 2005; Johnson, 2000). The ROC intervention's focus is monitoring and learning about hunger cues alongside cues to stop eating, which can help improve sensitivity to hunger and satiety perceptions.

To target children's decreased sensitivity to internal hunger and satiety cues, the ROC intervention uses principles from Craighead and Allen's (1995) Appetite Awareness Training intervention, which helps children monitor and learn about hunger cues alongside cues to stop eating. To monitor hunger, group leaders help parents and children find their diaphragm by taking a deep breath and then find their stomach, which sits just below the diaphragm. Parents and children then take deep breaths, focusing on their diaphragm and stomach for a few moments, and then they rate their hunger along a scale ranging from 1 (*very hungry* or "*starving*") to 5 (*very full* or "*stuffed*"), with concrete sensations provided. It is recommended that they begin eating at 2 and stop eating when they reach 4, and practice monitoring their hunger at the beginning, middle, and end of each meal twice daily.

1. *Starving:* "Your stomach may hurt, you may have a headache, feel a little weak, or be a little shaky or jittery."
2. *Hungry:* "Your stomach is gently growling and feels empty; you may feel a little low in energy."
3. *Neutral:* "You have taken the edge off your hunger and have more energy but still do not feel satisfied."
4. *Satisfied:* "You feel energetic and alert, ready to take on your next task." (participants are instructed that it may take 20 minutes for the feeling of fullness to register in their brain).
5. *Stuffed:* "You feel uncomfortable and tired. You may find it hard to move. You may feel low energy—not the jittery feeling of starving but the low energy of fullness."

To decrease eating in response to external food cues in the absence of hunger, the ROC intervention uses cue exposure with response prevention (Monti & Rohsenow, 1999). This extinguishes the relationship between physiological responses to the cue (in this case, food) and the behavior (consumption of food). Boutelle, Zucker, Peterson, Rydell, Cafri, and Harnack (2011) used the Pavlov classical conditioning study to illustrate the process. Initially, Pavlov's dogs did not salivate when they heard the bell. Only after he paired the bell with food did the dogs salivate when they heard the bell (cue-behavior formation). Pavlov then stopped feeding dogs when sounding the bell, and after several exposures of hearing the bell without the food, the dogs stopped salivating on hearing the bell (cue-behavior extinction). To illustrate this, the leader provides a practical scenario of eating popcorn at the movies. Eating popcorn at the movies often makes people crave popcorn when they are at the movie theater. However, going to the movies enough times without having popcorn will decrease their craving for popcorn. This teaches children (and parents) that if they do not respond to cravings, then the cravings will decrease over time.

Boutelle, Zucker, Peterson, Rydell, Cafri, and Harnack (2011) created the concept of the "Volcravo" rating scale to help assess food cravings for the cue exposure with response prevention treatment. A picture of an erupting volcano is provided to the left of a scale, ranging from 1 (*at bottom ground of volcano*) to 5 (*at the top where lava is spurting out*). The key term used in Volcravo is *craving*, which is described to parents and children as "wanting to eat when not physically hungry." A craving rating of 1 represents "I'm having so much fun with my friends, so I don't care about the cake" (or whatever food the child craves). A craving rating of 2 corresponds with "That cake looks so good, but I'm going to keep hanging out with my friends." A craving rating of 3 represents "Wow, that cake looks so tasty. I wish I had a piece." A craving rating of 4 corresponds with "I really want that cake! It's hard to stop thinking about it!" Last, a craving rating of 5 represents "GET OUT OF MY WAY! I WANT CAKE!" Children are provided a "toolbox" of coping skills to "ride the craving wave" during cue exposures.

Parents and children are asked to bring in foods that the child finds absolutely irresistible, one by one, each week for 7 weeks. For this to be effective, children should not consume this target food within 24 hr of the group, and they should not be physically hungry before or during the session. In the group, children are told to hold the chosen food and then rate their craving on Volcravo. Second, they are told to smell the food and then rate their craving. Third, they are told to taste the food by taking only two bites and then rate their craving. They put the food aside (but still within sight) and rate their cravings over time, every few minutes (the leader prompts the child when it is time to rate their craving). Children are encouraged to focus on the food until their cravings go below a 2 on Volcravo. Then children throw the food away. Twice daily, parents help children practice their craving monitoring.

Sessions are divided into two parts. The first part of the session is 45 min, and participants are divided into a parents-only group and a kids-only group. The content across the groups is similar, except that the materials for the children's group are presented in the form of age-appropriate games and discussion. After the main 45-min session, parents and children are reunited to participate in experiential eating practices for an additional 30 min.

After an overview of the program (Week 1), program leaders cover one "tricky hunger" per week. Tricky hungers are ways to understand high-risk situations to overeat. A coping skill is paired with each tricky hunger to provide a toolbox to "ride the craving wave." The first tricky hunger (Week 2) is "ignoring fullness," emphasizing that when biological signals to stop eating are weak, the result is often overeating. This tricky hunger is paired with parenting skills for the parent group, including positive reinforcement and role modeling (practice ROC intervention concepts and label their own tricky hunger in front of their children). The second tricky hunger presented (Week 3) is "getting too hungry." The coping skill of stimulus control is reviewed: Parents are urged to feed children every 3 to 4 hr, create a single "special" eating place such as the kitchen table, eliminate distractions during eating (no TV or electronic devices), choose mealtimes when most of the family can sit down together and talk, make fruits and vegetables visible and easily accessible, use smaller plates, and decrease the variety of prepackaged snack foods in the home. The third tricky hunger (Week 4) is "feeding your moods." Leaders provide tips for parents to help when their child eats for emotional reasons. Leaders cover coping skills such as deep breathing, muscle relaxation, and imagery. During the in vivo session for Weeks 1 through 4, parents and children eat dinner together and monitor their hunger throughout the meal.

The fourth tricky hunger (Week 5) is "eating too fast." Leaders teach coping skills of delay (techniques that children can use to distract themselves from eating when not hungry) and mindful eating. The fifth tricky hunger (Week 6) is "eating because it's there." Leaders train parents and children to differentiate between cravings and true hunger and discuss substituting activities (e.g., playing basketball, engaging in "volcanic blasts" or brief bursts of physical activity that have been shown to help reduce cravings; J. Z. Daniel, Cropley, & Fife-Shaw, 2006). The sixth tricky hunger (Week 7) discusses the marketing and media tricks to increase cravings (e.g., using colors, sounds, actors, cool packaging) so consumers will purchase their food. The seventh tricky hunger (Week 8) is the "Who cares?" response, or making the decision to give up control when eating (e.g., "I ate a brownie. There goes my diet; what the heck, I'll just eat the whole pan"). A coping skill that children can use is to enlist a "super-fuel superhero" to help them combat this tricky hunger. The eighth tricky hunger (Week 9) is "eating for entertainment or boredom." Leaders recommend that parents guide children to another activity, consistently label the boredom, label their craving as a tricky hunger, and suggest that they use their "distraction" coping skills. The ninth tricky hunger (Week 10) is "eating because other people are." Leaders review assertiveness skills for refusing food, and parents are encouraged to role model this behavior for children and help them "cruise" (i.e., check out all food options before making a decision). "Food rules" that dictate what and how much to eat are the 10th and final tricky hunger (Week 11). Leaders recommend replacing food rules with flexible guidelines and monitoring of hunger level. Cue exposure occurs for Weeks 5 through 10: During the in vivo session, children bring the first of their favorite foods in and hold, smell, taste two bites of, and ultimately put aside this food. At each step, they rate their craving on the Volcravo scale. Leaders encourage parents and children to practice cue exposure for at least 10 min at their home.

During Week 12, leaders help parents and children plan for high-risk situations. They also discuss relapse prevention and goals. During Week 13, leaders review the intervention and further discuss relapse prevention. The in vivo segments for these 2 weeks consist of families bringing in their dinner, rating their hunger throughout the dinner, and then doing a cue exposure exercise. During the final week (Week 14), leaders help parents and children plan their "next steps." Parents and children have a graduation buffet, where they practice their hunger monitoring and cue exposure skills. Leaders encourage parents and children to use self-motivational statements, such as "I am stronger than this craving. It can't control me."

The ROC intervention has begun to be evaluated for efficacy. Boutelle, Zucker, Peterson, Rydell, Cafri, and Harnack (2011) found preliminary support for Volcravo and Children's Appetite Awareness Training (CAAT), which were tested separately among 36 parent–child pairs who were randomly assigned to either intervention. Children were, on average, 10 years old, overweight, and ate in the absence of hunger. Both Volcravo and CAAT were well tolerated and had reasonable acceptability ratings from both parents and children. Volcravo, but not CAAT, reduced eating in the absence of hunger—a significant reduction was found at postintervention and 6 months after the termination of the intervention. Both resulted in decreases in overeating and binge eating in children. Children receiving Volcravo did not experience a change in their body mass index (BMI) until the 1-year post treatment assessment, whereas children receiving CAAT did not experience a decline in BMI. However, children consumed an average of 270 calories less in laboratory evaluation postintervention, which potentially could result in lack of gain of 28 lb per year. An integrated (Volcravo and CAAT) program still needs to be evaluated.

Although Boutelle, Zucker, Peterson, Rydell, Cafri, and Harnack (2011) originally designed the ROC intervention for parents and children, it could be tailored to the school setting. First, school personnel could send letters to parents to see whether they are concerned about their child's eating, for example, they notice their child eating in the absence of hunger, eating out of boredom, eating fast, craving foods frequently, eating when stressed or sad, or gaining weight at an accelerated pace, and whether they and their child are interested in joining an intervention. The letters should be sent home in a sealed envelope to reduce information dissemination about the program among students (to reduce the stigmatization of children who join the program). Also for this reason, the letter should request that parents who are not interested in joining (or do not have a reason to join) this group do not speak about the program to their children.

The program could be run in the evening after school hours, exactly how Boutelle et al. (2011) designed it. Area psychologists or health educators could implement the manualized program for students and parents. Teachers should be encouraged to sit in on the parent group to learn the concepts of the ROC intervention so that they do not unintentionally engage in behaviors or send messages that are inconsistent with the program's concepts. Alternatively, the concepts discussed in the parent group could be repeated in another group for teachers only. Perhaps a video also could be shown to teachers to illustrate cue exposure and response prevention treatment in action, or they could have a separate in vivo session, whereby they practice cue exposure with their favorite foods to see how this approach works.

Another option would be to implement this program after school in the evening (for the main intervention with parent and child groups and in vivo sessions) and within school (for the concepts to be comprehensively reviewed and practiced). The evening session could mirror Boutelle et al.'s (2011) design. Because it would be challenging for children to implement these skills at home without the knowledge and support of their caregivers, parents should be strongly encouraged to participate in the evening groups and in vivo sessions. Designing a third evening group for school personnel would help teachers and administrators understand the intervention, send messages congruent with the intervention to students, and be able to review and practice the concepts with students. Teacher-specific material, such as how to reinforce the coping skills and curriculum content, should also be integrated. School personnel would need to find an alternative way to disseminate the information contained in parent groups to parents who choose not to attend the evening sessions. When reviewing the material in school, teachers would need to cover how students can talk to their parents about the program concepts and send reading material and handouts home with the students.

If the program concepts are covered within the school day, including all students (not just those who eat in the absence of hunger and are overweight) is strongly recommended. Separating out heavy students for this intervention likely would increase stigma and teasing and would be impractical. Students who are not heavy or at risk for eating problems could also learn valuable coping skills that could help them maintain their connection to their internal hunger and satiety cues and buffer the development of eating problems in the future.

Integrating the ROC intervention in schools could reinforce the skills and strategies used, providing a common language among students, school personnel, and parents. Teachers may find it to be most helpful to reinforce and practice hunger monitoring right before lunch and cue exposure right after lunch. To practice cue exposure, children could bring a treat (although teachers should have some extra treats on hand for students who forget to bring one). Hunger monitoring also could be practiced during lunch, guided by a teacher. Students who have "graduated" from the program could serve as peer facilitators for younger students, reinforcing the concepts for both older and younger students. This strategy may help older children to continue using their internal hunger and satiety cues to guide their eating and their coping skills to combat the tricky hungers. Older students could also serve as role models, providing inspiration and motivation for the younger students. Younger students would benefit from seeing and hearing the older students' successes as well as how they worked through the challenges. Such tiered peer-mentoring programs have been found to be beneficial for older and younger students (Becker, Smith, & Ciao, 2006).

Third, the ROC intervention could be implemented solely within the school curriculum, involving all students. Prior to this, teachers would have to be trained to deliver the intervention to children. Before the first week, teachers could provide parents with information about the intervention, such as its purpose, the intent behind each of the exercises, weekly activities, and how parents can practice and reinforce the skills learned at school to home.

Teachers could integrate each session into their curriculum: one session and in vivo exercise per week. The presentation, coping skills, and hunger ratings could be covered before lunch, and teachers can encourage children to practice their hunger ratings during lunch throughout the week. They could guide them through hunger monitoring throughout lunch. Cue exposure and response prevention could be practiced after lunch. Regular opportunities to use the various coping skills could be integrated into the curriculum. Teachers could role model how students could talk to their parents about the program concepts and send reading material and handouts home with the students.

Fourth, the ROC intervention could be implemented in an after-school program, involving all enrolled students. Similar to carrying out this intervention within the school curriculum, administrators would need to be trained to deliver the intervention to children. Program administrators could provide parents with information about the intervention and how to practice the skills with their children. One session and in vivo exercise could be delivered once a week. Children could bring two snacks (if the after-school program does not provide snacks) and practice hunger ratings before and during eating the first snack. Twenty minutes later, they could take the second snack and practice their cue exposure response prevention skills. Administrators should have some extra snacks on hand for students who forget them. Further, administrators could practice with students how to talk with their parents about the program as well as send reading material and handouts home with the students.

CONCLUSION: WHICH PROGRAMS SHOULD YOUR SCHOOL SYSTEM CHOOSE?

Your choice of programs to be implemented at your school may largely depend on grade level (elementary, middle, or high school), cost of the program–funding of the school, student need, whether there is a community center available and willing to host a program, the overall indentation of the program within the school day, and the type of program desired (e.g., after school, incorporated into existing classes, reserved sections of time for the program). Table 7.1 serves as a guide to determine the best program for your school.

As examples of how to choose the appropriate programs for your school, we turn to the case studies presented in the Introduction to this volume. City Central is an elementary school that has a diverse student body, limited funding, no wellness policy, high childhood overweight–obesity rates, and is centered in a community that has high crime rates. Therefore, the best programs for this school may be the ROC intervention, which addresses eating in the absence of hunger, and Healthy Body Image, which includes an appreciation of body and cultural diversity within its activities. The ROC intervention would help students who, like Jared, eat for emotional reasons and have a hard time waiting out food cravings. Via the ROC program, these students would learn how to reconnect to their physiological hunger and satiety cues. The Healthy Body Image program would help students like Jacqueline who have been bullied about weight and have a hard time seeing their identity as more than their appearance. Both programs are relatively inexpensive to purchase and administer. Parents in the PTA at City Central want a school-based program that helps families support the physical and psychological health of their children, and the ROC, with its emphasis on incorporating parents into the program (which could be delivered in the evenings after school), would be ideal. Teachers can be involved and help children practice the techniques. Furthermore, teachers can deliver the Healthy Body Image program within the school. Both programs reinforce the school's newly developed wellness policy (see Chapter 3). Social studies teachers can also read *All Made Up* to the students and get them involved in age-appropriate media activism activities.

Students at Bayside, a suburban, upper middle class, predominantly White high school, have a tendency to display ED symptomatology and a greater preoccupation with losing weight–body fat than those at other typical high schools. Students like Kara and Ben would benefit from an after-school secondary–tertiary prevention program such as the Body Project, which would have them argue against the thin and mesomorphic ideals. Our modified version of Stice and Presnell's (2007) follow-up program (i.e., the Healthy Ideal) could be administered to students to encourage their focus on health and not weight and on eating according to their hunger and satiety cues. Also, supplemental media literacy materials such as *Cover Girl Culture* and *Seeing Through the Media Matrix* could be age-appropriate tools to help students at Bayside learn about the media tricks that prompt them to be dissatisfied with their bodies and hear students their age and body image experts contextualize rather than internalize media images. Furthermore, activities from Teaching Tolerance and Making Your Own Media could be integrated to help students appreciate individual differences in weight and appearance and combat media messages that encourage them to internalize societal body ideals. Following the transcontextual approach, the parent version of *Seeing Through the Media Matrix* could be delivered to parents by school personnel through links to the nearby youth bureau–community center in the evenings. This interactive video could help parents counteract media messages and align themselves with media literacy activities at school or align themselves with media messages.

Middle schools, on the basis of their funding, student demographic, community resources, and other nuances (e.g., whether they want after-school programs or programs integrated throughout lessons), could also incorporate many of these programs and resources. In fact, most of the programs and resources in this chapter are geared toward middle school students. If funds allow, Media Smart would be a great resource that is likely to yield beneficial and lasting effects, given its extant empirical support. Everybody's Different would allow educators flexibility in delivery as well as provide guidance with a teacher training program. All-girl middle schools and middle schools that host organizations for girls (e.g., Girl Scouts) may want to choose Full of Ourselves. Middle school students would further benefit from many of the supplemental materials discussed in this chapter, including *Cover Girl Culture*, *Seeing Through the Media Matrix*, Make Your Own Media, and Teaching Tolerance to counteract internalization of media messages and ideals as well as bullying and teasing based on weight or other social factors (e.g., cultural differences).

Nevertheless, the overall success of the program and resources hinges on the school's ability to disseminate its information to students' families and have families be receptive to such information. Regardless of which program and resources are administered, it is important that schools inform parents on topics within the program in a respectful way. Whenever possible, parents should be integrated into an interactive program (as is done in the ROC evening intervention and *Seeing Through the Media Matrix*). School-based family programs have been effective for encouraging children's literacy (Burningham & Dever, 2005), and a similar approach could be used to integrate parents in preventative intervention for body- and eating-related concerns (see Chapter 3 for detailed suggestions). Information should not be delivered with the tone "you are raising your child wrong," but with support (e.g., "We are all in this together for the health of all of our children") and assurance that empirically supported interventions are delivered. Lifting the focus from weight to health could help transfer parents' guilt (if any) to constructive action (e.g., from "I made my child fat" to "Let me take part in helping my child be healthy and have a positive body image") while also respecting cultural food practices and body diversity. Further, perhaps having parents who have internalized media appearance ideals participate in cognitive dissonance interventions like the Body Project may help disentangle them from internalizing media messages and images. If available, such programs can be delivered via community-based centers. Phone applications could also deliver information to parents. For example, the Media Smart program created a phone application that could be used to integrate parents into the program content and engage them in the activities.

8

SCREENING, ASSESSING, AND SUPPORTING STUDENTS WITH EATING AND BODY IMAGE PROBLEMS

School personnel are often the first line of defense against emerging disorder. However, few educational publications offer information and guidance as to how school personnel can be part of prevention and intervention efforts aimed at emerging disorders (C. Cook-Cottone, 2009; Haines, Neumark-Sztainer, & Thiel, 2007). Therefore, this chapter provides (a) tools school personnel can use to screen for eating disorder (ED) symptomatology among students and (b) directions for facilitating referral of students with EDs and supporting their educational needs during their treatment.

SCREENING AND ASSESSMENT

When presenting screening and assessment tools, we focus on their psychometric properties in children and adolescents, how to administer them, and how to interpret their scores. In this chapter, we also present instruments

DOI: 10.1037/14180-009
Healthy Eating in Schools: Evidence-Based Interventions to Help Kids Thrive, by C. P. Cook-Cottone,
E. Tribole, and T. L. Tylka

that assess students' levels of risk (i.e., eating in the absence of hunger, negative body image, internalization of the thin ideal) and protective factors (i.e., intuitive eating and body appreciation) of ED symptomatology so that school personnel better understand where their students stand on these factors. This information could be used to help identify the best prevention program (see Chapter 7) to fit their school's needs as well as identify those at risk for EDs.

Eating Disorder Symptomatology

Having screening tools available that are able to detect students who have active ED symptoms is a clear priority because of the damaging physical and psychological effects of these disorders, which often worsen and become more difficult to treat over time (Berkman, Lohr, & Bulik, 2007). Fortunately, instruments that account for children's distractibility and reading level are available for school personnel to screen and assess ED symptoms in students (Ricciardelli & McCabe, 2001). The SCOFF (Hill, Reid, Morgan, & Lacey, 2010; Morgan, Reid, & Lacey, 1999) and an adapted version of the Eating Attitudes Test–26 (EAT-26; Garner, Olmsted, Bohr, & Garfinkel, 1982) for children—the Children's EAT (ChEAT; Maloney, McGuire, & Daniels, 1988)—are two instruments that could be used by school personnel to achieve these goals. These instruments can facilitate appropriate school response and treatment referral for students with active EDs. But given the gravity of these disorders and the known struggles in treatment (e.g., resistance to recovery), we recommend that schools bring in an outside professional specifically trained in ED recovery assist these students (C. Cook-Cottone, 2009; Yager & O'Dea, 2005). Nevertheless, the school still plays two integral roles: acting as a liaison to detect students with EDs and connect them to outside professionals for help; and offering support, ensuring that the student's treatment has as minimal of an adverse impact on her or his education as possible.

The SCOFF

This brief five-item screening instrument assesses the core features of EDs (Hill et al., 2010; Morgan et al., 1999). It was designed to be acceptable and unobtrusive. It can be administered to students easily in either written or verbal format with language understandable to even young students. SCOFF is an acronym for the instrument's items. S stands for "Do you make yourself *SICK* (vomit) because you feel uncomfortably full?" C stands for "Do you worry that you have lost *CONTROL* over how much you eat?" O stands for "Have you recently lost more than *ONE* stone (or 15 pounds) in a 3-month period?" F stands for "Do you believe yourself to be *FAT* when others say you are thin?" The final F stands for "Would you say that *FOOD* dominates your life?" On the basis of sensitivity and specificity indexes, the authors set a cutoff of two or more positive questions, suggesting that any student that has two or more yes answers should receive further evaluation and treatment.

Children's Eating Attitudes Test

The original ChEAT contains 26 items (see Appendix B) that assess a variety of attitudes and behaviors associated with anorexia and bulimia in children (Maloney et al., 1988). Each item is rated on the following scale: *always, usually, often, sometimes, rarely,* and *never; always* is recoded to a score of 3, *usually* is recoded to a score of 2, and *often* is recoded to a score of 1. The remaining three choices receive a score of 0. ChEAT scores can range from 0 to 78, with a cutoff specified at 20 (Maloney et al., 1988). Thus, it is recommended that educators assist children who score ≥ 20 in receiving external help for their disordered eating symptoms.

The psychometric properties of the total scale have been upheld with elementary, middle, and high school children. Three items (3, 19, and 25), however, appear to be problematic, with low item-total correlations ($rs < .30$; Smolak & Levine, 1994). In a sample of middle school girls (M age = 13.2), alpha was .87 for the 26-item ChEAT and .89 for the 23-item ChEAT (all items except 3, 19, and 25), with both versions being moderately correlated in a positive direction with weight management and body dissatisfaction (Smolak & Levine, 1994). Factor analyses have failed to yield internally consistent subscales; for this reason, only total scores should be used (Anton et al., 2006; Ranzenhofer et al., 2008). Validity has been demonstrated for the ChEAT total score in that it was positively related to dieting, eating restraint, disinhibited eating, depression, and anxiety (Ranzenhofer et al., 2008). Average scores on the ChEAT seem to vary with the sample, with a mean of 15.74 (SD = 12.42) obtained for a sample of middle school girls (Smolak & Levine, 1994), a mean of 11.90 (SD = 10.8) obtained for a sample of high school girls (Rosen, Silberg, & Gross, 1988), and a mean of 12.6 (SD = 9.6) obtained for a sample of elementary school children (Anton et al., 2006). Overweight children reported higher ChEAT total scores than did nonoverweight children (M = 9.9, SD = 7.4 vs. M = 6.6, SD = 7.8, respectively; Ranzenhofer et al., 2008).

Eating in the Absence of Hunger

If children eat in the absence of hunger (EAH), then they are likely susceptible to eating when surrounded by tasty food and during emotional distress. Given the frequency of these events in most children's lives, EAH could contribute to excess body weight (Shunk & Birch, 2004). There are promising findings that young children who engage in EAH can be trained to use their internal hunger and satiety cues to regulate their food intake

(Johnson, 2000). Students who engage in EAH may also benefit from emotional-regulation skills and behavioral skills to control stress, resist tasty foods, and choose meaningful activities that leave them fulfilled rather than bored or tired. School psychologists, counselors, and other school personnel could teach students these skills, either one on one or in small, workshop-type groups. Therefore, it would be useful for school personnel to have a psychometrically sound tool to identify students that engage in EAH. This measure also could be used to gauge the effectiveness of school programs to increase intuitive eating, such as the Regulation of Cues intervention and Everybody's Different (see Chapter 7, this volume; Boutelle et al., 2011). Next, we present such a measure.

The Eating in the Absence of Hunger Questionnaire for Children (EAH-C; Tanofsky-Kraff et al., 2008) is a 14-item measure that can be administered to children ages 6 and older. Children are instructed to "imagine that you are eating a meal or snack at home, school, or in a restaurant. Imagine that you eat enough of your meal so that you are no longer hungry" (Tanofsky-Kraff et al., 2008, p. 150). Children are then presented with seven items with the stem "In this situation, how often do you keep eating because . . ." with the seven item fillers being (a) food looks, tastes, or smells so good; (b) others are still eating; (c) feeling sad or depressed; (d) feeling bored; (e) feeling angry or frustrated; (f) feeling tired; and (g) feeling anxious or nervous. Next, children are asked, "Now imagine that you finished eating a meal or snack some time ago and you are not yet hungry." The stem for the remaining seven items is "In this situation, how often do you start eating because . . ." (Tanofsky-Kraff et al., 2008, p. 150), and the seven item fillers shown above are provided once again. For each of the 14 items, children select the frequency with which they eat past their satiety cues and in the absence of hunger on a 5-point scale, ranging from 1 (*never*) to 5 (*always*).

On the basis of a sample of young children and teenagers, the EAH-C was found to have three factors–subscales that are internally consistent and stable across time (average period between administrations was 150 days; Tanofsky-Kraff et al., 2008). The negative affect eating subscale has six items ($\alpha = .88$, time $r = .65$) representing EAH in response to being sad or depressed, angry or frustrated, and anxious or nervous (filler items c, e, and g for both stems). The external eating subscale contains four items ($\alpha = .80$, time $r = .69$) representing EAH in response to foods looking, tasting, or smelling good and when others are eating (filler items a and b for both stems). Last, the fatigue–boredom eating subscale includes four items ($\alpha = .83$, time $r = .70$) representing EAH in response to feeling bored and tired (filler items d and f for both stems). The EAH-C subscales' construct validity was supported through their significant positive correlations with emotional eating, depression, and state and trait anxiety. Overall and subscale means and standard deviations were not reported; however, if children have an average score of > 3.0, then it can be assumed that this child sometimes eats in the absence of hunger and is in need of intervention.

Intuitive Eating

Individuals who are aware of and use their internal hunger and satiety cues to guide their eating behavior clearly reported better physical and psychological health (Tylka, 2006). A measure of intuitive eating in children could be used as a pre- and posttest of the Regulation of Cues intervention (Boutelle, Zucker, Peterson, & Rydell, 2011), a program we advocate for helping children connect with their internal hunger and satiety cues (see Chapter 7, this volume).

The Intuitive Eating Scale (IES) and recently the Intuitive Eating Scale–2 (IES-2; Tylka & Kroon Van Diest, 2012) have been developed and validated with several samples of young adult women and men (Kroon Van Diest & Tylka, 2010; Tylka, 2006), demonstrating that intuitive eating coincides with a myriad of positive psychological and physical outcomes, such as higher positive affect, life satisfaction, self-esteem, proactive coping, optimism, and body appreciation as well as lower media-ideal internalization, pressures to be thin, depression, BMI, and eating pathology. Recently, a version of the original IES was adapted for middle school children (the IES for Adolescents [see Appendix C]; Dockendorff, Petrie, Greenleaf, & Martin, 2011) for readability and relevance, as children often are not the ones controlling food selection and availability for their household.

The IES for Adolescents is a 17-item measure of four separate but interrelated characteristics of intuitive eating: unconditional permission to eat (UPE; readiness to eat in response to physiological hunger cues and whatever food is desired without classifying it as good or bad; six items), eating for physical rather than emotional reasons (EPR; use food to satisfy a physical hunger drive rather than to cope with emotional fluctuations, distress, or both; five items), awareness of internal hunger and satiety cues (AIC; three items), and trust in internal hunger and satiety cues to guide eating behavior (TIC; three items). All items are rated along a scale ranging from 1 (*strongly disagree*) to 5 (*strongly agree*). Item responses are averaged.

The IES for Adolescents yielded reliable and valid scores in middle school children (6th–8th grades, average age = 12.5 years; Dockendorff et al., 2011). Three of the four subscale scores were internally consistent: Cronbach's alphas were .78 for UPE, .85 for EPR, .75 for TIC, and .60 for AIC; alpha for the total IES was .75. (An α below .70 suggests low internal consistency reliability [Nunnally & Bernstein, 1994]; thus, we suggest that the AIC subscale should not interpreted on its own.) In terms of validity, the total IES for Adolescents score and the UPE, EPR, and TIC subscale scores were negatively related to BMI, negative affect, internalization of media standards for attractiveness, and perceived pressure to diet. The total score and these three subscales were positively related to body satisfaction, positive affect, and (with the exception of UPE) subjective well-being.

Average scores are 3.63 (SD = 0.54) for the overall IES, 3.34 (SD = 0.82) for UPE, and 3.51 (SD = 0.98) for TIC (Dockendorff et al., 2011). Girls and boys differed on EPR, with means being 3.68 (SD = 1.04) for girls and 4.06 (SD = 0.86) for boys (overall M = 3.91, SD = 0.99). Scores ± 1 SD could be used to identify students high and low on the overall score or particular intuitive eating dimension. Therefore, if girls and boys fall below 3.09 for the overall IES, 2.52 for UPE, 2.53 for TIC, and either 2.64 (girls) or 3.20 (boys) for EPR, then they could be classified as scoring low on intuitive eating.

Body Image

When choosing and administering body image instruments, school personnel must be aware of the degree to which students can reflect on their body, which may be difficult for students younger than age 8 (B. K. Mendelson, White, & Mendelson, 1996). School personnel also must consider the different body ideals of girls and boys and the implications of these differences for accurate and valid assessment of body image. When measuring girls' body satisfaction, body fat–thinness should be the main dimension of assessment; if body areas are specifically mentioned, they should be the hips, thighs, buttocks, and the abdomen (Gardner, Sorter, & Friedman, 1997). When measuring boys' body satisfaction, muscularity and body fat–leanness should be the primary dimensions of assessment; if body areas are specifically mentioned, they should be the arms, chest, shoulders, and the abdomen (Tylka, Bergeron, & Schwartz, 2005). Another potential issue is the nature of the questions. Wording questions or items in a highly negative manner (e.g., "I think my stomach is too fat") may spike distress in students. Rather, we recommend that questions be worded in a neutral or positive manner.

Questionnaires are the preferred method of body image assessment over figure rating scales for students. In figure rating scales, children are asked to indicate their perceived and ideal body size through a set of figure drawings ranging in size from very thin to obese (Collins, 1991). These scales will not measure children's degree of body image investment; they simply measure the extent to which students are aware that their body deviates from ideal media images of girls–women and boys–men. Figural rating scales also do not take into account muscularity (an important characteristic of the media body ideal for boys and men) and breast size independent of body fat (an important characteristic of the media body ideal for girls and women).

In this section, we cover the Body Appreciation Scale (BAS; Avalos et al., 2005) and the Body-Esteem Scale for Children (BES-C; B. K. Mendelson et al., 1996). We chose these measures because of their popularity, availability, and ease of administration and scoring. In describing these measures, we considered the gender inclusiveness of their items, whether they are worded neutrally or positively, their psychometric properties with children and adolescents, and whether their items are appropriate for children's reading level.

Body Appreciation Scale

The BAS (see Appendix D) is a 13-item survey that measures favorable opinions of the body (despite weight–body shape and perceived imperfections), awareness and attention to the body's needs, engagement in healthy behaviors to take care of the body, and protecting the body through rejecting unrealistic media body ideals. All items are designed to be gender neutral: all items mention "body" and "body shape or weight." One item has two question stems: one for girls–women (e.g., "I do not allow unrealistically thin images of women presented in the media to affect my attitudes toward my body") and the other for boys–men (e.g., "I do not allow unrealistically muscular images of men presented in the media to affect my attitudes toward my body"), making this item gender inclusive. All items are worded positively and are rated along a scale ranging from 1 (*never*) to 5 (*always*). Scoring is simple: Average the item responses. Although no cutoffs are specified, girls' (ages 12–20) mean was 3.78 ($SD = 0.8$), and boys' (ages 12–20) mean was 4.00 ($SD = 0.7$; Lobera & Bolaños Ríos, 2011). Scores ±1 SD could be used to identify students low on body appreciation (i.e., 2.98 for girls and 3.30 for boys).

The BAS's psychometric properties have been supported for adolescents. It has demonstrated a unidimensional factor structure in a sample of adolescent girls and boys (ages 12–20) from Spain (Lobera & Bolaños Ríos, 2011). In that sample, the BAS items were internally consistent (Cronbach's $\alpha = .91$), stable across two administrations 3 weeks apart ($r = .87$), and positively related to adaptive coping and self-esteem and negatively related to weight concerns, weight loss behaviors, and body concerns.

Whereas the BAS appears to be at a reading level that is appropriate for adolescents ages 12 and older, its items were not designed specifically for young children. If administered to children younger than 12 years old, some items would need to be modified. Appendix D contains suggested modifications to the items and response scale. Even with these modifications, however, the BAS probably would not be appropriate for children under age 8. It is important to recognize that this modified format has not been tested yet; therefore, the items should be considered tentative until psychometric evidence is accrued for children younger than age 12.

Body Esteem Scales for Children and Adolescents

The BES-C was designed for children. It contains 20 items with two answer options: yes or no. These items can be found on the website http://obesity.thehealthwell.info/body-esteem-scale-children-mendelson-white or in B. K. Mendelson et al. (1996). It is fairly gender neutral; however, one item mentions thinness (e.g., "I wish I were thinner"), and two items mention weight without including body size, which favor girls' body image concerns. Although some items on the BES-C are worded negatively (e.g., "My looks upset me"), most are worded positively (e.g., "I'm proud of my body").

Thirteen items form an appearance factor (e.g., "I like what I see when I look in the mirror"), three items form a weight factor (e.g., "My weight makes me happy"), and two items form a peer attribution factor (e.g., "Other people make fun of the way I look"); the remaining two items are not included in any factor (B. K. Mendelson et al., 1996). After negatively worded items (e.g., Items 4, 5, 7, 8, 11, 12, 13, 16, 17, 20) are reverse scored (i.e., yes becomes no, and vice versa), items within each factor are summed to form subscale scores. (Note that there is a typographical error on Item 10: "I really like what I weight" should be "I really like what I weigh.")

Some psychometric evidence for the BES-C exists for children ages 8 to 13 (B. K. Mendelson et al., 1996). The appearance and weight factors have adequate internal consistency reliability (Cronbach's α = .77 and .87) but moderate-to-low test–retest reliability over a 2-year period (r is between .34 and .57). Actual weight was negatively related to both subscales; however, the appearance subscale did not predict unique variance in actual weight above and beyond the weight subscale, suggesting discriminant validity for the weight subscale. Construct validity evidence further was reported for the appearance subscale in that it accounted for unique variance in self-esteem; however, the weight subscale did not. The attribution factor does not have adequate psychometric properties and therefore is not considered further.

Although cutoff values are not specified, girls ages 8 to 13 have means of 8.9 to 10.6 (SD = 3.6) on the appearance subscale and 1.7 to 2.2 (SD = 1.2) on the weight subscale, whereas boys ages 8 to 13 have means of 10.7 to 11.4 (SD = 2.2) on the appearance subscale and 2.0 to 2.7 (SD = 0.9) on the weight subscale. Scores ±1 SD could be used to identify students high and low on appearance and weight body esteem; in other words, girls who score below a 6.0 on appearance and under 1.0 on weight and boys who score below a 9.0 on appearance and 1.0 on weight could be classified as having low body esteem.

Differing from the yes versus no format of the BES-C, the Body-Esteem Scale for Adolescents and Adults (BES-AA; B. K. Mendelson et al., 2001) adopts a 5-point scale: 0 (*never*), 1 (*seldom*), 2 (*sometimes*), 3 (*often*), and 4 (*always*). B. K. Mendelson et al. (2001) also modified some items and added items on the weight and attribution subscales to improve their psychometrics.

The BES-AA contains 23 items and can be found in *Exacting Beauty: Theory, Assessment, and Treatment of Body Image Disturbance* (Thompson, Heinberg, Altabe, & Tantleff-Dunn, 1999). The appearance subscale contains 10 items (Items 1, 6, 7,* 9,* 11,* 13,* 15, 17,* 21,* 23; $\alpha = .92$), the weight subscale includes eight items (Items 3, 4,* 8, 10, 16, 18,* 19,* 22; $\alpha = .94$) and the attribution subscale contains five items (Items 2, 5, 12, 14, 20; $\alpha = .81$), with alphas obtained from a large sample of adolescents and young adults ranging from 12 to 25. Items with an asterisk are negatively worded items that need to be reverse scored before computing subscale scores; after these items are reverse scored, subscale items are averaged. Subscale means are often in the 1.8-to-2.3 ($SD = 1.0$) range for girls ages 12 to 18 and in the 2.7-to-3.2 ($SD = 0.9$) range for boys ages 12 to 18, and scores ±1 SD could be used to identify students high and low on body esteem. If mean subscale scores fall below 1.3 for girls and 2.2 for boys, then they could be classified with low body esteem.

BES-AA subscale scores were stable over a 3-month period (appearance $r = .89$, weight $r = .92$, attribution $r = .83$). Validity evidence also was accrued (B. K. Mendelson et al., 2001). Specifically, girls and women scored higher than boys and men; the weight subscale was related to appearance-based self-esteem; the appearance subscale was related to overall, appearance-based, social, and romantic self-esteem; and the attribution subscale was related to appearance-based, friend, social, and romantic self-esteem. It should be noted, however, that the BES-AA is not gender neutral; it is designed more for girls and women, who tend to focus on their weight, than for boys and men, who tend to focus on body shape (Tylka et al., 2005). Moreover, the number of negatively worded items may increase distress in students.

Internalization of Media Appearance Ideals

The tendency to internalize media appearance ideals and use these ideals as the standard from which to evaluate your body is a central risk factor for EDs (Stice, 2002). Many ED prevention programs explicitly target this variable, such as Media Smart (Wilksch, Tiggemann, & Wade, 2006) and the Body Project (Stice & Presnell, 2007). For more information on these programs, please see Chapter 7, this volume. A measure of internalization of media ideals that yields reliable and valid scores would be useful for schools that wish to assess initial levels of this variable within their students or track students' progress (i.e., changes in levels of internalization) within ED prevention programs.

The leading measure of internalization of media ideals is the 30-item Sociocultural Attitudes Towards Appearance Questionnaire–3 (SATAQ-3; Thompson, van den Berg, Roehrig, Guarda, & Heinberg, 2004), and its psychometric properties have been extensively supported with college women. Recently, Wilksch and Wade (2012) explored its factor structure as well as the reliability and validity of its scores among eighth-grade girls and boys. They altered a few items so they were gender neutral in language. They revealed that a 19-item abbreviated measure provided a better fit to adolescents' data than its original 30-item version; thus, we recommend that the 19-item version be administered to children as young as eighth grade. This measure is presented in Appendix E.

The SATAQ-3 for Adolescents assesses four distinct but interrelated aspects of internalization of media appearance ideals: information (seven items; the extent to which adolescents use media for information on what is attractive), pressures (five items; the degree to which adolescents feel pressured by the media to change their appearance), internalization athlete (three items; how much adolescents aspire to look like athletes in the media), and internalization general (four items; how much adolescents wish they looked like models and actors glamorized by the media). All items are rated along a scale ranging from 1 (*definitely disagree*) to 5 (*definitely agree*). Subscale item responses are averaged, and a total score can be calculated by averaging all 19 items.

All SATAQ-3 subscales were internally consistent among adolescents. For girls and boys, respectively, Cronbach's alphas were .93 and .95 for the total 19-item SATAQ-3, .90 and .94 for information, .86 and .88 for pressures, .85 and .83 for internalization athlete, and .90 and .88 for internalization general (Wilksch & Wade, 2012). One-month test–retest estimates ranged from .54 to .73. In terms of validity, the total SATAQ-3 and subscales were each positively related to body dissatisfaction and dietary restraint.

Average scores are 2.78 (*SD* = 0.81) among girls and 2.11 (*SD* = 0.79) among boys for the total SATAQ-3 score, 2.77 (*SD* = 0.91) among girls and 2.14 (*SD* = 0.94) among boys for information, 2.74 (*SD* = 1.02) among girls and 1.85 (*SD* = 0.82) among boys for pressures, 3.10 (*SD* = 1.10) among girls and 2.24 (*SD* = 0.97) among boys for internalization general, and 2.52 (*SD* = 1.03) among girls and 2.34 (*SD* = 1.04) among boys for internalization athlete (Wilksch & Wade, 2012). Scores ± 1 *SD* could be used to identify students high and low on the total SATAQ-3 score or the particular internalization dimensions. Although it would be useful to explore each dimension, we recommend that school personnel use total SATAQ-3 scores to gauge students' internalization of media appearance ideals. Thus, if girls fall above 3.59 and boys fall above 2.90 for the total SATAQ-3, then they are high on internalization of media appearance ideals.

EATING DISORDER TREATMENT

Children and adolescents with clinical level EDs require comprehensive and multifaceted care, requiring the efficient integration of mental health, medical–nutrition, and school practices (American Academy of Pediatrics,

2003; Scime et al., 2006). Treatment may be done either on an inpatient or outpatient basis, depending on the level of symptomatology and the patient's health status (C. Cook-Cottone, 2009; C. Cook-Cottone & Scime, 2006).

Next, we outline what can be experienced in the treatment of children and adolescents with disordered eating behavior. For children falling within the overweight and obese categories, like Jared, interventions such as the ROC would be beneficial if they have an elevated EAH-C score. For all children, regardless of weight, consultation with their pediatrician and consequent nutritional intervention (if needed) paired with daily physical activity (at least 1 hr per day) is recommended. It is important to recognize that some children of ideal weight can be malnourished and have poor eating habits, and some heavy children can have healthy eating habits. Severe restriction of food intake as a treatment should be avoided (Bacon, 2010). Educators and parents should question pediatricians who offer this treatment option, as restriction has not been shown to promote lasting weight loss and is associated with decreased well-being among children and adults. They should keep pediatricians abreast of the whole-school approach to healthy eating and body acceptance and only choose pediatricians who work within this approach. Perhaps educators could devise a pamphlet for pediatricians describing the whole-school approach (samples of these descriptions are included in the handbooks for the prevention programs described in Chapter 7, this volume).

The Treatment Team

Both Kara and Ben present with clinical level disorder and require a treatment team. The treatment of disordered eating uses a multidisciplinary team that specializes in the treatment of eating issues (C. Cook-Cottone, 2009). Members of the team address health status and medication issues, nutrition and meal planning, and psychosocial treatment (American Psychiatric Association Work Group on Eating Disorders, 2000; C. Cook-Cottone, 2009; Yager & O'Dea, 2005). Outpatient medical treatment typically involves attention to the patient's holistic wellness and the monitoring and treatment of physiological status (e.g., electrolyte levels, weight, vital signs, medications). A nutritionist often works with the patient to develop a nutrition plan to address restriction and chaotic eating patterns that can trigger bingeing-and-purging cycles as well as connect with natural hunger and satiety cues (Ozier & Henry, 2011).

Psychosocial issues are typically addressed by a licensed mental health professional with training in the treatment of EDs (i.e., psychologist, mental health counselor, social worker; C. Cook-Cottone, 2009). The psychological treatment of disordered eating typically involves a functional analysis of the role of the disordered eating in the client's life (e.g., regulate emotions, avoid distress or uncomfortable mood states). Therapy sessions often address emotional regulation; comorbid depression and anxiety; interpersonal issues, skills, and skill application deficits; cognitive distortions; meal plan compliance; and mind–body attunement (C. Cook-Cottone & Scime, 2006). Further, the treatment of anorexia nervosa, as in the case of Kara, often includes both individual and family therapy (APAWGED, 2000). Although further replication of the method is still needed, the Maudsely Method of family therapy has been found effective for adolescent patients with anorexia nervosa (A. Smith & Cook-Cottone, 2011). This three-phase treatment method uses the family as a resource in treatment. The family serves as a support in the refeeding and weight restoration process at home (Phase 1). In Phase 2, the treating therapist helps the family negotiate new patterns of relationships as the control over eating is transitioned back to the patient. The third and final phase involves a focus on the patients as they work to establish healthy adolescent development. Phase 3 ends with termination of therapeutic services (A. Smith & Cook-Cottone, 2011). Ben's family can discuss the various treatment options for bulimia nervosa. Treatments for bulimia nervosa and binge-eating disorder often include cognitive behavioral, dialectical behavior, or cognitive emotional behavioral therapy (see Chapter 6, this volume, for a review of mindfulness-based and mindfulness-informed therapies) or individual psychotherapy modalities augmented with group therapy and support groups (C. Cook-Cottone, 2009; Wilson, Grilo, & Vitousek, 2007). In more recent times, yoga has been added as a supplemental treatment to enhance treatment outcomes for anorexia, bulimia, and binge-eating disorder (C. Cook-Cottone, Beck, & Kane, 2008), which is also discussed more in Chapter 6.

School Personnel and Treatment

Adequate support in the school setting can be a critical part of the treatment and recovery process (Manley, Rickson, & Standeven, 2000). For example, school personnel can provide valuable support for students during treatment through provision of course work and guidance for hospitalized students (C. Cook-Cottone, 2009; Yager & O'Dea, 2005). An effective and supportive home–treatment–school bridge is critical for continued academic growth and healing (C. Cook-Cottone, 2009a). In cases like Kara's, school support and back-to-school transition can be a critical aspect of ongoing recovery.

Support of the treatment of disordered eating can be most effectively done within the context of a prevention-oriented school atmosphere already promoting (a) zero tolerance of in-school advertising, body teasing, harassment, and gender-biased discourse, as well as (b) healthy nutritional behaviors and opportunities for positive physical and expressive experiences (e.g., soccer, yoga classes, track, swimming, art, and music; C. Cook-Cottone, 2009).

To facilitate a timely referral process and support students in treatment, every school should have a resource or go-to person to handle ED concerns (Yager & O'Dea, 2005). Responsibilities associated with this role include being knowledgeable about how to approach individuals at risk for an ED; organizing inservices and booster sessions that provide information on healthy eating, body acceptance, and disordered eating for other school personnel; communicating with parents; and making referrals to appropriate professionals (C. Cook-Cottone & Scime, 2006; Yager & O'Dea, 2005). Often this individual is a school psychologist, counselor, or social worker (C. Cook-Cottone, 2009).

When a student in the school is in treatment for disordered eating, the school referral and treatment coordinator should communicate with the treatment team and coordinate the necessary treatments and supports in the school (Manley et al., 2000). Releases of information should be completed for all members of the treatment team. This role is important, as consistent communication with treatment providers helps in meeting the student's academic, social–emotional, and physical needs. In some cases, educational classification (e.g., other health impaired) or a Section 504 plan and services may be required. In cases of an extended inpatient hospitalization, academic consultation with treatment facilities educational staff may also be necessary (C. Cook-Cottone & Scime, 2006).

The school referral and treatment coordinator may also act as a student advocate. Advocacy issues might include eliciting support for accommodations, describing medication side effects to increase teacher empathy, and helping students negotiate scheduling complications (C. Cook-Cottone, 2009). For example, attending treatment team appointments (e.g., psychologist, nutritionist, and medical team members) and occasional visits to other medical specialists (e.g., psychiatrist), students may have from three to five weekly appointments. This can be socially and psychologically stressful, disrupting to academics, and frustrating for school personnel (Manley et al., 2000). By working with the family, treatment team members, and teachers, the treatment coordinator can help create a schedule that minimizes academic impact and stress.

If students require hospitalization or day treatment, their reentry to school is an important transition. Providing support for this transition is vital to recovery (Manley et al., 2000). The treatment coordinator should work with the treatment team and the school to plan for reintegration and address the student's medical, psychological, and academic needs (C. Cook-Cottone & Scime, 2006). Student needs may include supportive counseling, medical monitoring, release from physical education classes, meal monitoring, and communication with the treatment team and family. Special academic accommodations may be necessary, such as reduced workload, alternative assignments for some physical education requirements, extended time on assignments and tests, peer tutoring for missed coursework, copies of class notes, and access to quiet study locations (Manley et al., 2000). Given the medical complications sometimes involved in more chronic or severe cases, the school nurse plays an important role in the reintegration of students (C. Cook-Cottone & Scime, 2006). For example, the school nurse may be needed to check pulse, blood pressure, or other medical issues. The school nurse also manages the medical releases and restriction information for activities and meals. Some students prefer the school nurse for mandated meal monitoring (C. Cook-Cottone & Scime, 2006).

In-school counseling can nicely augment school efforts (C. Cook-Cottone & Scime, 2006). Helpful techniques include relaxation work; supportive and reflective listening; and short-term, solution-focused, or problem-solving approaches for in-school issues. In addition, the treatment team psychologist may have specific objectives with which he or she would like the individual to assist within the school setting.

Other Areas of School Support for Those With Disordered Eating

Support during meals can be very helpful. It is often very difficult for these students to eat on their own because eating healthy portions can be very scary for them. Teachers, the treatment coordinator, or both, can review the school lunch plan with these students, helping them to identify hearty and healthy choices. Teachers can support snack breaks and offer to be a meal buddy for kids struggling to eat (C. Cook-Cottone, 2009).

Often alternative assignments are required. Physical education teachers can provide alternative activities for students who cannot partake in physically demanding tasks (there are often medical restrictions for exceptionally low-weight patients). It will be important to allow alternative assignments for class activities that may be triggers for those with EDs, such as weighing in, coeducation swimming classes, or calorie counting in nutrition class (C. Cook-Cottone & Scime, 2006).

Students in treatment require flexibility and support with academic assignments and attendance. Treatment often involves frequent doctors' appointments (up to five a week), and school personnel must work to be understanding and supportive (C. Cook-Cottone, 2009). Children and adolescents in treatment often worry that teachers are angry about absences. They can experience additional distress that distracts them from recovery and increases their resistance to necessary treatment sessions (C. Cook-Cottone & Scime, 2006).

CONCLUSION

This chapter discussed several instruments that can be used to estimate how students feel about their bodies and their eating behaviors, which will be useful in determining where students lie on the two perpendicular dimensions of our model (see Figure 1.4). These instruments also can be used as screening tools to facilitate appropriate school response (e.g., interventions to increase positive body image and intuitive eating and decrease eating in the absence of hunger) and treatment referral (for those with EDs). We offer a guide for how school personnel can facilitate this treatment referral as well as make school a supportive, safe, and accommodating place in which these students can recover.

9

FEDERAL SCHOOL FOOD POLICIES AND PROFESSIONAL GUIDELINES

This chapter addresses policy and how policy may enhance, and/or obstruct your journey. As school personnel, you are fully versed in the challenge of federal, state, and local mandates. You have experienced the tension between your goal to ensure the education of students and the goals of policy. You know that sometimes there is perfect alignment, and sometimes you succeed in educating students despite policy. Addressing food and body issues in school can add to this challenging balance. It is worth the effort, and the effort will, in fact, improve your effectiveness in your ultimate goal to educate students. This chapter provides the history and context of policy along with tools to help you better negotiate this challenge.

The primary mandate for schools is the education of our youth. This charge has been the principal focus of federal, state, and local educational policies for centuries. However, as history shows, preparing students for academic achievement requires a comprehensive approach that includes health

DOI: 10.1037/14180-010
Healthy Eating in Schools: Evidence-Based Interventions to Help Kids Thrive, by C. P. Cook-Cottone, E. Tribole, and T. L. Tylka

and well-being (*A Blueprint for Reform: The Reauthorization of the Elementary and Secondary Education Act*, U.S. Department of Education, 2010; S. L. Roberts, 2002). School personnel vary in their knowledge of initiatives and policies that focus on cultivating healthy students. For some schools, like Bayside High School (see Introduction, this volume), administrators, teachers, staff, and school families are fully versed on policies and guidelines and are actively complying and even surpassing recommendations. For other schools, like City Central Elementary School (see the Introduction), there are so many other challenges that many families and even some school personnel would be surprised at the extent to which food, physical activity, and school wellness practices are addressed in policy and mandates.

Legislators, policymakers, and researchers agree that schools can have a substantial influence on the promotion of healthy dietary, exercise, and body acceptance behaviors (Centers for Disease Control and Prevention [CDC], 2011b; French, Story, & Fulkerson, 2002; Healthy, Hunger-Free Kids Act of 2010; O'Toole, Anderson, Miller, & Guthrie, 2007; U.S. Department of Education, 2010; World Health Organization, 2011). A school can be a critical health-promoting influence in a student's life. Most agree that the development of healthy eating, exercise, and body-related behaviors can only occur in a school environment with accessible, affordable, and nutritious food choices; opportunities to engage in physical activity; and a culture of acceptance of all types and sizes of bodies (Bromfield, 2009; Story, Kaphingst, Robinson-O'Brien, & Glanz, 2008). As policy increasingly integrates a more holistic view in support of the healthy student, school personnel can enthusiastically enact innovative changes within their schools that are consistent with guidelines and policies. With needs high, such actions will serve to support and enhance student health and reduce risk (U.S. Department of Education, 2010).

Attempts to influence school practices come from many directions and perspectives. Advocacy groups, parent groups, and government agencies have provided guidelines and recommendations addressing the food and body issues that affect many aspects of the school day. Some of the influences are positive (e.g., limitations on nonnutritious, competitive foods); some increase risk (e.g., public weighing and assessing body mass index [BMI] without intervention resources; Bacon, 2010). Either way, the impact of legislation and policy can be substantial. Over the past century, agencies, professional organizations, businesses, researchers, and citizen groups have engaged in the debate on how food and the body should be addressed in schools. Taking a needs-based approach, many organizations have active initiatives designed to inform legislation and policy in general (e.g., American Dietetic Association [ADA], CDC, Institute of Medicine [IOM]).

Generally, the nature of food and body policy and legislation has changed over the years in accordance with the needs of the population. This can be seen most clearly in the response to higher obesity rates and the ongoing and fast-paced changes in federal, state, and district policies (Story et al., 2009). Adjusting to the shifts in need, professional organizations have broadened their approach to childhood nutrition from targeting underconsumption and nutritional deficiencies to addressing overconsumption and reduced physical activity (ADA, 2008; Healthy, Hunger-Free Kids Act of 2010).

Schools are now encouraged to address the factors associated with higher obesity rates, as well as the long-standing needs associated with the over 12 million children who remain "food insecure" (i.e., not having adequate quantities of food available on a consistent basis, sufficient resources to obtain nutritious food, or knowledge on nutritional use of food; ADA, 2008; Healthy, Hunger-Free Kids Act of 2010). Recommendations have focused on healthy eating and a balanced approach to exercise. Illustrating specific recommendations, the ADA (2008) identified critical nutritional concerns for children ages 2 to 11 years that include excessive intake of dietary fat and inadequate intake of foods rich in calcium, fiber, vitamin E, folate, iron, magnesium, and potassium. Public health has historically addressed community health concerns through regulatory and policy mechanisms (e.g., vitamin D and rickets, dental caries and fluoridation of water, smoking and clean air policy; Dietz, Bland, Gortmaker, Molloy, & Schmid, 2002). Effective policy must be socioecological and address access to healthy and appealing food, access to safe places for children to play and exercise, and require daily physical activity and physical education in our schools (Dietz et al., 2002). Accordingly, legislation, policy, and debate have focused on many related aspects of the school day. Problems are easy to identify.

Presenting children with a healthy food and fitness environment is a necessity because making healthy choices is about more than willpower. Currently, children can eat two and sometimes three meals a day at school through the school meals program (O'Toole et al., 2007; Story et al., 2008). Schools have a long history of competitive foods (i.e., foods that compete with school meals program) or a la carte food sales that offer calorie-dense and less nutritious choices (French et al., 2002; O'Toole et al., 2007; Story et al., 2008). For several decades, vending machines have been an established part of some schools' fundraising initiatives (O'Toole et al., 2007). It has been commonplace for school stores, concession stands, and bake sales to offer candy bars, nonnutritious snacks, and desserts. School birthday and holiday parties nearly always involve high-sugar and high-carbohydrate sweets and drinks (French et al., 2002; O'Toole et al., 2007). As one school administrator noted, "Baked goods, pastries, and desserts for birthdays and holiday parties stream through the school doors every day." Fundraisers, especially those offered around winter and spring holidays, often involve candy. In some schools, educational lessons incorporate foodstuffs to increase students' interest in the activities (e.g., art lessons on cake decorating, math with candy). On the positive side, media literacy and nutrition curriculum are more commonplace than ever before, some schools have food gardens and garden clubs, and others offer yoga classes to students before or after school. Federal, state, and local policies have attempted to provide structure and support to school-based initiatives and have moved more closely toward empirically supported practices.

In this chapter, we review some of the more central policies and initiatives relevant to creating a "healthy food and body" school environment that supports the healthy student. This information can help school personnel working to make healthy changes in their school community by providing policy and guideline rationale for their initiatives. It was the practice of using policy to initiate change that made a difference at Bayside High School. Parents were able to advocate for fundraising efforts to follow district wellness and nutrition standards only after citing competitive foods legislation (Healthy, Hunger-Free Kids Act of 2010, § 206). At City Central Elementary School, the parents who want to convene a school wellness committee to develop a school wellness policy can explain to administrators that such policy is required by the Healthy, Hunger-Free Kids Act, § 9A. With problematic obesity rates at City Central, their new wellness committee can also look into the Nutrition Education and Obesity Prevention Grant program (Healthy, Hunger-Free Kids Act, § 241), a school and farm cooperative (§ 243), or organic foods (§ 210). Even the overwhelmed city school district cannot dismiss a group coming forward with action plans that are consistent with federal policy or potential grant funding.

SCHOOL POLICIES ASSOCIATED WITH EATING, FOOD, AND BODIES

School policies associated with the development of healthy students often function to cultivate a healthier school community overall. For example, there are a variety of specific recommendations and requirements often associated with funds for federal programs (e.g., not using food as a reward, restricting competitive nonnutritive foods, and providing water). There are also funds allocated for programmatic efforts (e.g., organic food programs, farm-to-school programs) that require grant applications. It is important to note, because guidelines are always in flux and vary by district and state, that this chapter purposefully not does not include each and every federal, state, and local guideline. Rather, key policies and policy-targeted areas are highlighted to illustrate their evolving nature over the years, challenges faced, and the role in school-based efforts to support healthy students.

Currently, school food policy and practice address a range of issues, including school meals programs, high obesity rates, and competitive foods in schools. Although most policies and guidelines serve to address the needs of children, some of these initiatives have been in response to other national needs and concerns outside of the well-being and academic success of students. As you will read in the history of the school lunch programs, federal initiatives have involved other issues, such as national security (i.e., physical fitness of young soldiers) and crop surpluses. It is important for school personnel, as citizens, to remain engaged in evolving policy and continuously ensure that these initiatives function primarily to serve students.

School Food Programs

As the first schools were built in the United States, the provision and regulation of food began schoolhouse by schoolhouse. Even back then, educators knew that a learning student is a nourished and healthy student. Families and communities provided the food as students took meals to school or walked home to eat. As the nation grew and developed, issues associated with poverty, war efforts, and agricultural surpluses changed the landscape. Over time, the provision and regulation of food in the schools was addressed by cities, states, and eventually, the federal government.

The national child nutrition programs have been viewed as among the greatest success stories of the U.S. domestic food and nutrition assistance programs (S. L. Roberts, 2002). Social histories of America in the early 1900s documented children of poverty who were unable to learn because of malnutrition and starvation. Early pilot programs in New York City (offering 3-cent lunches) documented improved physical status within 3 months. Around this same time period, other urban school feeding programs developed in large cities such as Boston and Philadelphia. In rural areas, there was a community approach as the school heating stove was sometimes used as a kitchen stove (S. L. Roberts, 2002). Children added their food from home to a community pot, and all would eat no matter what they brought. As history shows, whenever there is need, a market arises. Small-scale vendors began marketing food of variable quality to children for pennies. In 1909, William Penn High School in Philadelphia ran the first William Penn lunch program to provide healthy alternatives to the foodstuffs being sold to the children for profit (S. L. Roberts, 2002). Yet, despite great public need and malnutrition, the federal government was reluctant to get involved.

During the Great Depression and over the next 10 years, malnutrition in children became a growing public concern. As we continue to see today, it took a combination of other public challenges for the federal government to make a move. Millions of Americans were starving and substantial agricultural surpluses aggregated as a result of farmers being unable to find markets for their food. Initiation of a federal school feeding program was viewed as a way to address the needs of hungry children and help get rid of surplus farm commodities (S. L. Roberts, 2002). The U.S. Department of Agriculture (USDA) purchased surplus food, distributed the food to school children, and hired unemployed women to work under the Work Projects Administration. By 1942, 6 million children were fed annually, and both health professionals and educators were seeing results. Nevertheless, over time this program came to be viewed as a way to help farmers and put the unemployed to work, rather than a program with a primary goal of feeding children (S. L. Roberts, 2002).

Reports coming from military officials helped to shift opinions back in favor of school lunch programs. During World War II, Selective Service administrators reported that over 150,000 casualties were attributable to mal-nutrition in the services' young men. The malnutrition of children was now seen as a threat to national security. Amidst the debate, in 1946, the Richard B. Russell National School Lunch Act was passed, addressing the funding of school meals. Still part of current law, the National School Lunch Act, passed by Congress as a national security initiative, served to (a) protect the health and well-being of the nation's children and (b) encourage the consumption of nutritious food including agricultural commodities (S. L. Roberts, 2002). These initial central purposes continue to guide today's school food legislation.

School food programs are administered by the USDA's Food and Nutrition Service (FNS). Following a 1968 CBS documentary entitled *Hunger in America,* President Nixon responded to public concern for the needs of children through the establishment of the FNS (S. L. Roberts, 2002). Evolving from this initial legislation, the National School Lunch Program (NSLP) and the School Breakfast Program (SBP) are key components of federal policy designed to safeguard and promote the nutritional well-being of the nation's children (http://www.fns.usda.gov/). Today's school food pro-grams essentially function to address what Congress identified in 1946 as contributing factors to poor nutrition among children: (a) economic barriers, (b) lack of nutritional knowledge, and (c) access to healthy foods at school (S. L. Roberts, 2002). To be specific, the NSLP is a federally assisted meal program that operates in both public and nonprofit private schools, as well as residential care institutions, and provides either low-cost or free lunches to children at school (Li & Hooker, 2010). Added during the 1966 revisions of the legislation, the SBP functions much like the NSLP and offers free or reduced-price breakfasts to eligible children (Burgeson, Wechsler, Brener, Young, & Spain, 2001; S. L. Roberts, 2002).

In 1994, Congress passed the Healthy Meals for Healthy Americans Act. In 1995, regulations for the act were released mandating that school breakfasts and lunches must meet Dietary Guidelines for Americans (DGA; O'Toole et al., 2007). This resulted in decreases in levels of fat and saturated fat relative to calorie content in lunches offered to students, with overall totals for breakfasts and lunches remaining above DGA-recommended targets (O'Toole et al., 2007). In previous legislation, after-school programs in several states (e.g., Delaware, New York, Pennsylvania) were authorized by Congress to serve dinner as well as snacks in areas in which over 50% of the children qualified for free or reduced-price meals (Story et al., 2008).

The most recent legislation associated specifically with school-lunch programs is the Healthy, Hunger-Free Kids Act of 2010 and the Elementary and Secondary Education Act (ESEA) of 2010. The ESEA, which spells out the Department of Education's "blueprint for reform," is currently being reauthorized. The proposed reauthorization calls for fostering healthy students and specifically provides for competitive grants to improve school capacity in a variety of areas, including physical and mental health and well-being, nutrition education, healthy eating, and physical fitness. These proposed changes are addressed in relevant sections within this chapter as the implications affect several domains in the support of the healthy student. The Healthy, Hunger-Free Kids Act is organized around several goals: (a) reduction of childhood hunger, (b) reduction of childhood obesity, (c) improvement in the diets of children, (d) improvement in the management and integrity of child nutrition programs, and (e) support of programs that are consistent with the above goals (e.g., the farmer market nutrition program). Within the context of federal guidance, school food programs are operated through state agencies that have agreements with the local school systems (http://www.fns.usda.gov/).

In more general terms, the Healthy, Hunger-Free Kids Act of 2010 authorizes funding for federal school meal and child nutrition programs and increases access to healthy food for low-income children. Consistent with the Child Nutrition and WIC Reauthorization Act of 2004, the Healthy, Hunger-Free Kids Act requires each local educational agency receiving funds for USDA Child Nutrition Program to establish a local school wellness policy (O'Toole et al., 2007). Placing responsibility at the local level, this federal legislation requires schools to (a) create goals for nutrition education, physical activity, and other activities designed to promote student wellness; (b) develop and follow nutritional guidelines to ensure that the food choices available during the school day promote school health and reduce childhood obesity; (c) develop and utilize procedures for assessing how well the wellness policy has been implemented; and (d) encourage student, family, and community involvement. The act also provides additional funding to schools that meet updated nutritional standards (i.e., DGA) for federally subsidized lunches. Section 210 establishes a pilot program that awards competitive grants to school food authorities to increase the quantity of organic foods to children under the NSLP.

In a large national study of over 62,000 children, the use of free or reduced-price lunch or breakfast programs at public schools was found to be positively correlated with children's BMI (Li & Hooker, 2010). This finding held even when controlling for position on the socioeconomic scale. Over the years, the USDA has conducted studies of the NSLP and the SBP (O'Toole et al., 2007). The School Nutrition Dietary Assessment (SNDA) studies— that is, SNDA, 1991–1992 (Dwyer, 1995; Fox, Crepinsek, Connor, Battaglia, & McKinney, 2001; Story, 2009); and SNDA II, 1998–1999 (Fox et al., 2001; Story, 2009)—assessed the nutrients and foods provided by schools (public and private) participating in the NSLP and SBP and provided information about menu planning practices and the availability of meal plan alternatives (e.g., a la carte food sales, vending machines; O'Toole et al., 2007). Results of the SNDA indicated that school meals were failing to meet certain key nutritional goals (http://www.fns.usda.gov/). In response to these findings, in 1993 the USDA launched a reform of the school meals programs aimed at upgrading the nutritional content of school meals (http://www.fns.usda. gov/). Components of this reform are collectively referred to as the School Meals Initiative for Healthy Children (SMI; http://www.fns.usda.gov/).

In September 1996, FNS commenced a series of national studies of USDA's school-based child nutrition programs (http://www.fns.usda.gov/). The first report, published in 2000, examined the status of the SMI during the 1997–1998 school year and the actions taken by state agencies and school districts (http://www.fns.usda.gov/). The second report, published in 2001, built on the findings of the first year report while examining several new topics (http://www.fns.usda.gov/). The third report expanded on the findings of the first two reports in documenting the status of the SMI implementation and in assessing other topics of interest to FNS policymakers and program administrators (http://www.fns.usda.gov/).

Every 6 years, the CDC conducts the School Health Policies and Programs Study. The most recent study was conducted through phone interviews and mail questionnaires completed by state education agency personnel in all 50 states plus the District of Columbia among a nationally representative sample of school districts ($N = 445$) and computer-assisted personal interviews with a nationally representative sample of elementary, middle, and high schools ($N = 944$; O'Toole et al., 2007). The results of this study indicated that the nutrition services program practices in many schools across the nation continue to need improvement. According to the results, states varied, sometimes substantially, in how they implemented nutritional services for their students. For example, 4.0% of states required and 40.0% recommended that schools offer students a choice between two or more different nonfried vegetables each day for lunch. Also, 40.4% of districts and 41.3% of schools used ground turkey or lean ground beef instead of regular ground beef. Over 90% of districts and 87.4% of schools drain fat from browned meat (O'Toole et al., 2007).

Generally, findings indicated that few states required schools to restrict the availability of deep-fried foods, to prohibit the sale of foods that have low nutrient density in certain venues, or to make healthful beverages available when beverages were offered. Furthermore, although many schools did sell healthful foods and beverages outside of school nutrition programs, there were many that also sold items high in fat, sodium, and added sugars. The specific recommendations included increased implementation of food preparation practices that reduced the total fat, saturated fat, sodium, and added sugar content of school meals. The report also recommended that opportunities to eat and drink at school should be used to encourage greater daily consumption of fruits, vegetables, whole grains, and nonfat or low-fat dairy products (O'Toole et al., 2007).

The Healthy, Hunger-Free Kids Act of 2010, § 241, provides grants to states for the implementation of nutrition education and obesity prevention programs that promote healthy food choices as defined by the DGA. Those eligible for participation include (a) supplemental nutrition assistance program participants, (b) school lunch and breakfast plan participants, and (c) individuals who reside in a low-income community or are low-income individuals. Grantees are permitted to adopt individual and group-based nutrition education as well as community and public health approaches. In addition, school nutrition services staff can promote healthy eating through the foods they make available in the school cafeteria and the opportunities they have to reinforce nutrition education taught in the classroom (O'Toole et al., 2007).

Nutrition Education

Nutrition education in the schools has evolved over the years as nutrition has been embraced as a critical health practice. Most of us can remember taking a health class in high school. These days, nutrition education is not only offered in health classes, many schools also weave health education throughout the curriculum. Many schools offer nutrition modules within the health curriculum, with fewer offering nutrition education before or after school, within the context of parent workshops, or through partnerships with community organizations (Hammerschmidt, Tackett, Golzynski, & Golzynski, 2011). Some schools coordinate nutrition and physical activity programs with the curriculum offered in the classroom (Story et al., 2009). Teachers can help promote healthy eating by including behavior-focused nutritional education in the classroom curricula (O'Toole et al., 2007). See Part II of this book for a review of specific prevention intervention programs and descriptions of the nutritional educational components of these programs.

Most states require schools to provide health education; however, the amount of time spent on nutrition education varies substantially. The Healthy, Hunger-Free Kids Act of 2010 addresses nutrition education as it relates to a variety of areas addressed in the act (e.g., obesity, school gardens). Schools like City Central Elementary School should review the Healthy, Hunger-Free Kids Act for potential funding for nutrition education and prevention intervention programs. High-poverty schools with rising obesity rates are specially addressed in §241 of the act (i.e., Nutrition Education and Obesity Prevention Grant Program). There are also a variety of other federal awards, such as the Carol M. White Physical Education Program, administered through the Department of Education. With tens of millions of dollars awarded each year, these grants support school districts and community organizations who plan to implement comprehensive physical fitness and nutrition education programs to their students.

Competitive Foods at School

Competitive foods include foods available during school mealtimes that are in addition to, or outside of, the school meal program (O'Toole et al., 2007; Story et al., 2008). Schools addressing competitive foods are working to cultivate a healthy school environment. When this issue is not addressed, food and beverages that are not part of the school meal programs have often not been required to meet nutritional standards. As a result of inconsistent guidelines, these foods are often low in nutrient density and are high in fat, added sugar, and calories—thus adding a diet-related health risk (French et al., 2002; O'Toole et al., 2007; S. L. Roberts, 2002; Story et al., 2008). Some believe that the rise in obesity rates over the past decade can be, in part, attributed to the number of food options available throughout the school day (e.g., Story et al., 2008).

This can be a contentious issue, as financial recourses can be tightly tied to competitive food programs. In one of our case studies, City Central Elementary School, the school has signed a contract with a national soda chain. As a result, they have four vending machines, and they must sell the contracted brand of soda at every school event. City Central has a rising obesity problem and the families are already struggling to help the student make good choices. Access to soda after school and provision of soda at school events increases the challenge. This challenge exists for the legislators too. As it stands, they must choose sides between the beverage companies and the interests of the children. One option for City Central is to work with the beverage company and stock machines with brand-name waters and other healthier beverages.

There are additional issues associated with the provision of competitive foods. For example, some worry that because competitive foods are offered for additional money, children participating only in the school meal program may be stigmatized for eating the meals prepared for the "poor children" (O'Toole et al., 2007, p. 501). In this way, competitive foods contribute to the stigmatization of school meal programs and place the viability of meal programs at risk (S. L. Roberts, 2002). There is also a risk that the less nutritious competitive foods send a message that nutritious eating is an academic exercise and not an authentic daily practice supported by school administration (O'Toole et al., 2007).

Competitive foods were first addressed in the legislation within the 1970 amendment to the Child Nutrition Act (S. L. Roberts, 2002). According to the amendment, competitive foods were not allowed. However, over time these foods emerged in vending machines and snack shops as schools recognized the profits inherent in such ventures. There have been ongoing legal challenges to this aspect of the legislation (S. L. Roberts, 2002). For example, in 1972, an amendment to the act eliminated regulation of competitive foods; in 1980, the sale of foods with minimal nutritional value (FMNV) was not permitted in schools during the school day. In more recent times, legislation shifted the responsibility for articulating the rules for competitive foods to states, requiring that they at least prohibit sales of FMNV during breakfast or lunch periods. In 2008, Story et al. reported that about 90% of schools sold competitive foods. The nutritional quality of these foods has remained suspect. The Institute of Medicine (IOM) released a set of recommendations addressing competitive foods in the schools (O'Toole et al., 2007; Story et al., 2008). According to the recommendations, the federally reimbursable school nutrition programs should be the main source of food at school, and the competitive foods that are made available should consist of fruits, vegetables, whole grains, and nonfat–low-fat dairy products aligned with healthy eating patterns (Story et al., 2008). In some states and districts, the regulation associated with the offering of competitive foods in schools has been more stringent than USDA regulations, with many regulations being less stringent than IOM recommendations.

To illustrate this challenge, in 2003, the CSPI (2004) surveyed the contents of 1,420 vending machines in 251 schools across the country. The results indicated that the overwhelming majority of the options available in these machines were high in calories and low in nutrition, with 75% of the beverage options and 85% of snacks being of poor nutritional quality. The IOM nutritional standards for foods in schools are directed, in part, at products sold in vending machines and at school stores, as these products compete with healthier foods that meet specific nutritional guidelines and are provided by the school (USDA Team Nutrition, 2004).

Children's total energy intake has been found to be positively associated with soft drink consumption (ADA, 2008). Soft drink companies have a strong interest in marketing to children in an effort to create early brand loyalty. S. L. Roberts (2002) reported that soft drink companies often circumvent rules by donating soft drinks for free distribution at school. She cited the needs of cash-strapped school administrators accepting, even soliciting, agreements with food corporations in order to fund "everything from computers and musical instruments to art supplies and staff training" (S. L. Roberts, 2002, p. 606). Some schools have agreed to "pouring rights" contracts, articulating an exclusive agreement between a school or school district and a particular soft drink company (S. L. Roberts, 2002, p. 606). An exemplar of how far such agreements can go was covered by the *The New York Times* and *The Washington Post* in the late 1990s: A Colorado school district was paid $8 million for a 10-year agreement with Coca-Cola.

As also reported by the CSPI (2007), there has been a gradual strengthening of state nutritional policies over the past 10 years. The CSPI released its second State School Foods Report Card in 2007. The CSPI evaluated the school nutrition policies of all 50 states and the District of Columbia regarding food and beverages sold outside of the school lunch programs through vending machines, a la carte, school stores, and fundraisers based on five considerations: (a) beverage nutritional standards, (b) food nutritional standards, (c) grade levels to which policies apply, (d) time of day to which policies apply, and (e) locations to which policies apply. Results indicated that despite changes, there continues to be a fragmented, patchwork of policies across the nation that fails to meet students' needs in a timely manner. According to the report, 12 states (24%) have established a set of school food and beverage nutritional standards, and many of these address only foods and beverages sold in the cafeteria during meal periods or apply to foods and beverages sold up until the end of the last lunch period. Twenty-seven states prohibited the sales of sugary soft drinks in schools in at least some grade levels. At the time of the report, only seven states limited the sale of high-fat whole and 2% milk in schools, 16 states omitted sales of sports drinks, 12 states limited beverage portion size, and 14 states limited the portion size for snacks. Saturated fat was limited in snacks in 16 states, and trans fat was limited by 11 states. Overall, 26 states limited added sugars in school snack foods. Researchers indicated that many schools have been able to improve the nutritional quality of competitive foods without loss of revenue (see Story et al., 2009).

The Healthy, Hunger-Free Kids Act of 2010 has given the USDA authority to set national standards for all foods regularly sold in schools, including foods sold in vending machines, a la carte, and in school stores. Federal regulations on competitive foods include the prohibition of the sale of foods with minimal nutritional values in the food service area during school mealtimes (e.g., soft drinks, some candies, chewing gum; O'Toole et al., 2007). Of note, the Healthy, Hunger-Free Kids Act has not necessarily required food sold at school fundraisers to meet nutritional standards (see § 208).

Food as Reward

Using food as a reward or withholding food as a punishment is counter to an intuitive and healthy eating model. The CSPI (2007) acknowledged that there have been few studies conducted on the effect of using food rewards on children's long-term eating habits. The center suggested that the best policy is to not use food to reward children for good behavior or academic performance. They suggested that at minimum, children should not be rewarded using foods of poor nutritional quality. In § 221 of the Healthy, Hunger-Free Kids Act of 2010, it is estimated that reimbursable meals service should contribute to the development and socialization of the children enrolled in the program by providing that the food is not used as a punishment or reward. The CSPI (2007) offered a list of alternative rewards, including social rewards (e.g., praise, smiles), recognition (e.g., certificates, e-mail, photo, a recognition note), privileges (e.g., going first in line, choosing an activity, helping others), rewards for the class (e.g., extra recess, reading outdoors, free choice time at the end of the day), and school supplies (e.g., pencils, erasers, markers).

Farm-to-School Programs and Community–School Gardens

Fresh, locally grown food programs can improve the dietary intake of students (J. N. Davis, Ventura, Cook, Gyllenhamer, & Gatto, 2011). There have been a variety of programs with emerging data supporting both garden and farm-to-school programs. Both are addressed in some state policies as well as in the Healthy, Hunger-Free Kids Act of 2010 (§ 243, Access to Local Foods: farm-to-school program).

School garden programs typically involve an on-campus or local community garden that is cared for as part of coursework or an after-school gardening program. How the produce is used varies from participation in local farmers' markets to use in schools meals. Only a few states have state policy addressing school gardens (e.g., California, Hawaii, Washington). To illustrate, California's Education Code §§ 9000–9004 (2002) require the state's department of education to establish, develop, and implement an instructional school garden program that provides startup or expansion grants to school districts and county offices of education. According to the policy, schools may use the funds to do the following: (a) create an instructional school garden if one does not already exist, and (b) incorporate a school garden salad bar or compost program if a school garden already exists.

Farm-to-school programs link local farmers to schools to provide fresh, locally grown produce to school service cafeterias (Story et al., 2008). In its essence, the program was designed to support small farms by providing access to intuitional markets (i.e., schools) while improving the quality of the food provided to students. Although concerns have been raised in regard to the additional costs associated with preparation, these programs have provided schools with high-quality produce while supporting local agriculture. School and community garden programs provide an outdoor learning laboratory and a variety of curricular connections, ranging from biology to nutrition classes (Story et al., 2009).

These programs also hold promise in terms of increased number of school salad bars, improved participation in school food programs, and the promotion of healthy eating. The Healthy, Hunger-Free Kids Act of 2010 provides help for communities in establishing local farm-to-school networks, creation of school gardens, and use of more local foods in the school setting. The act authorizes appropriations for a pilot school and community garden grant program for high-poverty schools to provide students with hands-on vegetable gardening and nutrition education.

Access to Water

Beyond its other well-known essential health benefits (e.g., disease prevention, regularity, body temperature regulation), drinking water significantly elevates resting energy expenditure and may assist overweight children with weight loss (Dubnov-Raz, Constantini, Yariv, Nice, & Shapira, 2011). Accordingly, §203 of the Healthy, Hunger-Free Kids Act of 2010 requires participating schools to increase access to water at mealtimes and an expansion of access to drinking water in schools. Both City Central and Bayside could negotiate contracts with beverage companies to stock beverage machines with brand-name bottled water.

Physical Activity

In 1996, the U.S. Surgeon General's report on physical activity and health explicated substantial health benefits of regular physical activity for children and adolescents (Burgeson et al., 2001). For children and adolescents, benefits included building and strengthening bones, muscles, and joints; weight control; building of lean muscle; fat reduction; delayed development of high blood pressure; and reduction of anxious and depressive feelings. Surveys of school practices often revealed that many schools do not require physical education or offer additional opportunities for physical activity, with the percentage of schools declining after Grade 5 (Burgeson et al., 2001). The percentage of schools offering daily physical education classes is also low.

In 2005, the U.S. dietary guidelines included separate chapters that delineated specific guidelines for physical activity (ADA, 2008). These guidelines included a recommendation that children engage in at least 60 min of physical activity for most, and preferably all, days of the week. Despite the growing body of research, many states do not mandate quantity or quality of time spent in physical activity or have established fitness and performance standards (Story et al., 2009). Other areas relevant to policy that have been identified as critical to increasing daily physical activity include recess and walking or biking to school.

The Healthy, Hunger-Free Kids Act of 2010 sets basic standards for school wellness policies, including goals for physical activity (§ 221). Furthermore, the Omnibus Appropriations Act of 2009 allocated $78 million for the Carol M. White Physical Education Program established under No Child Left Behind (NCBL; Li & Hooker, 2010). This program was designed to initiate, expand, or improve physical education and afterschool activities for children in Grades K–12 in both schools and community-based organizations. Also, this act allocated $183 million for the Safe Routes to School program. This program aimed to help communities provide safer access to schools through bike lanes, trails, and sidewalks. In A *Blueprint for Reform* (ESEA, 2010), competitive grants are offered to support states, school districts, and their partners to address variety of issues, including physical fitness.

School Weighing Practices: To BMI or Not to BMI

In 2005, the IOM issued a call for the development of federal guidance for a BMI measurement program in schools (Nihiser et al., 2007). In 2007, the CDC provided a report designed to inform decision making on school-based BMI measurement programs. Guidance offered by the CDC indicated that BMI measurement programs in schools may be conducted for surveillance and screening purposes (Nihiser et al., 2007). For surveillance programs, BMIs are collected anonymously to assess the weight status of a specific population such as children in a school, district, or state to identify population trends or outcomes of interventions. For screening programs, BMIs are calculated to assess the weight status of individual students to identify those at risk, provide parents with information, and facilitate family decision making. Many states have implemented surveillance and screening programs.

The CDC (2007) and others (e.g., Bacon, 2010) have reported concerns associated with BMI measurement in schools. First, there is no clear body of evidence explaining the outcomes or use of BMI measurement programs in schools (Nihiser et al., 2007). The CDC has assessed that the practice of BMI measurement in schools meets only some of the criteria that the American Academy of Pediatrics (2004) created to help determine whether a school-based screening should be implemented for any health condition (e.g., Nihiser et al., 2007). To be specific, although BMI is often used as a measurement for obesity (a highly prevalent condition) and schools are a logical measurement site reaching nearly all youth, (a) there are no established, effective treatments of obesity available; (b) research has not established the efficacy and cost-effectiveness of BMI screening programs; and (c) often communities do not have the resources to help those at-risk access treatment (Nihiser et al., 2007). Furthermore, BMI does not account for lean muscle mass; therefore, children with substantial muscle (especially athletes) may have a higher BMI than even children who have excess body fat (Tylka, 2011b).

According to the CDC, concerns about school-based BMI screening programs include stigmatization, increased risk for harmful behaviors (e.g., disordered eating, emotional eating), lack of effectiveness, squandering of health promotions resources, and distraction from other school-based obesity prevention efforts. Also, BMI screening does not highlight those students who are not heavy but have poor eating and exercise habits (Bacon, 2010). Many girls with bulimia nervosa, for example, have an average BMI and will slip past the BMI screening process. There has been less concern over BMI surveillance programs (Nihiser et al., 2007).

The American Academic of Pediatrics recommended annual BMI measurements within the child's medical home (Nihiser et al., 2007). The U.S. Prevention Services Task Force (2010) indicated that there appears to be insufficient evidence to recommend for or against BMI screening programs for youth in clinical screenings as a means to prevent problematic health outcomes.

The CDC (2007) recommended that schools that choose to implement a BMI measurement program do so within a safe and supportive environment for students of all body sizes (Nihiser et al., 2007). For example, Gibbs et al. (2008) recommended that body heights and weights be collected on an individual basis rather than in front of peers, that results be screened in private to prevent peer comparison, and to focus on health and not solely BMI. It is also recommended that weight categories used with children and adolescents include "below healthy weight," "healthy weight," and "above a healthy weight" to avoid the stigma associated with overweight and obesity (Gibbs et al., 2008, p. 56). The CDC further recommended that BMI measurement programs obtain parental consent, establish safeguards to protect student privacy, obtain and use accurate equipment, accurately calculate and interpret the data, train staff in administering the program, use qualified staff (i.e., school nurse), avoid using BMI results to evaluate students or teacher performance, regularly evaluate the program to be sure it is meeting its intended outcomes and avoiding unintended consequences (Nihiser et al., 2007). Furthermore, schools that conduct BMI screening programs should have a comprehensive set of science-based strategies that promote physical activity and healthy eating. We recommend that these assessments be conducted only if deemed absolutely necessary by the school. If they are conducted, we recommend that they be done with sensitivity, confidentiality, and support for the students.

First Do No Harm: Policy on Bullying, Weighing, and Body-Related Talk

Every school prevention and intervention program should have a "First do no harm" principle at its core (Neumark-Sztainer et al., 2002; O'Dea, 2005). Even though schools may be well-intentioned and diligent about following the CDC recommendations when conducting BMI screenings, these screenings can still cause distress for students who find themselves in conversations with their peers and are prompted to share their BMI score or category. Simply weighing and measuring students can prime body talk, fat talk, and dieting talk (see Chapter 8, this volume). For this reason, we do not recommend BMI screenings within schools.

Both eating disordered and obesity prevention and intervention programs have the potential to unintentionally increase risk. A rigid focus on weight reduction and smaller body size can create an atmosphere that encourages *weightism*, or a systemic bias, even bullying, against those who are overweight and obese as well as a body comparison dynamic among students regardless of their body size (Bromfield, 2009; Neumark-Sztainer et al., 2002). Studies indicate that weight-related teasing is prevalent among adolescents and that bullying frequently targets students who deviate from the average weight range (Neumark-Sztainer et al., 2002). Neumark-Sztainer et al. (2002) also documented an association between weight-related teasing and eating disorders. Solutions should not marginalize overweight and obese children or encourage unhealthy weight reduction practices (Bromfield, 2009; Neumark-Sztainer et al., 2002).

Schools should maintain antibullying and inclusion policies and practices (Bromfield, 2009). A zero-tolerance policy should be enforced. Neumark-Sztainer et al. (2002) recommended clear-cut policies that do not allow weight teasing, accompanied by educational interventions in which both students and staff learn about the complex etiology of obesity and increase awareness of personal attitudes and behaviors toward people of different sizes (see Chapter 7, this volume). Prevention programs may also include information about the harmful effects of weight-related teasing and ways to intervene when teasing is witnessed (Neumark-Sztainer et al., 2002). Body talk, fat talk, and dieting talk should be defined for students so they can recognize this dialogue, and educators should show students how to use strategies to counter its effects (see Chapter 7).

Obesity and Policy

Be careful and do no harm: The focus of this text is on helping students internalize a sense of healthy and intuitive eating and practices of self-care, including physical activity that enhances health. The policies and guidelines described previously, excluding the use of BMI, are intended primarily to increase student health and reduce risk. We believe that addressing BMI or weight category as a target of intervention shifts goals away from healthy daily practice and toward an externalized benchmark that may or may not be correlated with the risk and health outcomes in the same manner that nutrition, physical activity, and stress reduction are. The Healthy, Hunger-Free Kids Act of 2010 and the blueprint for reform (ESEA, 2010) addressed the issue of obesity through provision of guidelines, the support of funds, or both, that serve to increase school's capacity to implement programs and change. Consider these policies as community tools. If the guideline is not working, challenge it. If it helps, reinforce it. Ultimately, use what is offered in the service of what will support students at your school.

CONCLUSION

School policy and professional guidelines that address eating, food, and body acceptance issues have evolved over the past 150 years. As the needs and challenges of the country have changed (e.g., from undernutrition and underweight to malnutrition and overweight–obesity issues), policies at local, state, and federal levels have shifted. It can be overwhelming and confusing for school personnel and administrators to develop and adhere to these sometimes complex and varied policies. Part II and Part III of this volume, as well as the Suggested Resources provided at the end of the book, can be your guide when developing, assessing, and revising local school policies and practices. Several organizations have developed sample policy and provide guidelines as to how to create local policy (e.g., The National Alliance for Nutrition and Activity). Furthermore, it is important for school personnel to take advantage of the funding opportunities available for those schools interested in taking new directions (e.g., developing relationships with local farms and creating a school and community garden). There are several award-winning school grants web pages and blogs that can guide you through the grant writing process (e.g., http://k12grants.org/). Schools that experience the most success are those that view policy changes as opportunities rather than roadblocks. It is your charge as a member of the school community to integrate policy consistent practices, innovation, and creativity to implement programs and practices at your school that can enhance health without increasing risk. This book will help you do that.

APPENDIX A: DEFINITIONS OF UNCOMMON DISORDERS OF EATING

It is important for school personnel to know the definitions and diagnostic criteria to effectively prevent, refer, and support the treatment of eating disorders (EDs; i.e., anorexia nervosa [AN], bulimia nervosa [BN], binge-eating disorder [BED], and eating disorder not otherwise specified [EDNOS]; see the Introduction for definitions of the major EDs [i.e., AN, BN, BED, EDNOS] and the DSM–IV–TR [American Psychiatric Association, 2000] and DSM-5 for diagnostic criteria). There are several less common EDs and conditions that are not the focus of this text (e.g., pica). These disorders are defined in this appendix to clarify the distinctions among the major EDs, overweight, obesity, and these other eating concerns.

OTHER EATING-RELATED DISORDERS DEFINED (IN ALPHABETICAL ORDER)

The following eating-related disorders are defined to help school personnel make distinctions among them and major EDs (i.e., AN, BN, BED, and EDNOS), overweight, and obesity. Notably, these specific disorders are not the focus of this text. When appropriate, specific readings are recommended.

Anorexia athletica has been described as a subclinical form of AN (Sundgot-Borgen & Torstveit, 2010). However, most athletes who meet criteria for anorexia athletica meet the criteria for AN (Sundgot-Borgen & Torstveit, 2010). Anorexia athletica is characterized by a pursuit of negative energy intake (i.e., burning off more calories than one is eating) and compulsive–obligatory exercise that is higher in intensity, frequency, and duration than what is recommended for good health. There may also be a continual pursuit of increasingly challenging athletic accomplishments with accompanying satisfaction in accomplishments. These individuals are at increased risk for injury and the *female athlete triad* (i.e., low energy availability, amenorrhea, and poor bone mineral density; Sundgot-Borgen & Torstveit, 2010).

Body dysmorphic disorder (BDD), although not an ED, is a disorder characterized by a preoccupation with an imagined or exaggerated physical anomaly (*DSM–IV–TR*; American Psychiatric Association, 2000). According to Altamura, Paluello, Mundo, Medda, and Mannu (2001), any aspect of appearance may be the basis of concern. Furthermore, preoccupation can manifest in recurrent mirror checking or other repetitive and/or ritualized behaviors. Boys and men who are preoccupied with gaining muscle mass and bodybuilding may develop *muscle dysmorphia*, which is a form of BDD (Leone, Sedory, & Gray, 2005; Olivardia, 2007). Prevalence estimates range from 5% (among women requesting aesthetic surgery procedures) to as high as 11.9% (among patients seeking dermatological treatment; Altamura et al., 2001; Phillips, Dufresne, Wilkel, & Vittorio, 2000).

Feeding disorder of infancy or early childhood is manifested by a persistent failure of the infant or child to eat adequately, accompanied by weight loss or a significant failure to gain weight (*DSM–IV–TR*; American Psychiatric Association, 2000). The disturbance cannot be because of an associated gastro-intestinal or other medical condition. Furthermore, it cannot be accounted for by another mental disorder or by a lack of available food. Children with this disorder may present with (a) a history of a delay or absence of feeding or eating skills; (b) problems managing or tolerating fluids; (c) a reluctance or refusal to eat due to taste, texture, or other sensory issues; (d) a lack of appetite or interest in food; or (e) the utilization of feeding behaviors to comfort, self-soothe, or self-stimulate (Bravender et al., 2010).

The female athlete triad was first identified in 1992 by the American College of Sports Medicine (ACSM) as an association of disordered eating, amenorrhea, and osteoporosis in athletes. In 2007, the ACSM broadened the definition of the triad's components and changed the term *disordered eating* to *energy availability*. The updated female athlete triad is defined as the interrelationships among energy intake (with or without ED), menstrual dysfunction, and low bone mineral density. Each of these components alone, or in combination, poses significant health risks, some of which are potentially irreversible (Nattiv et al., 2007). An athlete does not necessarily need to exhibit all three symptoms to be at risk for compromised health (Ozier & Henry, 2011).

Although prevalence studies on female school-age athletes are limited, the emerging trend is disturbing. One study found that a substantial number of high school athletes (78%) had one or more components of the female athlete triad (Hoch et al., 2009). A recent review of the literature by Thein-Nissenbaum and Carr (2011) found the prevalence of low energy intake and disordered eating ranged from 18% to 35%, and menstrual irregularities ranged from 19% to 54%, among female high school athletes. Furthermore, girls with one or more of the athlete triad components had injury rates 2 to 4 times higher, compared with female athletes without the triad symptoms. The reported injuries included stress fractures and musculoskeletal injury.

Sustained low energy availability, with or without disordered eating, impairs bone health and development indirectly and directly. Inadequate caloric intake indirectly impairs the protective effect of estrogen on bones, and it directly suppresses the hormones involved in bone formation, which increases the risk for stress fractures. Inadequate caloric intake also interferes with the growth and repair of muscles, contributing to the risk of athletic injury. According to the ACSM (Nattiv et al., 2007), there is critical need for prevention, early diagnosis, and treatment of female athlete triad; it is recommended that screening for the triad should occur at the preparticipation exam or annual health-screening exam.

Night-eating syndrome (NES) and *sleep-related eating disorder* (defined below) were defined primarily by researchers in the sleep and obesity fields and are distinct from BED (Allison, Grilo, Masheb, & Stunkard, 2005; Howell, Schenck, & Crow, 2009). The two main features that characterize NED are (a) wakeful eating that occurs after the individual's last meal and prior to final awakening and (b) hyperphagia (i.e., eating greater than one third of total daily calories after the evening meal; Howell et al., 2009; Lundgren et al., 2006). There is some evidence that the syndrome may involve alterations in the circadian rhythm. However, it is not known whether the altered circadian rhythm is a cause or an effect of night eating (Howell et al., 2009). NES is a chronic condition that occurs among normal weight, overweight, and obese individuals (Howell et al., 2009). Prevalence rates range from 1.5% in adults and 1.1% in pediatric populations. Notably, NES is associated with life stress, distress, insomnia, depression, substance abuse (most commonly alcohol), and increased body mass index (BMI; Howell et al., 2009; Lundgren et al., 2006).

Orthorexia nervosa is not an independent diagnostic category in the *DSM–IV–TR* (American Psychiatric Association, 2000). It has been defined as a chronic and intense obsession with healthy food (Donini, Marsili, Graziani, Imbriale, & Cannella, 2005). Pure or healthy foods include foods that are not genetically modified and are free of herbicides, pesticides, and other artificial substances (Fidan, Ertekin, Isikay, & Kirpinar, 2010). Individuals with orthorexia are more concerned with eating healthy and pure foods than the quantity or appearance of food (Fidan et al., 2010). It is important to make a distinction between those who desire to eat healthy foods and those who obsess about healthy foods, adhere to strict rules, lose a sense of moderation and balance, and withdraw from normal life activities as a result of their food obsessions and rigid and exclusionary eating behaviors (Donini et al., 2005; Fidan et al., 2010). Donini et al. (2005) reported that the orthorexic individual spends a great deal of time thinking about food and planning, purchasing, preparing, and consuming the food considered to be healthy.

Pica is defined as the "recurrent consumption of nonnutritive items" (Stiegler, 2005; p. 27). Pica is most often observed among individuals with autism and other developmental disabilities. School personnel should watch for the key sign, the consumption of nonfood items repeatedly over time despite efforts to reduce the behavior. It is important to make a distinction between pica and the normal exploration of objects by mouth that is seen in infants, toddlers, and some individuals with developmental disabilities (Stiegler, 2005). Also, if the behavior is culturally appropriate, it is not pica.

To illustrate, in some cultures, eating clay or soil is considered normal during certain life circumstances, such as pregnancy or illness (Stiegler, 2005). Finally, it is important to rule out a medical condition that may explain the symptom. For example, conditions such as anemia have been associated with nonfood cravings. (See Stiegler, 2005, for a complete review.)

Prader–Willi syndrome is a genetic disorder that affects multiple systems in the body and is marked by hyperphagia and lack of satiety in early childhood, adolescence, and adulthood (Cassidy & Driscoll, 2009). Other notable symptoms include hypotonia with poor suck and poor weight gain in infancy, mild mental retardation, hypogonadism, growth hormone insufficiencies, short stature, obesity, and behavioral and psychiatric disturbance. (See Cassidy and Driscoll, 2009, for a detailed description and review.)

According to the *DSM–IV–TR*, *rumination disorder* involves the repeated regurgitation and rechewing of food (American Psychiatric Association, 2000). Criteria require that this behavior must be present for at least one month following a period of normal functioning. Rumination disorder often occurs among those with pervasive developmental disorders and mental retardation (Bryant-Waugh, Markham, Kreipe, & Walsh, 2010). It has also been identified among patients with depressive, obsessive compulsive, and anxiety symptoms.

Sleep related eating disorder (SRED) has been characterized by recurrent episodes of arousal from nighttime sleep and consequent out-of-control or involuntary eating with adverse consequences (e.g., peculiar combinations of food, consumption of inedible substances, morning anorexia [i.e., restriction of food intake in the morning], dangerous food preparation, injury, and/or weight gain; Howell et al., 2009). A distinctive feature of SRED is *impaired consciousness* during the eating episode. SRED may be relatively common among individuals with EDs, with the prevalence rate among this population ranging from 8.7% to 16.7% (Howell et al., 2009). SRED has been associated with underlying sleep disorders (e.g., sleepwalking), restless leg syndrome, obstructive sleep apnea, depressed mood, dissociation, anxiety, withdrawal from substance abuse, and increased BMI.

APPENDIX B: CHILDREN'S EATING ATTITUDES TEST

1. I am scared about being overweight
2. I stay away from eating when I am hungry
3. I think about food a lot of the time
4. I have gone on eating binges where I feel that I might not be able to stop
5. I cut my food into small pieces
6. I am aware of the energy (calorie) content in foods that I eat
7. I try to stay away from foods such as breads, potatoes, and rice
8. I feel that others would like me to eat more
9. I vomit after I have eaten
10. I feel very guilty after eating
11. I think a lot about wanting to be thinner
12. I think about burning up energy (calories) when I exercise
13. Other people think I am too thin
14. I think a lot about having fat on my body
15. I take longer than others to eat my meals
16. I stay away from foods with sugar in them
17. I eat diet foods
18. I think that food controls my life
19. I can show self-control around food
20. I feel that others pressure me to eat
21. I give too much time and thought to food
22. I feel uncomfortable after eating sweets
23. I have been dieting
24. I like my stomach to be empty
25. I enjoy trying new rich foods[a]
26. I have the urge to vomit after eating

Note. Each item is rated and scored along this scale: *always* (3), *usually* (2), *often* (1), *sometimes* (0), *rarely* (0), and *never* (0). A total score is generated by summing all items; clinical cut-off score is specified at 20. From "Reliability Testing of a Children's Version of the Eating Attitude Test," by M. J. Maloney, J. B. McGuire, and S. R. Daniels, 1988, *Journal of the American Academy of Child and Adolescent Psychiatry, 27,* pp. 541–543. Copyright 1988 by Elsevier. Reprinted with permission.
[a]Reverse-scored item.

APPENDIX C: INTUITIVE EATING SCALE FOR ADOLESCENTS

1. I try to avoid certain foods high in fat, carbohydrates, or calories.[a]
2. I find myself eating when I'm feeling emotional (e.g., anxious, depressed, sad), even when I'm not physically hungry.[a]
3. I follow eating rules or dieting plans that dictate what, when, and/or how much to eat.[a]
4. I find myself eating when I am bored, even when I'm not physically hungry.[a]
5. I can tell when I'm slightly full.
6. I can tell when I'm slightly hungry.
7. I find myself eating when I am lonely, even when I'm not physically hungry.[a]
8. I trust my body to tell me when to eat.
9. I trust my body to tell me what to eat.
10. I trust my body to tell me how much to eat.
11. I have forbidden or "bad" foods that I don't allow myself to eat.[a]
12. When I'm eating, I can tell when I am getting full.
13. I use food to help me soothe my negative emotions, such as feeling sad or angry.[a]
14. I find myself eating when I am stressed out, even when I'm not physically hungry.[a]
15. I feel guilty if I eat a certain food that is high in calories, fat, or carbohydrates.[a]
16. I think of a certain food as "good" or "bad" depending on how much fat or how many calories it has in it.[a]
17. I don't trust myself around fattening or high calorie foods.[a]

Note. Each item is rated along this scale: 1 (*strongly disagree*), 2 (*disagree*), 3 (*neutral*), 4 (*agree*), 5 (*strongly agree*). After appropriate items are reverse scored, a total Intuitive Eating Scale (IES) score is obtained by averaging all items. For scoring Unconditional Permission to Eat (UPE), average items 1, 3, 11, 15, 16, and 17. For scoring Eating for Physical Reasons (EPR), average items 2, 4, 7, 13, and 14. For scoring Trust in Internal Cues (TIC), average items 8, 9, and 10.
[a]Reverse-scored item.

APPENDIX D: BODY APPRECIATION SCALE

1. I respect my body
2. I feel good about my body
3. On the whole, I am satisfied with my body
4. Despite its flaws, I accept my body for what it is
5. I feel that my body has at least some good qualities
6. I take a positive attitude toward my body
7. I am attentive to my body's needs
8. My self-worth is independent of my body shape or weight
9. I do not focus a lot of energy being concerned with my body shape or weight
10. My feelings toward my body are positive, for the most part
11. I engage in healthy behaviors to take care of my body
12. For girls: I do not allow unrealistically thin images of women presented in the media to affect my attitudes toward my body
    For boys: I do not allow unrealistically muscular images of men presented in the media to affect my attitudes toward my body
13. Despite its imperfections, I still like my body

Note. Each item is rated along this scale: 1 (*never*), 2 (*rarely*), 3 (*sometimes*), 4 (*often*), 5 (*always*). Items are averaged to obtain a total score. Items should be modified for children ages 8–12. We suggest the modifications for the following items: 1. I treat my body well, 2. I feel good about my body, 3. I am happy with my body, 4. I love my body even though it's not perfect, 5. I feel that my body has some good points, 6. I think good things about my body, 7. I take good care of my body, 8. I like myself in spite of my body shape or weight, 9. I think long and hard about my body shape or weight, 10. I feel positive about my body, 11. I do healthy things for my body, 12. I feel good about my body even when I see pictures of famous people, and 13. I would like my body even if I wasn't beautiful or handsome. Also, a 3-point scale (*never, sometimes, a lot*) is recommended. After *never* is scored as a 1, *sometimes* is scored as a 2, and *a lot* is scored as a 3, and Item 9 is reverse-scored, item values could be averaged. From "The Body Appreciation Scale: Development and Psychometric Evaluation," by L. Avalos, T. L. Tylka, and N. L. Wood-Barcalow, 2005, *Body Image, 2,* p. 289. Copyright 2005 by Elsevier. Reprinted with permission.

APPENDIX E: SOCIOCULTURAL ATTITUDES TOWARDS APPEARANCE QUESTIONNAIRE–3 (SATAQ-3; ADOLESCENT VERSION)

1. I would like my body to look like the people who are on TV.
2. TV commercials are an important source of information about fashion and "being attractive."
3. For girls: I've felt pressure from TV or magazines to look pretty. For boys: I've felt pressure from TV or magazines to look strong.
4. I would like my body to look like the models who appear in magazines.
5. Music videos on TV are an important source of information about fashion and "being attractive."
6. For girls: I've felt pressure from TV and magazines to be thin. For boys: I've felt pressure from TV or magazines to be muscular.
7. I would like my body to look like the people who are in movies.
8. Magazine articles are an important source of information about fashion and "being attractive."
9. I've felt pressure from TV or magazines to have a perfect body.
10. I wish I looked like the models in music videos.
11. Magazine advertisements are an important source of information about fashion and "being attractive."
12. I've felt pressure from TV or magazines to diet.
13. Pictures in magazines are an important source of information about fashion and "being attractive."
14. I wish I looked as athletic as sports stars.
15. I compare my body to that of people who are athletic.
16. Movies are an important source of information about fashion and "being attractive."
17. I've felt pressure from TV or magazines to change my appearance.
18. Movie stars are an important source of information about fashion and "being attractive."
19. I try to look like sports athletes.

Note. Each item is rated along this scale: 1 (*definitely disagree*), 2 (*disagree*), 3 (*neither disagree nor agree*), 4 (*agree*), 5 (*definitely agree*). Subscale items are averaged to obtain a total score. For the Information subscale, average items 2, 5, 8, 11, 13, 16, and 18. For the Pressure subscale, average items 3, 6, 9, 12, and 17. For the Internalization-Athlete subscale, average items 14, 15, and 19. For the Internalization-General subscale, average items 1, 4, 7, and 10. A total score can be calculated by averaging all 19 items. From "Examination of the Sociocultural Attitudes Towards Appearance Questionnaire-3 in a Mixed-Gender Young-Adolescent Sample," by S. M. Wilksch and T. D. Wade, 2012, *Psychological Assessment, 24*, pp. 354–355. doi:10.1037/a0025618. Copyright 2012 by the American Psychological Association.

SUGGESTED RESOURCES FOR SCHOOL PERSONNEL ON HEALTHY EATING

Authoritative Reports and Guidelines

American College of Sports Medicine (ACSM). *The Female Athlete Triad Position Stand.* http://journals.lww.com/acsm-msse/Fulltext/2007/10000/The_Female_Athlete_Triad.26.aspx

This 16-page paper describes the female athlete triad and provides evidence-based recommendations.

Centers for Disease Control and Prevention (CDC). *School Health Index: A Self-Assessment and Planning Guide.* http://www.cdc.gov/HealthyYouth/SHI/

This guide is designed to help schools establish effective policies on physical activity, nutrition, and other health issues.

CDC (September, 2011). *School Health Guidelines to Promote Healthy Eating and Physical Activity. Morbidity and Mortality Weekly Report, 60,* 1–76. http://www.cdc.gov/mmwr/pdf/rr/rr6005.pdf

CDC Coordinated School Health Program (CSHP). http://www.cdc.gov/healthy youth/cshp/components.htm

This program consists of 8 interactive components to help schools, districts, and states improve their school health programs: nutrition, health education, physical education, healthy school environment, health promotion for staff, counseling psychological services, and family community involvement.

Institute of Medicine (IOM; 2006). *Food Marketing to Children and Youth: Threat or Opportunity?* Washington, DC: The National Academies Press. http://www.nap.edu/catalog.php?record_id=11514

This 536-page report is available in pdf format.

IOM (2007). *Nutrition Standards for Foods in Schools: Leading the Way Toward Healthier Youth.* Washington, DC: The National Academies Press. http://www.nap.edu/catalog.php?record_id=11899

This 292-page report is available at no charge in pdf format.

IOM (2008). *Nutrition Standards and Meal Requirements for National School Lunch and Breakfast Programs.* Washington, DC: The National Academies Press. http://books.nap.edu/catalog.php?record_id=12512

This 192-page report is available free in pdf format.

IOM (2010). *School Meals: Building Blocks for Healthy Children.* Washington, DC: The National Academies Press. http://www.nap.edu/openbook.php?record_id=12751

This 395-page report is available free in pdf format.

An * denotes items that are available for a fee.

IOM (2011). *Hunger and Obesity: Understanding a Food Insecurity Paradigm: Workshop Summary.* Washington, DC: The National Academies Press. http://www.nap.edu/catalog.php?record_id=13102

> This 240-page report is available in pdf format.

NCAA Handbook: Managing the Female Athlete Triad. http://www.princeton.edu/uhs/pdfs/NCAA%20Managing%20the%20Female%20Athlete%20Triad.pdf

> This 53-page manual provides coaches with strategies to identify, manage, and prevent the Female Athlete Triad.

U.S. Department of Agriculture and U.S. Department of Health and Human Services (December, 2010). *Dietary Guidelines for Americans* (7th ed.). Washington, DC: Government Printing Office. http://health.gov/dietaryguidelines/dga2010/DietaryGuidelines2010.pdf

Curriculum, Lesson Plans, and Handouts

Accepting Size Differences. http://www.tolerance.org/activity/accepting-size-differences

> Three lesson plans for Grades 3–5, 6–8 and 9–12. Students learn to evaluate both their own biases related to size differences and the ways in which media shape those biases.

The Body Project (Stice & Presnell, 2007). http://www.bulimia.com/productdetails.cfm?PC=1557

> This handbook includes the lesson plans, activities, and scripts for The Body Project, a secondary prevention program that reduces students' internalization of media ideals, negative body image, and disordered eating (see Chapter 7, this volume).*

California Project Lean. http://www.californiaprojectlean.org/doc.asp?id=193#Nutr_and_PA_Lessons

> Research-based, user friendly toolkits, lesson plans, fact sheets, policy briefs, and recipes on topics such as school wellness, physical activity, safe routes to school, school food, and beverage standards. Includes materials in Spanish.

Ellyn Satter's Reproducible Education Resources. http://www.ellynsatter.com/links-i-82.html

> Newsletter and educational materials promote healthy eating and parent–child feeding dynamics for children.

Everybody's Different (O'Dea, 2007).

> This handbook includes the lesson plans, activities, and scripts for a primary prevention program that promotes students' self-esteem, body acceptance, body tolerance, health, and nutrition (see Chapter 7, this volume, for a more complete description).*

Food Psychology and Behavior Teacher ToolBox. http://foodpsychology.cornell.edu/toolbox/lesson-planning.html

> Created by Cornell's Food and Brand Lab, explores psychology and eating behavior via tips sheets, class modules, and teaching cartoons.

Fruits and Veggies Matter. http://www.fruitsandveggiesmatter.gov/health_professionals/educational_materials.html

Educational materials encourage kids and parents to eat more fruits and vegetables by exploring new tastes. Includes Leader's Guide, interactive worksheets, and recipe cards.

Full of Ourselves: A Wellness Program to Advance Girl Power, Health, and Leadership (Steiner-Adair & Sjostrom, 2006). http://www.catherinesteineradair.com/full-of-ourselves.php and http://jwa.org/feminism/_html/_pdf/JWA068a.pdf

This primary prevention program is designed to help girls combat the ubiquitous social and cultural pressures to focus on their appearance. It includes detailed lesson plans, handouts, and materials to enhance girls' appreciation for their bodies and relationships with both themselves and others (see Chapter 7, this volume, for a more complete description).*

Healthy Body Image: Teaching Kids to Eat and Love Their Bodies, Too! (Kater, 2005). http://www.bodyimagehealth.org/index.html

This primary prevention program includes detailed lesson plans, preparations, handouts, and materials for bolstering students' healthy body image and preventing unhealthy eating (see Chapter 7, this volume, for a more complete description).*

Healthy Buddies. http://www.healthybuddies.ca/program.htm

This peer-led program described in Chapter 4, this volume, promotes healthy attitudes and behaviors toward body image, nutrition, and activity. There are several free downloads, but there is a fee for the complete manualized program.

Jump Start Teens. http://www.californiaprojectlean.org/doc.asp?id=20

This student-tested program of eight lessons encourages teens to eat healthy and keep moving, which can integrated within language arts, math, science, and social studies.

New Moves. http://www.newmovesonline.com/materials.html

This evidenced-based program was created to prevent weight-related problems among high school girls (described in Chapter 4, this volume). The entire program can be downloaded. It includes lesson plans, teacher's guide, cookbook, reproducible worksheets (including Hunger Satiety Scale), and "Girl Pages," the student textbook.

Nutrition Detectives. http://davidkatzmd.com/nutritiondetectives.aspx

This 75-page teacher manual and PowerPoint evaluates nutrition issues and label reading. It was created and tested by Yale health advocate, David Katz, MD.

Reshaping Body Image. http://www.tolerance.org/activity/reshaping-body-image

Lesson plan and activity for Grades 9 to 12; it helps students dissect the current social norms about size and appearance. Includes a pdf handout and PowerPoint.

SPARK Physical Education. http://www.sparkpe.org/

SPARK was created to improve the health of students by disseminating evidence-based physical activity and nutrition programs that provide curriculum, staff development, follow-up support, and equipment to teachers of Pre-K through 12th-grade students. While this is a fee-based program, there are many free resources and sample lesson plans.*

Take 10! http://www.take10.net/whatistake10.asp?page=new

This is a classroom-based physical activity program for kindergarten to 5th grade, created by the International Life Sciences Institute's Center for Health Promotion, with the objective of adding 10-min periods of physical activity to the school day. The program links physical activity with academic learning objectives. Website includes "Teacher Toolbox," classroom tips, and sample materials.*

Eating Disorders Toolkit for Educators and Coaches. http://www.nationaleatingdisorders.org/information-resources/educator-toolkit.php

The National Eating Disorders Association created toolkits, one for educators and one aimed at coaches, providing information, curriculum, and resources in an easy-to-use format.

Organizations and Websites

Academy for Eating Disorders (AED). http://www.aedweb.org

International organization for health professionals and researchers specializing in eating disorders. Includes resources and information on eating disorders.

Academy of Nutrition and Dietetics. http://www.eatright.org

Formerly known as American Dietetic Association, this site contains well-documented information on food and nutrition and links to position papers.

American Public Health Association. http://www.apha.org/programs/resources/obesity/obesityparenttools.htm

Includes resources and tools for obesity prevention.

BAM! Body and Mind. http://www.bam.gov/

Created by the CDC for kids 9 to 13 years old. The site focuses health, stress and physical fitness—using kid-friendly lingo, games, quizzes, and other interactive features.

The Body Positive. http://www.bodypositive.com/

This website discusses how to promote positive body image and media literacy in children.

CDC: Division of Nutrition, Physical Activity, and Obesity. http://www.cdc.gov/nccdphp/dnpao/index.html

A comprehensive resource from the Centers for Disease Control and Prevention, including publications, social marketing resources, campaigns, policy resources and conferences.

CDC: Division of Adolescent and School Health (DASH). http://www.cdc.gov/healthyyouth/schoolhealth/index.htm

Several tools and resources: interactive tools including the School Health Index, Curriculum Analysis Tool, School Health Policies and Practices Study,

Coordinated School approaches, protocols, fact sheets, guidelines, and School Health Services Resources Tool.

The Center for Mindful Eating. http://www.tcme.org/

This multidisciplinary webpage is a forum for professionals interested in developing, deepening, and understanding the value and importance of mindful eating. It provides a wide variety of resources and training for those seeking up-to-date information about mindful eating practices, research, and education.

Cornell Center for Behavioral Economics in Child Nutrition Programs. http://ben. dyson.cornell.edu/index.html

The aim of this program is to help food service directors and policymakers design sustainable research-based lunchrooms that subtly guide healthier food choices. Includes free resources and tools for schools.

The Female Athlete Triad Coalition. http://www.femaleathletetriad.org/

This organization is dedicated to addressing unhealthy eating behaviors, hormonal irregularities, and bone health among female athletes and active women.

The Geena Davis Institute. http://www.seejane.org

The Geena Davis Institute spotlights gender inequalities at every media and entertainment company through research, education, training, strategic guidance, and advocacy programs (see "Jane"). Their mission is to work within the entertainment industry to dramatically alter how girls and women are reflected in media (e.g., improve gender balance, reduce stereotyping, and create a wide variety of female characters for entertainment targeting children ages 11 and under).

Girls Leadership Institute (GLI). http://www.girlsleadershipinstitute.org

Cofounded by bestselling author and girl-expert Rachel Simmons, GLI is a national nonprofit 501(c)(3) organization providing transformational programs to girls, their parents, and their educational communities. They teach the practices of emotional intelligence, assertive self-expression, and healthy relationships, giving girls the skills and confidence to live as leaders. They offer camps and workshops designed to teach girls, educators, and parents the core practices of emotional intelligence, healthy relationships, and assertive self-expression.

Hardy Girls Healthy Women. http://www.hghw.org

Hardy Girls Healthy Women (HGHW) is a nonprofit organization dedicated to the health and well-being of girls and women. Their vision is that all girls and women experience equality, independence, and safety in their everyday lives. To that end, their mission is to create opportunities, develop programs, and provide services that empower them. HGHW offers programming, resources, and services powered by the latest research in girls' development.

The National Alliance for Nutrition and Activity (NANA). http://www.nana coalition.org

NANA is made up of more than 300 organizations that advocate for federal policies and programs to promote healthy eating and physical activity. Resources for schools include model local school wellness policies on physical activity and nutrition, which are aligned with the Child Nutrition and WIC Reauthorization Act of 2004.

National Eating Disorders Awareness and Prevention (EDAP). http://www.national eatingdisorders.org/

This website supports individuals and families affected by eating disorders and serves as a catalyst for prevention, treatment, and access to quality care.

National Policy & Legal Analysis Network to Prevent Childhood Obesity. http://www.nplanonline.org/nplan/schools

Funded by the Robert Wood Johnson Foundation, this resource creates strong policy interventions to reverse childhood obesity. This site includes fact sheets, toolkits, training, and technical assistance to explain legal issues related to public health.

Powered by Girl (PBG). http://www.poweredbygirl.org

Powered by Girl is a girl-driven media activism site designed and maintained by the Girls Advisory Board of Hardy Girls Healthy Women and Women's, Gender, and Sexuality Studies students at Colby College. Integrating blogs and an ad gallery, PBG does more than question and analyze the media. The page creates opportunities for girls and women to think and work together, public spaces to critique and talk back, and tools to demand a more diverse and healthier set of messages.

The President's Challenge. http://www.presidentschallenge.org/tools-resources/docs/PresChal_booklet_10-11.pdf

President's Council on Fitness, Sports and Nutrition is dedicated to increasing the physical activity and fitness of America's youth. Includes free resources and tools.

The Rudd Center for Food Policy & Obesity. http://www.yaleruddcenter.org/

This nonprofit research and public policy organization is devoted to improving the world's diet, preventing obesity, and reducing weight stigma. Site includes free publications, podcasts, reports and seminars.

School Nutrition Association. http://www.schoolnutrition.org

This nonprofit organization works to ensure students have access to healthful school meals and nutrition education. There are several, free, downloadable lesson plans, but you will need to register (free) to access the materials.

Something Fishy. http://www.something-fishy.org/

Promotes awareness of eating disorders and includes a wide variety of resources for recovery and support.

SPARK: Sexualization Protest: Action Resistance Knowledge. http://www.spark summit.com

SPARK was designed to engage girls as part of the solution rather than to protect them from the problem. The web page offers media commentary (e.g., the Girls Library of Really?), personal stories, a research blog, a SPARKkit (i.e., recourse kit), and contests and other methods for taking action.

Teaching Tolerance. http://www.tolerance.org

>This nonprofit organization is dedicated to reducing prejudice and supporting equitable school experiences for children. It provides free educational materials to teachers and other school practitioners in the United States and abroad.

Team Nutrition Resource Library. http://teamnutrition.usda.gov/library.html

>Comprehensive listing of resources available through Team Nutrition to schools participating in the federal child nutrition programs. Available in Spanish.

USDA. Eat Smart. Play Hard. http://teamnutrition.usda.gov/Resources/eatsmart materials.html

>Campaign and resources encourage and teach children, parents, and caregivers to eat healthy and be physically active, consistent with the Dietary Guidelines for Americans.

USDA. Changing the Scene: Improving the School Nutrition Environment. http://www.fns.usda.gov/tn/resources/changing.html

>This toolkit was developed with input from 16 education, nutrition, and health organizations, and includes resources for promoting a healthy school environment.

USDA Center for Nutrition Policy and Promotion. http://www.cnpp.usda.gov/Publications.htm

>Provides several downloadable publications, including My Plate, U.S. Dietary Guidelines, and Healthy Eating Index.

Other Resources

Bullying: Guidelines for Teachers. http://www.tolerance.org/activity/bullying-guidelines-teachers

>Includes information on the issue of bullying and overweight students.

Constructive Classroom Rewards. http://cspinet.org/new/pdf/constructive_classroom_rewards.pdf

>This five-page guide lists nonfood reward ideas for student achievement and behavior.

Fitness File Software. http://www.presidentschallenge.org/tools-resources/tracking-software.shtml

>Free software for tracking students' progress and administering the Physical Fitness Test.

Kids Walk to School Program. http://www.cdc.gov/nccdphp/dnpa/kidswalk/index.htm

>This community-based program, created by the CDC, aims to increase physical activity by encouraging children to walk to and from school, in groups accompanied by adults. Free resources include PowerPoint and resource guide.

Let's Move In Schools (LMIS). http://www.letsmove.gov/schools

Provides several free resources to help increase physical activity in schools, created by the American Alliance for Health, Physical Education, Recreation and Dance.

Lunch Room Strategies. http://smarterlunchrooms.org.

A strategy guide for low-cost changes to improve the lunch room environment.

Youth Physical Activity Guidelines Toolkit. http://www.cdc.gov/HealthyYouth/physicalactivity/guidelines.htm#1

Provides strategies to support youth physical activity. Includes step-by-step guidance and customizable resources.

REFERENCES

Agras, W. S., Hammer, L. D., Huffman, L. C., Mascola, A., Bryson, S. W., & Danaher, C. (2012). Improving healthy eating in families with a toddler at risk for overweight: A cluster randomized controlled trial. *Journal of Developmental and Behavioral Pediatrics, 33*, 529–534. doi:10.1097/DBP.0b013e3182618e1f

Ahern, A. L., Bennett, K. M., & Hetherington, M. M. (2008). Internalization of the ultra-thin ideal: Positive implicit associations with underweight fashion models are associated with drive for thinness in young women. *Eating Disorders: The Journal of Treatment & Prevention, 16*, 294–307. doi:10.1080/10640260802115852

Albers, S. (2003). *Eating mindfully: How to end mindless eating and enjoy a balanced relationship with food*. Oakland, CA: New Harbinger.

Allen, K. L., Byrne, S. M., La Puma, M., McLean, N., & Davis, E. A. (2008). The onset and course of binge eating in 8- to 13-year-old healthy weight, overweight and obese children. *Eating Behaviors, 9*, 438–446. doi:10.1016/j.eatbeh.2008.07.008

Allison, K. C., Grilo, C. M., Masheb, R. M., & Stunkard, A. J. (2005). Binge eating disorder and night eating syndrome: A comparative study of disordered eating. *Journal of Consulting and Clinical Psychology, 73*, 1107–1115. doi:10.1037/0022-006X.73.6.1107

Altamura, C., Paluello, M. M., Mundo, E., Medda, S., & Mannu, P. (2001). Clinical and subclinical body dysmorphic disorder. *European Archives of Psychiatry and Clinical Neuroscience, 251*, 105–108. doi:10.1007/s004060170042

American Academy of Pediatrics. (2003). Identifying and treating eating disorders: Policy statement by the Committee on Adolescence. *Pediatrics, 111*, 204–211.

American Academy of Pediatrics. (2004). *School health: Policy & practice* (6th ed.). Elk Grove, IL: American Academy of Pediatrics.

American Dietetic Association. (2008). Position of the American Dietetic Association: Nutrition guidance for healthy children ages 2–11. *Journal of the American Dietetic Association, 108*, 1038–1047. doi:10.1016/j.jada.2008.04.005

American Psychiatric Association. (2000). *Diagnostic and statistical manual of mental disorders* (4th ed. text rev.). Washington, DC: Author.

American Psychiatric Association. (2011, November 13). *Diagnostic and Statistical Manual of Mental Disorders (DSM-5) development: Proposed revisions—eating disorders*. Retrieved from http://www.dsm5.org/Pages/Default.aspx

American Psychiatric Association Work Group on Eating Disorders. (2000). Practice guideline for the treatment of patients with eating disorders (revision). *The American Journal of Psychiatry, 157*, 1–39.

Anderson, P. M., & Butcher, K. F. (2005). *Reading, writing, and Raisinets: Are school finances contributing to children's obesity?* (Working Paper No. 11177). Retrieved from http://www.nber.org/papers/w11177

Anthamatten, P., Brink, L., Lampe, S., Greenwood, E., Kingston, B., & Nigg, C. (2011). An assessment of schoolyard renovation strategies to encourage children's physical activity. *The International Journal of Behavioral Nutrition and Physical Activity, 8*, 27–35. doi:10.1186/1479-5868-8-27

Anton, S. D., Han, H., Newton, R. L., Jr., Martin, C. K., York-Crowe, E., Stewart, T. M., & Williamson, D. A. (2006). Reformulation of the Children's Eating Attitudes Test (ChEAT): Factor structure and scoring method in a non-clinical population. *Eating and Weight Disorders, 11*, 201–210.

Arcelus, J., Mitchell, A. J., Wales, J., & Nielsen, A. (2011). Mortality rates in patients with anorexia nervosa and other eating disorders: A meta-analysis of 36 studies. *Archives of General Psychiatry, 68*, 724–731. doi:10.1001/archgenpsychiatry.2011.74

Aubie, C. D., & Jarry, J. L. (2009). Weight-related teasing increases eating in binge eaters. *Journal of Social and Clinical Psychology, 28*, 909–936. doi:10.1521/jscp.2009.28.7.909

Augustus-Horvath, C. L., & Tylka, T. L. (2011). The acceptance model of intuitive eating: A comparison of women in emerging adulthood, early adulthood, and middle adulthood. *Journal of Counseling Psychology, 58*, 110–125. doi:10.1037/a0022129

Austin, S. B. (2011). The blind spot in the drive for childhood obesity prevention: Bringing eating disorders prevention into focus as a public health priority. *American Journal of Public Health, 101*, e1–e4. doi:10.2105/AJPH.2011.300182

Austin, S. B., Field, A. E., Wiecha, J., Peterson, K. E., & Gortmaker, S. L. (2005). The impact of a school-based obesity prevention trial on disordered weight-control behaviors in early adolescent girls. *Archives of Pediatrics & Adolescent Medicine, 159*, 225–230. doi:10.1001/archpedi.159.3.225

Austin, S. B., Kim, J., Wiecha, J., Troped, P. J., Feldman, H. A., & Peterson, K. E. (2007). School-based overweight preventive intervention lowers incidence of disordered weight-control behaviors in early adolescent girls. *Archives of Pediatrics & Adolescent Medicine, 161*, 865–869. doi:10.1001/archpedi.161.9.865

Avalos, L., & Tylka, T. L. (2006). Exploring a model of intuitive eating with college women. *Journal of Counseling Psychology, 53*, 486–497. doi:10.1037/0022-0167.53.4.486

Avalos, L., Tylka, T. L., & Wood-Barcalow, N. L. (2005). The Body Appreciation Scale: Development and psychometric evaluation. *Body Image, 2*, 285–297. doi:10.1016/j.bodyim.2005.06.002

Bacon, L. (2010). *Health at every size: The surprising truth about your weight.* Dallas, TX: BenBella Books.

Bacon, L., Keim, N. L., Van Loan, M. D., Derricote, M., Gale, B., Kazaks, A., & Stern, J. S. (2002). Evaluating a "non-diet" wellness intervention for improvement of metabolic fitness, psychological well-being and eating and activity behaviors. *International Journal of Obesity and Related Metabolic Disorders, 26*, 854–865.

Bacon, L., Stern, J. S., Van Loan, M. D., & Keim, N. L. (2005). Size acceptance and intuitive eating improve health for obese, female chronic dieters. *Journal of the American Dietetic Association, 105,* 929–936. doi:10.1016/j.jada.2005.03.011

Baer, R. A., Fischer, S., & Huss, D. B. (2005). Mindfulness-based cognitive therapy applied to binge eating: A case study. *Cognitive and Behavioral Practice, 12,* 351–358. doi:10.1016/S1077-7229(05)80057-4

Baker, J. H., Maes, H. H., Lissner, L., Aggen, S. H., Lichtenstein, P., & Kendler, K. S. (2009). Genetic risk factors for disordered eating in adolescent males and females. *Journal of Abnormal Psychology, 118,* 576–586. doi:10.1037/a0016314

Barlett, C. P., Vowels, C. L., & Saucier, D. A. (2008). Meta-analyses of the effects of media images on men's body-image concerns. *Journal of Social and Clinical Psychology, 27,* 279–310. doi:10.1521/jscp.2008.27.3.279

Barr-Anderson, D. J., Neumark-Sztainer, D., Schmitz, K. H., Ward, D. S., Conway, T. L., Pratt, C., . . . Pate, R. R. (2008). But I like PE: Factors associated with enjoyment of physical education class in middle school girls. *Research Quarterly for Exercise and Sport, 79,* 18–27. doi:10.5641/193250308X13086 753542735

Batsell, W. R., Jr., Brown, A. S., Ansfield, M. E., & Paschall, G. Y. (2002). "You will eat all of that!": A retrospective analysis of forced consumption episodes. *Appetite, 38,* 211–219. doi:10.1006/appe.2001.0482

Baumrind, D. (1966). Effects of authoritative parental control on child behavior. *Child Development, 37,* 887–907. doi:10.2307/1126611

Bean, M. K., Stewart, K., & Olbrisch, M. E. (2008). Obesity in America: Implications for clinical and health psychologists. *Journal of Clinical Psychology in Medical Settings, 15,* 214–224. doi:10.1007/s10880-008-9124-9

Becker, A. E., Burwell, R. A., Herzog, D. B., Hamburg, P., & Gilman, S. E. (2002). Eating behaviours and attitudes following prolonged exposure to television among ethnic Fijian adolescent girls. *The British Journal of Psychiatry, 180,* 509–514. doi:10.1192/bjp.180.6.509

Becker, C. B., Smith, L. M., & Ciao, A. C. (2006). Peer-facilitated eating disorder prevention: A randomized effectiveness trial of cognitive dissonance and media advocacy. *Journal of Counseling Psychology, 53,* 550–555. doi:10.1037/0022-0167.53.4.550

Becker, C. B., & Stice, E. (2008). *Sorority body image program: Group leader guide.* New York, NY: Oxford University Press.

Beets, M. W., Beighle, A., Erwin, H. E., & Huberty, J. L. (2009). After-school program impact on physical activity and fitness: A meta-analysis. *American Journal of Preventive Medicine, 36,* 527–537. doi:10.1016/j.amepre.2009.01.033

Berkman, N. D., Lohr, K. N., & Bulik, C. M. (2007). Outcomes of eating disorders: A systematic review of the literature. *International Journal of Eating Disorders, 40,* 293–309. doi:10.1002/eat.20369

Birch, L. L., & Fisher, J. O. (2000). Mothers' child-feeding practices influence daughters' eating and weight. *The American Journal of Clinical Nutrition, 71,* 1054–1061.

Birch, L. L., Fisher, J. O., & Davison, K. K. (2003). Learning to overeat: Maternal use of restrictive feeding practices promotes girls' eating in the absence of hunger. *The American Journal of Clinical Nutrition, 78,* 215–220.

Birch, L. L., Johnson, C., & Fisher, J. O. (1995). Children's eating: The development of food-acceptance patterns. *Young Children, 50,* 71–78.

Birch, L. L., Johnson, S. L., Andresen, G., Peters, J. C., & Schulte, M. C. (1991, January 24). The variability of young children's energy intake. *The New England Journal of Medicine, 324,* 232–235. doi:10.1056/NEJM199101243240405

Birch, L. L., Parker, L., & Burns, A. (Eds.). (2011). *Early childhood obesity prevention policies.* Washington, DC: National Academies Press.

Bloom, T., Sharpe, L., Heriot, S., Zucker, N., & Craighead, L. (2005, June). *Children's Appetite Awareness Training (CAAT): A cognitive-behavioral intervention in the treatment of childhood obesity.* Paper presented at the World Health Organization Expert Meeting on Childhood Obesity, Kobe, Japan.

Boudette, R. (2006). Question & answer: Yoga in the treatment of disordered eating and body image disturbance. How can the practice of yoga be helpful in recovery from an eating disorder? *Eating Disorders: The Journal of Treatment & Prevention, 14,* 167–170. doi:10.1080/10640260500536334

Boutelle, K., Zucker, N., Peterson, C., & Rydell, S. (2011, April). *Regulation of cues for childhood overeating: The ROC intervention.* Paper presented at the annual Academy for Eating Disorders International Conference, Miami, FL.

Boutelle, K. N., Zucker, N. L., Peterson, C. B., Rydell, S. A., Cafri, G., & Harnack, L. (2011). Two novel treatments to reduce overeating in overweight children: A randomized controlled trial. *Journal of Consulting and Clinical Psychology, 79,* 759–771. doi:10.1037/a0025713

Brannan, M. E., & Petrie, T. A. (2008). Moderators of the body dissatisfaction-eating disorder symptomatology relationship: Replication and extension. *Journal of Counseling Psychology, 55,* 263–275. doi:10.1037/0022-0167.55.2.263

Brashich, A. (2006). *All made up: A girl's guide to seeing through celebrity hype and celebrating real beauty.* New York, NY: Walker and Company.

Bratman, S. (2001). *Health food junkies: Orthorexia nervosa: Overcoming the obsession with healthful eating.* New York, NY: Broadway.

Bravender, T., Bryant-Waugh, R., Herzog, D., Katzman, D., Kriepe, R. D., Lask, B., . . . Zucker, N. (2010). Classification of eating disturbance in children and adolescents: Proposed changes for the DSM-V. *European Eating Disorders Review, 18,* 79–89. doi:10.1002/erv.994

Briefel, R. R., Crepinsek, M. K., Cabili, C., Wilson, A., & Gleason, P. M. (2009). School food environments and practices affect dietary behaviors of U.S. public school children. *Journal of the American Dietetic Association, 109,* S91–S107. doi:10.1016/j.jada.2008.10.059

Briggs, M. (2010). Position of the American Dietetic Association, School Nutrition Association, and Society for Nutrition Education: Comprehensive school nutrition services. *Journal of the American Dietetic Association, 110*, 1738–1749. doi:10.1016/j.jada.2010.08.035

Bromfield, P. V. (2009). Childhood obesity: Psychosocial outcomes and the role of weight bias and stigma. *Educational Psychology in Practice, 25*, 193–209. doi:10.1080/02667360903151759

Brown, K. A., Ogden, J., Vogele, C., & Gibson, E. L. (2008). The role of parental control practices in explaining children's diet and BMI. *Appetite, 50*, 252–259. doi:10.1016/j.appet.2007.07.010

Bruch, H. (1962). Perceptual and conceptual disturbance is anorexia nervosa. *Psychonomic Medicine, 24*, 187–194.

Bruch, H. (1973). *Eating disorders: Obesity, anorexia nervosa, and the person within.* New York, NY: Basic Books.

Bryant-Waugh, R., Markham, L., Kreipe, R. E., & Walsh, B. T. (2010). Feeding and eating disorders in childhood. *International Journal of Eating Disorders, 43*, 98–111.

Bulik, C. M., Sullivan, P. F., Fear, J. L., & Pickering, A. (2000). Outcome of anorexia nervosa: Eating attitudes, personality, and parental bonding. *International Journal of Eating Disorders, 28*, 139–147. doi:10.1002/1098-108X(200009)28:2<139::AID-EAT2>3.0.CO;2-G

Burgeson, C. R., Wechsler, H., Brener, N. D., Young, J. C., & Spain, C. G. (2001). Physical education and activity: Results from the School Health Policies and Programs Study 2000. *The Journal of School Health, 71*, 279–293. doi:10.1111/j.1746-1561.2001.tb03505.x

Burke, C. A. (2010). Mindfulness-based approaches with children and adolescents: A preliminary review of current research in an emergent field. *Journal of Child and Family Studies, 19*, 133–144. doi:10.1007/s10826-009-9282-x

Burningham, L., & Dever, M. T. (2005). An interactive model to foster family literacy. *Young Children, 60*, 87–94.

Callahan, C. (2008). *Dialectic behavioral therapy for children and adolescents.* Eau Claire, WI: PESI.

Calogero, R. M., Herbozo, S., & Thompson, J. K. (2009). Complimentary weightism: The potential costs of appearance-related commentary for women's self-objectification. *Psychology of Women Quarterly, 33*, 120–132. doi:10.1111/j.1471-6402.2008.01479.x

Calogero, R. M., & Pedrotty, K. (2007). Daily practices for mindful exercise. In L. L'Abate, D. Embry, & M. Baggett (Eds.), *Handbook of low-cost preventive interventions for physical and mental health: Theory, research, and practice* (pp. 141–160). New York, NY: Springer-Verlag.

Caprio, S., Daniels, S. R., Drewnowski, A., Kaufman, F. R., Palinkas, L. A., Rosenbloom, A. L., & Schwimmer, J. B. (2008). Influence of race, ethnicity, and culture on childhood obesity: Implications for prevention and treatment: A consensus of shaping America's health and obesity society. *Diabetes Care, 31,* 2211–2221. doi: 10.2337/dc08-9024

Carei, T. R., Fyfe-Johnson, A. L., Breuner, C. C., & Brown, M. A. (2009). Randomized controlled clinical trial of yoga in the treatment of eating disorders. *The Journal of Adolescent Health, 46,* 346–351.

Carpenter, K. M., Hasin, D. S., Allison, D. B., & Faith, M. S. (2000). Relationships between obesity and *DSM–IV* major depressive disorder, suicide ideation, and suicide attempts: Results from a general population study. *American Journal of Public Health, 90,* 251–257. doi:10.2105/AJPH.90.2.251

Carper, J. L., Fisher, J. O., & Birch, L. L. (2000). Young girls' emerging dietary restraint and disinhibition are related to parental control in child feeding. *Appetite, 35,* 121–129. doi:10.1006/appe.2000.0343

Cash, T. F. (2008). *The body image workbook: An eight-step program for learning to like your looks* (2nd ed.). Oakland, CA: New Harbinger.

Cassidy, S. B., & Driscoll, D. J. (2009). Prader-Willi syndrome. *European Journal of Human Genetics, 17,* 3–13. doi:10.1038/ejhg.2008.165

Center for Science in the Public Interest. (2004). *Dispensing junk: How school vending undermines efforts to feed children well.* Retrieved from http://www.cspinet.org/schoolfoods

Center for Science in the Public Interest. (2007). *School foods report card.* Retrieved from http://www.cspinet.org/nutritionpolicy/sf_reportcard.pdf

Centers for Disease Control and Prevention. (2005). *School health index: A self-assessment and planning guide. Elementary school version.* Atlanta, GA: U.S. Department of Health and Human Services.

Centers for Disease Control and Prevention. (2009). *Youth physical activity: The role of schools.* Atlanta, GA: U.S. Department of Health and Human Services. Retrieved from http://www.cdc.gov/HealthyYouth

Centers for Disease Control and Prevention. (2010a). *The association between school-based physical activity, including physical education, and academic performance.* Atlanta, GA: Department of Health and Human Services.

Centers for Disease Control and Prevention. (2010b). *Healthy weight—It's not a diet, it's a lifestyle!: About BMI for children and teens.* Retrieved from http://www.cdc.gov/healthyweight/assessing/bmi/childrens_bmi/about_childrens_bmi.html

Centers for Disease Control and Prevention. (2011a). *Children's food environment state indicator report.* Retrieved from http://www.cdc.gov/obesity/downloads/ChildrensFoodEnvironment.pdf

Centers for Disease Control and Prevention. (2011b). School health guidelines to promote healthy eating and physical activity. *Morbidity and Mortality Weekly Report (MMWR), 60,* 1–76.

Chaput, J. P., Klingenberg, L., Rosenkilde, M., Gilbert, J. A., Tremblay, A., & Sjodin, A. (2011). Physical activity plays an important role in body weight regulation. *Journal of Obesity, 2011,* 1–11. doi:10.1155/2011/360257

Child Nutrition and WIC Reauthorization Act of 2004. Pub. L. No. 108-265, 118 Stat. 729.

Ciampolini, M., & Bianchi, R. (2006). Training to estimate blood glucose and to form associations with initial hunger. *Nutrition & Metabolism, 3,* 42. doi:10.1186/1743-7075-3-42

Ciampolini, M., Lovell-Smith, D., Bianchi, R., de Pont, B., Sifone, M., van Weeren, M., . . . Pietrobelli, A. (2010). *Sustained self-regulation of energy intake: Initial hunger improves insulin sensitivity.* doi:10.1155/2010/286952

Clark, N. (Director). (2009). *Cover girl culture: Awakening the media generation* [motion picture]. United States: Women Make Movies.

Clark, N. (Director). (2011). *Seeing through the media matrix: A companion guide to cover girl culture* [motion picture]. United States: Women Make Movies.

Claus, L., Braet, C., & Decaluwe, V. (2006). Dieting history in obese youngsters with and without disordered eating. *International Journal of Eating Disorders, 39,* 721–728. doi:10.1002/eat.20295

Collins, M. E. (1991). Body figure perceptions and preferences among preadolescent children. *International Journal of Eating Disorders, 10,* 199–208. doi:10.1002/1098-108X(199103)10:2<199::AID-EAT2260100209>3.0.CO;2-D

Cook-Cottone, C. (2006a). The attuned representation model for the primary prevention of eating disorders: An overview for school psychologists. *Psychology in the Schools, 43,* 223–230. doi:10.1002/pits.20139

Cook-Cottone, C. (2006b). *The brain owner's manual for kids: Helping the feeling and thinking parts work together.* Buffalo, NY: Growing and Learning Press.

Cook-Cottone, C. (2009). Eating disorders in childhood: Prevention and treatment supports. *Childhood Education, 85,* 300–306. doi:10.1080/00094056.2009.10521701

Cook-Cottone, C., Beck, M., & Kane, L. (2008). Manualized-group treatment of eating disorders: Attunement in mind, body, and relationship (AMBR). *Journal for Specialists in Group Work, 33,* 61–83. doi:10.1080/01933920701798570

Cook-Cottone, C., Jones, L. A., & Haugli, S. (2010). Prevention of eating disorders among minority youth: A matched-sample repeated measures study. *Eating Disorders: The Journal of Treatment & Prevention, 18,* 361–376. doi:10.1080/10640 266.2010.511894

Cook-Cottone, C., & Scime, M. (2006). The prevention and treatment of eating disorders: An overview for school psychologists. *The Communiqué, 34,* 38–40. Retrieved from http://www.nasponline.org/publications/cq/cq345eatingdis orders.aspx

Cook-Cottone, C. P. (2009). The neuropsychology of eating disorders in women. In E. Fletcher-Janzen (Ed.), *Neuropsychology of women* (pp. 1–33). New York, NY: Springer. doi:10.1007/978-0-387-76908-0_9

Corstorphine, E. (2006). Cognitive-emotional-behavioral therapy for the eating disorders: Working with beliefs about emotions. *European Eating Disorders Review, 14,* 448–461. doi:10.1002/erv.747

Craighead, L. W., & Allen, H. N. (1995). Appetite awareness training: A cognitive behavioral intervention for binge eating. *Cognitive and Behavioral Practice, 2,* 249–270.

Crisp, A. H., Callender, J. S., Halek, C., & Hsu, L. K. (1992). Long-term mortality in anorexia nervosa. A 20-year follow-up of the St George's and Aberdeen cohorts. *The British Journal of Psychiatry, 161,* 104–107. doi:10.1192/bjp.161.1.104

Crow, S., Eisenberg, M. E., Story, M., & Neumark-Sztainer, D. (2008). Are body dissatisfaction, eating disturbance, and body mass index predictors of suicidal behavior in adolescents? A longitudinal study. *Journal of Consulting and Clinical Psychology, 76,* 887–892. doi:10.1037/a0012783

Crow, S. J., Peterson, C. B., Swanson, S. A., Raymond, N. C., Specker, S., Eckert, E. D., & Mitchell, J. E. (2009). Increased mortality in bulimia nervosa and other eating disorders. *The American Journal of Psychiatry, 166,* 1342–1346. doi:10.1176/appi.ajp.2009.09020247

Culbert, K. M., Burt, S. A., McGue, M., Iacono, W. G., & Klump, K. L. (2009). Puberty and the genetic diathesis of disordered eating attitudes and behaviors. *Journal of Abnormal Psychology, 118,* 788–796. doi:10.1037/a0017207

Daniel, J. Z., Cropley, M., & Fife-Schaw, C. R. (2006). The effect of exercise in reducing desire to smoke and cigarette withdrawal symptoms is not caused by distraction. *Addiction, 101,* 1187–1192.

Daniel, S., & Bridges, S. K. (2010). The drive for muscularity in men: Media influences and objectification theory. *Body Image, 7,* 32–38. doi:10.1016/j.bodyim.2009.08.003

Daníelsdóttir, S., Burgard, D., & Oliver-Pyatt, W. (2010). AED Guidelines for childhood obesity prevention programs. Retrieved from http://www.aedweb.org/AM/Template.cfm?Section=Advocacy&Template=/CM/ContentDisplay.cfm&ContentID=1659

Darby, A., Hay, P., Mond, J., Quirk, F., Buttner, P., & Kennedy, L. (2009). The rising prevalence of comorbid obesity and eating disorder behaviors from 1995 to 2005. *International Journal of Eating Disorders, 42,* 104–108. doi:10.1002/eat.20601

Das, U. N. (2010). Obesity: Genes, brain, gut, and environment. *Nutrition, 26,* 459–473. doi:10.1016/j.nut.2009.09.020

Dave, D., & Rashad, I. (2009). Overweight status, self-perception, and suicidal behaviors among adolescents. *Social Science & Medicine, 68,* 1685–1691. doi:10.1016/j.socscimed.2009.02.015

Davis, C. (1997). Normal and neurotic perfectionism in eating disorders: An interactive model. *International Journal of Eating Disorders, 22,* 421–426. doi:10.1002/(SICI)1098-108X(199712)22:4<421::AID-EAT7>3.0.CO;2-O

Davis, J. N., Ventura, E. E., Cook, L. T., Gylenhammer, L. E., & Gatto, N. M. (2011). LA Sprouts: A gardening, nutrition, and cooking intervention for Latino youth improves diet and reduces obesity. *Journal of the American Dietetic Association, 111,* 1224–1230. doi:10.1016/j.jada.2011.05.009

Davison, K. K., Cutting, T. M., & Birch, L. L. (2003). Parents' activity-related parenting practices predict girls' physical activity. *Medicine and Science in Sports and Exercise, 35*, 1589–1595. doi:10.1249/01.MSS.0000084524.19408.0C

de Graaf, C., Blom, W. A., Smeets, P. A., Stafleu, A., & Hendriks, H. F. (2004). Biomarkers of satiation and satiety. *The American Journal of Clinical Nutrition, 79*, 946–961.

Devlin, M. J., Goldfein, J. A., & Dobrow, I. (2003). What is this thing called BED? Current status of binge eating disorder nosology. *International Journal of Eating Disorders, 34*, S2–S18. doi:10.1002/eat.10201

Dietz, W. H., Bland, M. G., Gortmaker, S. L., Molloy, M., & Schmid, T. L. (2002). Policy tools for the childhood obesity epidemic. *The Journal of Law, Medicine & Ethics, 30*, 83–87.

Dishman, R. K., Motl, R. W., Sallis, J. F., Dunn, A. L., Birnbaum, A. S., Welk, G. J., . . . Jobe, J. B. (2005). Self-management strategies mediate self-efficacy and physical activity. *American Journal of Preventive Medicine, 29*, 10–18. doi:10.1016/j.amepre.2005.03.012

Dockendorff, S. A., Petrie, T. A., Greenleaf, C., & Martin, S. (2011, August). *Intuitive Eating Scale for Adolescents: Factorial and construct validity.* Paper presented at the 119th Annual Convention of the American Psychological Association, Washington, DC.

Donini, L. M., Marsili, D., Graziani, M. P., Imbriale, M., & Cannella, C. (2005). Orthorexia nervosa: Validation of a diagnosis questionnaire. *Eating and Weight Disorders, 10*, e28–e32.

Donnelly, J. E., Greene, J. L., Gibson, C. A., Smith, B. K., Washburn, R. A., Sullivan, D. K., . . . Ryan, J. J. (2009). Physical activity across the curriculum (PAAC): A randomized controlled trial to promote physical activity and diminish overweight and obesity in elementary school children. *Preventive Medicine, 49*, 336–341. doi:10.1016/j.ypmed.2009.07.022

Donnelly, J. E., & Lambourne, K. (2011). Classroom-based physical activity, cognition, and academic achievement. *Preventive Medicine, 52*, S36–S42. doi:10.1016/j.ypmed.2011.01.021

Dorjee, D. (2010). Kinds and dimensions of mindfulness: Why it is important to distinguish them. *Mindfulness, 1*, 152–160. doi:10.1007/s12671-010-0016-3

Douglass, L. (2007). How did we get here? A history of yoga in America, 1800–1970. *International Journal of Yoga Therapy, 17*, 35–42.

Douglass, L. (2009). Yoga as an intervention in the treatment of eating disorders: Does it help? *Eating Disorders: The Journal of Treatment & Prevention, 17*, 126–139. doi:10.1080/10640260802714555

Dubnov-Raz, G., Constantini, N., Yariv, H., Nice, S., & Shapira, N. (2011). Influence of water drinking on resting energy expenditure in overweight children. *International Journal of Obesity, 35*, 1295–1300. doi:10.1038/ijo.2011.130

Dwyer, J. (1995). The School Nutrition Dietary Assessment Study. *American Journal of Clinical Nutrition, 61*, 173S–257S.

Eddy, K. T., Keel, P. K., Dorer, D. J., Delinsky, S. S., Franko, D. L., & Herzog, D. B. (2002). Longitudinal comparison of anorexia nervosa subtypes. *International Journal of Eating Disorders, 31,* 191–201. doi:10.1002/eat.10016

Eneli, I. U., Crum, P. A., & Tylka, T. L. (2008). The trust model: A different feeding paradigm for managing childhood obesity. *Obesity, 16,* 2197–2204. doi:10.1038/oby.2008.378

Eriksson, L., Baigi, A., Marklund, B., & Lindgren, E. C. (2008). Social physique anxiety and sociocultural attitudes toward appearance impact on orthorexia test in fitness participants. *Scandinavian Journal of Medicine & Science in Sports, 18,* 389–394. doi:10.1111/j.1600-0838.2007.00723.x

Erlanson-Albertsson, C. (2005). [Sugar triggers our reward-system. Sweets release opiates which stimulates the appetite for sucrose—insulin can depress it]. *Lakartidningen, 102,* 1620–1622, 1625, 1627. Retrieved from http://www.ncbi.nlm.nih.gov/pubmed/15962882

Fairburn, C. G., Cooper, Z., Doll, H. A., Norman, P., & O'Connor, M. (2000). The natural course of bulimia nervosa and binge eating disorder in young women. *Archives of General Psychiatry, 57,* 659–665. doi:10.1001/archpsyc.57.7.659

Farley, T. A., Meriwether, R. A., Baker, E. T., Watkins, L. T., Johnson, C. C., & Webber, L. S. (2007). Safe play spaces to promote physical activity in inner-city children: Results from a pilot study of an environmental intervention. *American Journal of Public Health, 97,* 1625–1631. doi:10.2105/AJPH.2006.092692

Fichter, M. M., & Quadflieg, N. (2004). Twelve-year course and outcome of bulimia nervosa. *Psychological Medicine, 34,* 1395–1406. doi:10.1017/S0033291704002673

Fidan, T., Ertekin, V., Isikay, S., & Kirpinar, I. (2010). Prevalence of orthorexia among medical students in Erzurum, Turkey. *Comprehensive Psychiatry, 51,* 49–54. doi:10.1016/j.comppsych.2009.03.001

Field, A. E., Austin, S. B., Taylor, C. B., Malspeis, S., Rosner, B., Rockett, H. R., . . . Colditz, G. A. (2003). Relation between dieting and weight change among preadolescents and adolescents. *Pediatrics, 112,* 900–906. doi:10.1542/peds.112.4.900

Fisher, J. O., & Birch, L. L. (1999). Restricting access to palatable foods affects children's behavioral response, food selection, and intake. *The American Journal of Clinical Nutrition, 69,* 1264–1272.

Fisher, J. O., & Birch, L. L. (2000). Parents' restrictive feeding practices are associated with young girls' negative self-evaluation of eating. *Journal of the American Dietetic Association, 100,* 1341–1346. doi:10.1016/S0002-8223(00)00378-3

Fisher, J. O., & Birch, L. L. (2002). Eating in the absence of hunger and overweight in girls from 5 to 7 y of age. *The American Journal of Clinical Nutrition, 76,* 226–231.

Flegal, K. M., Carroll, M. D., Ogden, C. L., & Curtin, L. R. (2010). Prevalence and trends in obesity among U.S. adults, 1999-2008. *JAMA, 303,* 235–241. doi:10.1001/jama.2009.2014

Flook, L., Smalley, S. L., Kitil, M. J., Galla, B. M., Kaiser-Greenland, S., Locke, J., . . . Kasari, C. (2010). Effects of mindful awareness practices on executive functions in elementary school children. *Journal of Applied School Psychology, 26,* 70–95. doi:10.1080/15377900903379125

Fox, M. K., Crepinsek, M. K., Connor, P., Battaglia, M., & McKinney, P. (2001). *School Nutrition Dietary Assessment Study–II: Summary of Findings.* Alexandria, VA: U.S. Department of Agriculture, Food and Nutrition Service, Office of Analysis, Nutrition and Evaluation.

Franks, A., Kelder, S., Dino, G., Horn, K., Gortmaker, S., Wiecha, J., & Simoes, E. (2007). School-based programs: Lessons learned from CATCH, Planet Health, and Not-On-Tobacco. *Preventing Chronic Disease, 4,* A33.

Franks, P. W., Hanson, R. L., Knowler, W. C., Sievers, M. L., Bennett, P. H., & Looker, H. C. (2010, February 11). Childhood obesity, other cardiovascular risk factors, and premature death. *The New England Journal of Medicine, 362,* 485–493. doi:10.1056/NEJMoa0904130

Fredrickson, B. L., & Losada, M. F. (2005). Positive affect and the complex dynamics of human flourishing. *American Psychologist, 60,* 678–686. doi:10.1037/0003-066X.60.7.678

Fredrickson, B. L., & Roberts, T.-A. (1997). Objectification theory: Toward understanding women's lived experiences and mental health risks. *Psychology of Women Quarterly, 21,* 173–206. doi:10.1111/j.1471-6402.1997.tb00108.x

French, S. A., Story, M., & Fulkerson, J. A. (2002). School food policies and practices: A state-wide survey of secondary school principals. *Journal of the American Dietetic Association, 102,* 1785–1789. doi:10.1016/S0002-8223(02)90382-2

Frisén, A., & Holmqvist, K. (2010). What characterizes early adolescents with a positive body image? A qualitative investigation of Swedish girls and boys. *Body Image, 7,* 205–212. doi:10.1016/j.bodyim.2010.04.001

Gagnon-Girouard, M. P., Begin, C., Provencher, V., Tremblay, A., Boivin, S., & Lemieux, S. (2009). Can we apply the dual-pathway model of overeating to a population of weight-preoccupied overweight women? *International Journal of Eating Disorders, 42,* 244–252. doi:10.1002/eat.20614

Galantino, M. L., Galbavy, R., & Quinn, L. (2008). Therapeutic effects of yoga for children: A systematic review of the literature. *Pediatric Physical Therapy, 20,* 66–80. doi:10.1097/PEP.0b013e31815f1208

Galloway, A. T., Farrow, C. V., & Martz, D. M. (2010). Retrospective reports of child feeding practices, current eating behaviors, and BMI in college students. *Obesity, 18,* 1330–1335. doi:10.1038/oby.2009.393

Galloway, A. T., Fiorito, L. M., Francis, L. A., & Birch, L. L. (2006). "Finish your soup": Counterproductive effects of pressuring children to eat on intake and affect. *Appetite, 46,* 318–323. doi:10.1016/j.appet.2006.01.019

Gardner, R. M., Sorter, R. G., & Friedman, B. N. (1997). Developmental changes in children's body images. *Journal of Social Behavior & Personality, 12,* 1019–1036.

Garner, D. M., Olmsted, M. P., Bohr, Y., & Garfinkel, P. E. (1982). The Eating Attitudes Test: Psychometric features and clinical correlates. *Psychological Medicine, 12,* 871–878. doi:10.1017/S0033291700049163

Gast, J., Madanat, H., & Nielson, A. C. (2012). Are men more intuitive when it comes to eating and physical activity? *American Journal of Men's Health, 6*, 164–171.

Gibbs, L., O'Connor, T., Waters, E., Booth, M., Walsh, O., Green, J., . . . Swinburn, B. (2008). Addressing the potential adverse effects of school-based BMI assessments on children's wellbeing. *International Journal of Pediatric Obesity, 3*, 52–57. doi:10.1080/17477160701645202

Gibson, C. A., Smith, B. K., DuBose, K. D., Greene, J. L., Bailey, B. W., Williams, S. L., . . . Donnelly, J. E. (2008). Physical activity across the curriculum: Year one process evaluation results. *The International Journal of Behavioral Nutrition and Physical Activity, 5*, 36. Retrieved from http://www.ijbnpa.org/content/5/1/36 doi:10.1186/1479-5868-5-36

Gillberg, C., Råstam, M., & Gillberg, I. C. (1994). Anorexia nervosa: Physical health and neurodevelopment at 16 and 21 years. *Developmental Medicine & Child Neurology, 36*, 567–575. doi:10.1111/j.1469-8749.1994.tb11893.x

Goossens, l., Braet, C., Vlierberghe, L. V., & Meis, S. (2009). Loss of control over eating in overweight youngsters: The role of anxiety, depression and emotional eating. *European Eating Disorders Review, 17*, 68-78.

Gopher Sport. (2006). Creating an active, safe & friendly playground. *Active and healthy schools program manual: A road map to make your school environment active & healthy* (pp. 29–37). Retrieved from http://www.gophersport.com/files/pdf/GS38452_ActiveHealthyManual.pdf

Gortmaker, S. L., Peterson, K., Wiecha, J., Sobol, A. M., Dixit, S., Fox M. K., & Laird N. (1999). Reducing obesity via a school-based interdisciplinary intervention among youth. *Archives of Pediatrics & Adolescent Medicine, 9*, 409–418.

Grabovac, A. D., Lau, M. A., & Willett, B. R. (2011). Mechanisms of mindfulness: A Buddhist psychological model. *Mindfulness*. Retrieved from doi:10.1007/s12671-011-0054-5

Greco, L. A., & Hayes, S. C. (2008). *Acceptance and mindfulness treatments for children and adolescents: A practitioner's guide*. Oakland, CA: New Harbingers Press.

Grilo, C. M., Hrabosky, J. I., White, M. A., Allison, K. C., Stunkard, A. J., & Masheb, R. M. (2008). Overvaluation of shape and weight in binge eating disorder and overweight controls: Refinement of a diagnostic construct. *Journal of Abnormal Psychology, 117*, 414–419. doi:10.1037/0021-843X.117.2.414

Guarracino, J. L., Savino, S., & Edelstein, S. (2006). Yoga participation is beneficial in obesity prevention, hypertension control, and possible quality of life. *Topics in Clinical Nutrition, 21*, 108–113.

Haines, J., & Neumark-Sztainer, D. (2006). Prevention of obesity and eating disorders: A consideration of shared risk factors. *Health Education Research, 21*, 770–782. doi:10.1093/her/cyl094

Haines, J., Neumark-Sztainer, D., & Thiel, L. (2007). Addressing weight-related issues in an elementary school: What do students, parents, and school staff recommend? *Eating Disorders: The Journal of Treatment & Prevention, 15,* 5–21. doi:10.1080/10640260601044428

Halmi, K. A., Eckert, E., Marchi, P., Sampugnaro, V., Apple, R., & Cohen, J. (1991). Comorbidity of psychiatric diagnoses in anorexia nervosa. *Archives of General Psychiatry, 48,* 712–718. doi:10.1001/archpsyc.1991.01810320036006

Hammerschmidt, P., Tackett, W., Golzynski, M., & Golzynski, D. (2011). Barriers to and facilitators of healthful eating and physical activity in low-income schools. *Journal of Nutrition Education and Behavior, 43,* 63–68. doi:10.1016/j.jneb.2009.11.008

Harris, J. L., Schwartz, M. B., Brownell, K. D., Sarda, V., Ustjanauskas, A., Javadizadeh, J., & Ohri-Vachaspati, P. (2010). *Evaluating fast food nutrition and marketing to youth.* New Haven, CT: Yale Rudd Center for Food Policy & Obesity.

Hawks, S. R., Madanat, H., Hawks, J., & Harris, A. (2005). The relationship between intuitive eating and health indicators among college women. *American Journal of Health Education, 36,* 331–336.

Hawks, S. R., Merrill, R. M., & Madanat, H. N. (2004). The Intuitive Eating Validation Scale: Preliminary validation. *American Journal of Health Education, 35,* 90–98.

Hawks, S. R., Merrill, R. M., Madanat, H. N., Miyagawa, T., Suwanteerangkul, J., Guarin, C. M., & Shaofang, C. (2004). Intuitive eating and the nutrition transition in Asia. *Asia Pacific Journal of Clinical Nutrition, 13,* 194–203.

Haworth-Hoeppner, S. (2000). The critical shapes of body image: The role of culture and family in the production of eating disorders. *Journal of Marriage and the Family, 62,* 212–227. doi:10.1111/j.1741-3737.2000.00212.x

Hay, P. J., & Sachdev, P. (2011). Brain dysfunction in anorexia nervosa: Cause or consequence of undernutiriton? *Current Opinion in Psychiatry, 24,* 251–256. doi:10.1097/YCO.0b013e3283453775

Hayes, D. (2010). Childhood obesity: Helping without harming. *Infant, Child, &. Adolescent Nutrition, 2,* 145–146. doi:10.1177/1941406410372324

Haynos, A. F., & Fruzzetti, A. E. (2011). Anorexia nervosa as a disorder of emotion dysregulation: Evidence and treatment implications. *Clinical Psychology: Science and Practice, 18,* 183–202. doi:10.1111/j.1468-2850.2011.01250.x

Hays, N. P., & Roberts, S. B. (2008). Aspects of eating behaviors "disinhibition" and "restraint" are related to weight gain and BMI in women. *Obesity, 16,* 52–58. doi:10.1038/oby.2007.12

Healthy, Hunger-Free Kids Act of 2010. Pub. L. No. 111-296, 124 Stat. 3183.

Healthy Meals for Healthy Americans Act of 1994, Pub. L. No. 103-448, 108 Stat. 4699

Heffner, M., Sperry, J., Eifert, G. H., & Detweiler, M. (2002). Acceptance and commitment therapy in the treatment of an adolescent female with anorexia nervosa: A case example. *Cognitive and Behavioral Practice, 9,* 232–236. doi:10.1016/S1077-7229(02)80053-0

Herman, C. P., & Polivy, J. (1983). A boundary model for the regulation of eating. In A. J. Stunkard & E. Stella (Eds.), *Eating and its disorders* (pp. 141–156). New York, NY: Raven.

Herman, C. P., Polivy, J., Lank, C. N., & Heatherton, T. F. (1987). Anxiety, hunger, and eating behavior. *Journal of Abnormal Psychology, 96,* 264–269. doi:10.1037/0021-843X.96.3.264

Hetherington, M., Rolls, B. J., & Burley, V. J. (1989). The time course of sensory-specific satiety. *Appetite, 12,* 57–68. doi:10.1016/0195-6663(89)90068-8

Hill, L. S., Reid, F., Morgan, J. F., & Lacey, J. H. (2010). SCOFF, the development of an eating disorder screening questionnaire. *International Journal of Eating Disorders, 43,* 344–351.

Hirsch, T. G. (1999). *Relational identity, psychological differentiation, perceived social support, and eating attitudes in college women.* Unpublished doctoral dissertation, Temple University, Philadelphia, PA.

Hoch, A. Z., Pajewski, N. M., Moraski, L. A., Carrera, G. F., Wilson, C. R., Hoffmann, R. G., . . . Gutterman, D. D. (2009). Prevalence of the female athlete triad in high school athletes and sedentary students. *Clinical Journal of Sport Medicine, 19,* 421–428. doi:10.1097/JSM.0b013e3181b8c136

Hoek, H. W., & van Hoeken, D. (2003). Review of the prevalence and incidence of eating disorders. *International Journal of Eating Disorders, 34,* 383–396. doi:10.1002/eat.10222

Howell, M. J., Schenck, C. H., & Crow, S. J. (2009). A review of nighttime eating disorders. *Sleep Medicine Reviews, 13,* 23–34. doi:10.1016/j.smrv.2008.07.005

Huberty, J. L., Siahpush, M., Beighle, A., Fuhrmeister, E., Silva, P., & Welk, G. (2011). Ready for recess: A pilot study to increase physical activity in elementary school children. *The Journal of School Health, 81,* 251–257. doi:10.1111/j.1746-1561.2011.00591.x

Hudson, J. I., Hiripi, E., Pope, H. G., Jr., & Kessler, R. C. (2007). The prevalence and correlates of eating disorders in the National Comorbidity Survey Replication. *Biological Psychiatry, 61,* 348–358. doi:10.1016/j.biopsych.2006.03.040

Huppert, F. A., & Johnson, D. M. (2010). A controlled trial of mindfulness training in schools: The importance of practice for an impact on well-being. *The Journal of Positive Psychology, 5,* 264–274. doi:10.1080/17439761003794148

Institute of Medicine. (2007). *Nutrition standards for foods in schools: Leading the way toward healthier youth.* Washington, DC: National Academies Press.

Institute of Medicine. (2008). *Nutrition standards and meal requirements for national school lunch and breakfast programs.* Washington, DC: National Academies Press.

Institute of Medicine. (2010). *School meals: Building blocks for healthy children.* Washington, DC: National Academies Press.

Johnson, S. L. (2000). Improving preschoolers' self-regulation of energy intake. *Pediatrics, 106,* 1429–1435. doi:10.1542/peds.106.6.1429

Kater, K. (2005). *Healthy body image: Teaching kids to eat and love their bodies too!* (2nd ed.). Seattle, WA: National Eating Disorders Association.

Kater, K., Rohwer, J., & Levine, M. P. (2000). An elementary school project for developing healthy body image and reducing risk factors for unhealthy and disordered eating. *Eating Disorders: The Journal of Treatment & Prevention, 8,* 3–16. doi:10.1080/10640260008251208

Kater, K. J., Rohwer, J., & Londre, K. (2002). Evaluation of an upper elementary school program to prevent body image, eating, and weight concerns. *The Journal of School Health, 72,* 199–204. doi:10.1111/j.1746-1561.2002.tb06546.x

Katz, D. L., O'Connell, M., Njike, V. Y., Yeh, M. C., & Nawaz, H. (2008). Strategies for the prevention and control of obesity in the school setting: Systematic review and meta-analysis. *International Journal of Obesity, 32,* 1780–1789. doi:10.1038/ijo.2008.158

Kaye, W. (2008). Neurobiology of anorexia and bulimia nervosa. *Physiology & Behavior, 94,* 121–135. doi:10.1016/j.physbeh.2007.11.037

Kemp, E., Bui, M., & Grier, S. (2011). Eating their feelings: Examining emotional eating in at-risk groups in the United States. *Journal of Consumer Policy, 34,* 211–229. doi:10.1007/s10603-010-9149-y

Kessler, D. A. (2009). *The end of overeating. Taking control of the insatiable American appetite.* Emmaus, PA: Rodale.

Keys, A., Brozek, J., Henschel, A., Mickelsen, O., & Taylor, H. L. (1950). *The biology of human starvation* (Vol. 1–2). Minneapolis, MN: University of Minnesota Press.

King, G. A., Herman, C. P., & Polivy, J. (1987). Food perception in dieters and nondieters. *Appetite, 8,* 147–158. doi:10.1016/S0195-6663(87)80007-7

King, N. A., Caudwell, P. P., Hopkins, M., Stubbs, J. R., Naslund, E., & Blundell, J. E. (2009). Dual-process action of exercise on appetite control: Increase in orexigenic drive but improvement in meal-induced satiety. *The American Journal of Clinical Nutrition, 90,* 921–927. doi:10.3945/ajcn.2009.27706

Klump, K. L., Suisman, J. L., Burt, S. A., McGue, M., & Iacono, W. G. (2009). Genetic and environmental influences on disordered eating: An adoption study. *Journal of Abnormal Psychology, 118,* 797–805. doi:10.1037/a0017204

Kral, T. V., & Faith, M. S. (2009). Influences on child eating and weight development from a behavioral genetics perspective. *Journal of Pediatric Psychology, 34,* 596–605. doi:10.1093/jpepsy/jsn037

Kristeller, J. L., & Wolever, R. Q. (2010). Mindfulness-based eating awareness training for treating binge eating disorder: The conceptual foundation. *Eating Disorders: The Journal of Treatment & Prevention, 19,* 49–61. doi:10.1080/10640266.2011.533605

Kroon Van Diest, A. M., & Tylka, T. (2010). The Caregiver Eating Messages Scale: Development and psychometric investigation. *Body Image, 7,* 317–326. doi:10.1016/j.bodyim.2010.06.002

Kropski, J. A., Keckley, P. H., & Jensen, G. L. (2008). School-based obesity prevention programs: An evidence-based review. *Obesity*, *16*, 1009–1018. doi:10.1038/oby.2008.29

Kubik, M. Y., Lytle, L. L., & Story, M. (2005). Schoolwide food practices are associated with body mass index in middle school students. *Archives of Pediatrics & Adolescent Medicine*, *159*, 1111–1114. doi:10.1001/archpedi.159.12.1111

LaFontaine, T. (2008). Physical activity: The epidemic of obesity and overweight among youth: Trends, consequences, and interventions. *American Journal of Lifestyle Medicine*, *2*, 30–36. doi:10.1177/1559827607309688

Lee, Y., Mitchell, D. C., Smiciklas-Wright, H., & Birch, L. L. (2001). Diet quality, nutrient intake, weight status, and feeding environments of girls meeting or exceeding recommendations for total dietary fat of the American Academy of Pediatrics. *Pediatrics*, *107*, e95. doi:10.1542/peds.107.6.e95

Lemmens, S. G., Rutters, F., Born, J. M., & Westerterp-Plantenga, M. S. (2011). Stress augments food "wanting" and energy intake in visceral overweight subjects in the absence of hunger. *Physiology & Behavior*, *103*, 157–163. doi:10.1016/j.physbeh.2011.01.009

Leone, J. E., Sedory, E. J., & Gray, K. A. (2005). Recognition and treatment of muscle dysmorphia and related body image disorders. *Journal of Athletic Training*, *40*, 352–359.

Levine, M. P., Piran, N., & Stoddard, C. (1999). Mission more probable: Media literacy, activism, and advocacy in the prevention of eating disorders. In N. Piran, M. P. Levine, & C. Steiner-Adair (Eds.), *Preventing eating disorders: A handbook of interventions and special challenges* (pp. 3–25). Philadelphia, PA: Brunner/Mazel.

Li, J., & Hooker, N. H. (2010). Childhood obesity and schools: Evidence from the national survey of children's health. *The Journal of School Health*, *80*, 96–103. doi:10.1111/j.1746-1561.2009.00471.x

Lightwood, J., Bibbins-Domingo, K., Coxson, P., Wang, Y. C., Williams, L., & Goldman, L. (2009). Forecasting the future economic burden of current adolescent overweight: An estimate of the coronary heart disease policy model. *American Journal of Public Health*, *99*, 2230–2237. doi:10.2105/AJPH.2008.152595

Linehan, M. (1993). *Cognitive-behavioral treatment of borderline personality disorder*. New York, NY: Guilford Press.

Liu, A. (2007). *Gaining: The truth about life after eating disorders*. New York, NY: Warner Books.

Lobera, I. J., & Bolaños Ríos, P. (2011). Spanish version of the Body Appreciation Scale (BAS) for adolescents. *The Spanish Journal of Psychology*, *14*, 411–420. doi:10.5209/rev_SJOP.2011.v14.n1.37

Loos, R. J. F., & Bouchard, C. (2003). Obesity—is it a genetic disorder? *Journal of Internal Medicine*, *254*, 401–425. doi:10.1046/j.1365-2796.2003.01242.x

Lundgren, J. D., Allison, K. C., Crow, S., O'Reardon, J. P., Berg, K. C., Galbraith, J., . . . Stunkard, A. J. (2006). Prevalence of the night eating syndrome in a psychiatric population. *The American Journal of Psychiatry, 163,* 156–158. doi:10.1176/appi.ajp.163.1.156

Macklem, G. L. (2008). *Practitioner's guide to emotion regulation in school-aged children.* New York, NY: Springer Verlag.

Madanat, H. N., & Hawks, S. R. (2004). Validation of the Arabic version of the Intuitive Eating Scale. *Promotion & Education, 11,* 152–157.

Maloney, M. J., McGuire, J. B., & Daniels, S. R. (1988). Reliability testing of a children's version of the Eating Attitude Test. *Journal of the American Academy of Child & Adolescent Psychiatry, 27,* 541–543. doi:10.1097/00004583-198809000-00004

Manley, R. S., Rickson, H., & Standeven, B. (2000). Children and adolescents with eating disorders: Strategies for teachers and school counselors. *Intervention in School and Clinic, 35,* 228–231. doi:10.1177/105345120003500405

Mann, T., Nolen-Hoeksema, S., Huang, K., Burgard, D., Wright, A., & Hanson, K. (1997). Are two interventions worse than none? Joint primary and secondary prevention of eating disorders in college females. *Health Psychology, 16,* 215–225. doi:10.1037/0278-6133.16.3.215

Mann, T., Tomiyama, A. J., Westling, E., Lew, A. M., Samuels, B., & Chatman, J. (2007). Medicare's search for effective obesity treatments: Diets are not the answer. *American Psychologist, 62,* 220–233. doi:10.1037/0003-066X.62.3.220

Martins, V. J. B., Toledo Florêncio, T. M. M., Grillo, L. P., & do Carmo, P. F. (2011). Long-lasting effects of undernutrition. *International Journal of Environmental Research and Public Health, 8,* 1817–1846. doi:10.3390/ijerph8061817

McAleese, J. D., & Rankin, L. J. (2007). Garden-based nutrition education affects fruit and vegetable consumption in sixth-grade adolescents. *Journal of the American Dietetic Association, 107,* 662–665. doi:10.1016/j.jada.2007.01.015

McCreary, D. R., Hildebrandt, T. B., Heinberg, L. J., Boroughs, M., & Thompson, J. K. (2007). A review of body image influences on men's fitness goals and supplement use. *American Journal of Men's Health, 1,* 307–316. doi:10.1177/1557988306309408

McEwen, B. S. (2008). Central effects of stress hormones in health and disease: Understanding the protective and damaging effects of stress and stress mediators. *European Journal of Pharmacology, 583,* 174–185. doi:10.1016/j.ejphar.2007.11.071

McGuire, K. A., & Ross, R. (2011). Incidental physical activity is positively associated with cardiorespiratory fitness. *Medicine and Science in Sports and Exercise, 43,* 2189–2194. doi:10.1249/MSS.0b013e31821e4ff2

McKenzie, T. L., Sallis, J. L., & Rosengard, P. (2009). Beyond the stucco tower: Design, development, and dissemination of the SPARK physical education programs. *Quest, 61,* 114–127. doi:10.1080/00336297.2009.10483606

McKnight Investigators. (2003). Risk factors for the onset of eating disorders in adolescent girls: Results of the McKnight longitudinal risk factor study. *The American Journal of Psychiatry, 160,* 248–254. doi:10.1176/appi.ajp.160.2.248

Mehling, W. E., Gopisetty, V., Daubenmier, J., Price, C. J., Hecht, F. M., & Stewart, A. (2009). Body awareness: Construct and self-report measures. *PLoS ONE, 4,* e5614. doi:10.1371/journal.pone.0005614

Mendelson, B. K., Mendelson, M. J., & White, D. R. (2001). Body-esteem scale for adolescents and adults. *Journal of Personality Assessment, 76,* 90–106. doi:10.1207/S15327752JPA7601_6

Mendelson, B. K., White, D. R., & Mendelson, M. J. (1996). Self-esteem and body esteem: Effects of gender, age, and weight. *Journal of Applied Developmental Psychology, 17,* 321–346. doi:10.1016/S0193-3973(96)90030-1

Mendelson, T., Greenberg, M. T., Dariotis, J. K., Gould, L. F., Rhoades, B. L., & Leaf, P. J. (2010). Feasibility and preliminary outcomes of a school-based mindfulness intervention for urban youth. *Journal of Abnormal Child Psychology, 38,* 985–994. doi:10.1007/s10802-010-9418-x

Monti, P. M., & Rohsenow, D. J. (1999). Coping-skills training and cue-exposure therapy in the treatment of alcoholism. *Alcohol Research & Health, 23,* 107–115.

Moon, A., & Berenbaum, H. (2009). Emotional awareness and emotional eating. *Cognition and Emotion, 23,* 417–429. doi:10.1080/02699930801961798

Moradi, B., Dirks, D., & Matteson, A. V. (2005). Roles of sexual objectification experiences and internalization of standards of beauty in eating disorder symptomatology: A test and extension of objectification theory. *Journal of Counseling Psychology, 52,* 420–428. doi:10.1037/0022-0167.52.3.420

Morgan, J. F., Reid, F., & Lacey, J. H. (1999). The SCOFF questionnaire: Assessment of a new screening tool for eating disorders. *British Medical Journal, 319,* 1467–1468. doi:10.1136/bmj.319.7223.1467

Mussap, A. J. (2007). The relationship between feminine gender role stress and disordered eating symptomatology in women. *Stress and Health, 23,* 343–348. doi:10.1002/smi.1152

National Association for Sport and Physical Education. (2008). *Comprehensive school physical activity programs* [Position statement]. Retrieved from http://www.aahperd.org/naspe/standards/upload/Comprehensive-School-Physical-Activity-Programs2-2008.pdf

Nattiv, A., Loucks, A. B., Manore, M. M., Sanborn, C. F., Sundgot-Borgen, J., Warren, M. P., & American College of Sports Medicine. (2007). American College of Sports Medicine position stand. The female athlete triad. *Medicine and Science in Sports and Exercise, 39,* 1867–1882. doi:10.1249/mss.0b013e318149f111

Neumark-Sztainer, D. (2005). Can we simultaneously work toward the prevention of obesity and EDs in children and adolescents? *International Journal of Eating Disorders, 38,* 220–227. doi:10.1002/eat.20181

Neumark-Sztainer, D. (2011). Obesity and body image in youth. In T. F. Cash & L. Smolak (Eds.), *Body image: A handbook of science, practice, and prevention* (2nd ed., pp. 180–188). New York, NY: Guilford Press.

Neumark-Sztainer, D., Bauer, K. W., Friend, S., Hannan, P. J., Story, M., & Berge, J. M. (2010). Family weight talk and dieting: How much do they matter for body dissatisfaction and disordered eating behaviors in adolescent girls? *Journal of Adolescent Health, 47*, 270–276. doi:10.1016/j.jadohealth.2010.02.001

Neumark-Sztainer, D., Falkner, N., Story, M., Perry, C., Hannan, P., & Mulert, S. (2002). Weight-teasing among adolescents: Correlations with weight status and disordered eating behaviors. *International Journal of Obesity, 26*, 123–131. doi:10.1038/sj.ijo.0801853

Neumark-Sztainer, D., Hannan, P. J., Story, M., Croll, J., & Perry, C. (2003). Family meal patterns: Associations with sociodemographic characteristics and improved dietary intake among adolescents. *Journal of the American Dietetic Association, 103*, 317–322. doi:10.1053/jada.2003.50048

Neumark-Sztainer, D., Story, M., & Coller, T. (1999). Perceptions of secondary school staff toward the implementation of school-based activities to prevent weight-related disorders: A needs assessment. *American Journal of Health Promotion, 13*, 153–156. doi:10.4278/0890-1171-13.3.153

Neumark-Sztainer, D., Story, M., Hannan, P. J., Tharp, T., & Rex, J. (2003). Factors associated with changes in physical activity: A cohort study of inactive adolescent girls. *Archives of Pediatrics & Adolescent Medicine, 157*, 803–810. doi:10.1001/archpedi.157.8.803

Neumark-Sztainer, D., Wall, M., Guo, J., Story, M., Haines, J., & Eisenberg, M. (2006). Obesity, disordered eating, and eating disorders in a longitudinal study of adolescents: How do dieters fare 5 years later? *Journal of the American Dietetic Association, 106*, 559–568. doi:10.1016/j.jada.2006.01.003

Neumark-Sztainer, D., Wall, M., Larson, N. I., Eisenberg, M. E., & Loth, K. (2011). Dieting and disordered eating behaviors from adolescence to young adulthood: Findings from a 10-year longitudinal study. *Journal of the American Dietetic Association, 111*, 1004–1011. doi:10.1016/j.jada.2011.04.012

Neumark-Sztainer, D. R., Friend, S. E., Flattum, C. F., Hannan, P. J., Story, M. T., Bauer, K. W., . . . Petrich, C. A. (2010). New moves—Preventing weight-related problems in adolescent girls: A group-randomized study. *American Journal of Preventive Medicine, 39*, 421–432. doi:10.1016/j.amepre.2010.07.017

Nihiser, A. J., Lee, S. M., Wechsler, H., McKenna, M., Odom, E., Reinold, C., . . . Grummer-Strawn, L. (2007). Body mass index measurement in schools. *The Journal of School Health, 77*, 651–671. doi:10.1111/j.1746-1561.2007.00249.x

Norman, G. J., Schmid, B. A., Sallis, J. F., Calfas, K. J., & Patrick, K. (2005). Psychosocial and environmental correlates of adolescent sedentary behaviors. *Pediatrics, 116*, 908–916. doi:10.1542/peds.2004-1814

Nunnally, J., & Bernstein, I. H. (1994). *Psychometric theory*. New York, NY: McGraw-Hill.

Nutrition Labeling and Education Act of 1990, Pub. L. No. 101-535, 104 Stat. 2353

O'Dea, J. A. (2003). Why do kids eat healthful food? Perceived benefits of and barriers to healthful eating and physical activity among children and adolescents. *Journal of the American Dietetic Association, 103*, 497–501.

O'Dea, J. A. (2005). Prevention of child obesity: "First, do no harm." *Health Education Research, 20*, 259–265. doi:10.1093/her/cyg116

O'Dea, J. A. (2007). *Everybody's different: A positive approach to teaching about health, puberty, body image, nutrition, self-esteem, and obesity prevention.* Victoria, Australia: Australian Council for Educational Research Press.

O'Dea, J. A., & Abraham, S. (2000). Improving the body image, eating attitudes, and behaviors of young male and female adolescents: A new educational approach that focuses on self-esteem. *International Journal of Eating Disorders, 28*, 43–57. doi:10.1002/(SICI)1098-108X(200007)28:1<43::AID-EAT6>3.0.CO;2-D

O'Dea, J. A., & Yager, Z. (2011). School-based psychoeducational approaches to prevention. In T. F. Cash & L. Smolak (Eds.), *Body image: A handbook of science, practice, and prevention* (2nd ed., pp. 434–441). New York, NY: Guilford Press.

Ogden, C., & Carroll, M. D. (2010). *Prevalence of obesity among children and adolescents: United States, trends 1963–1965 through 2007–2008.* Washington, DC: National Center for Health Statistics, Centers for Disease Control and Prevention.

Ogden, J., Reynolds, R., & Smith, A. (2006). Expanding the concept of parental control: A role for overt and covert control in children's snacking behaviour? *Appetite, 47*, 100–106. doi:10.1016/j.appet.2006.03.330

Olivardia, R. (2007). Muscle dysmorphia: Characteristics, assessment and treatment. In J. K. Thompson & G. Cafri (Eds.), *The muscular ideal: Psychological, social, and medical perspectives* (pp. 123–139). Washington, DC: American Psychological Association. doi:10.1037/11581-006

Omnibus Appropriations Act, 2009, Pub. L. No. 111-8, 123 Stat. 524

O'Toole, T. P., Anderson, S., Miller, C., & Guthrie, J. (2007). Nutrition services and foods and beverages available at school: Results from the School Health Policies and Programs Study 2006. *The Journal of School Health, 77*, 500–521. doi:10.1111/j.1746-1561.2007.00232.x

Ozier, A. D., & Henry, B. W. (2011). Position of the American Dietetic Association: Nutrition intervention in the treatment of eating disorders. *Journal of the American Dietetic Association, 111*, 1236–1241. doi:10.1016/j.jada.2011.06.016

Partnership for Prevention. (2008). *School-based physical education: Working with schools to increase physical activity among children and adolescents in physical education classes—An action guide.* Washington, DC: Author.

Pate, R. R., Saunders, R., Dishman, R. K., Addy, C., Dowda, M., & Ward, D. S. (2007). Long-term effects of a physical activity intervention in high school girls. *American Journal of Preventive Medicine, 33*, 276–280. doi:10.1016/j.amepre.2007.06.005

Pate, R. R., Ward, D. S., Saunders, R. D., Felton, G., Dishman, R. K., & Dowda, D. (2005). Promotion of physical activity among high-school girls: A randomized controlled trial. *American Journal of Public Health, 95*, 1582–1587. doi:10.2105/AJPH.2004.045807

Patel, P., Wheatcroft, R., Park, R. J., & Stein, A. (2002). The children of mothers with eating disorders. *Clinical Child and Family Psychology Review, 5*, 1–19. doi:10.1023/A:1014524207660

Patton, G. C., Selzer, R., Coffey, C., Carlin, J. B., & Wolfe, R. (1999). Onset of adolescent eating disorders: Population based cohort study over 3 years. *British Medical Journal, 318*, 765–768. doi:10.1136/bmj.318.7186.765

Paxton, S. J. (2011). Public policy approaches to prevention. In T. F. Cash & L. Smolak (Eds.), *Body image: A handbook of science, practice, and prevention* (2nd ed., pp. 460–468). New York, NY: Guilford Press.

Phillips, K. A., Dufresne, R. G., Jr., Wilkel, C. S., & Vittorio, C. C. (2000). Rate of body dysmorphic disorder in dermatology patients. *Journal of the American Academy of Dermatology, 42*, 436–441. doi:10.1016/S0190-9622(00)90215-9

Pietiläinen, K. H., Saarni, S. E., Kaprio, J., & Rissanen, A. (2011). Does dieting make you fat? A twin study. *International Journal of Obesity, 36*, 456–464. doi:10.1038/ijo.2011.160

Piran, N. (1999). *The whole-school approach to the prevention of body weight and preoccupation.* Paper presented at the second annual Harvard Eating Disorders Center Conference for Educators, Boston, MA.

Polivy, J. (1996). Psychological consequences of food restriction. *Journal of the American Dietetic Association, 96*, 589–592. doi:10.1016/S0002-8223(96)00161-7

Polivy, J., & Herman, C. P. (1999). Distress and eating: Why do dieters overeat? *International Journal of Eating Disorders, 26*, 153–164. doi:10.1002/(SICI)1098-108X(199909)26:2<153::AID-EAT4>3.0.CO;2-R

Proulx, K. (2007). Experiences of women with bulimia nervosa in a mindfulness-based eating disorder treatment group. *Eating Disorders: The Journal of Treatment & Prevention, 16*, 52–72. doi:10.1080/10640260701773496

Raby, T., & Cook-Cottone, C. P. (2012). *Girls growing in wellness and balance: Efficacy of parent workshops.* Manuscript in preparation.

Ranzenhofer, L. M., Tanofsky-Kraff, M., Menzie, C. M., Gustafson, J. K., Rutledge, M. S., Keil, M. F., . . . Yanovski, J. A. (2008). Structure analysis of the Children's Eating Attitudes Test in overweight and at-risk for overweight children and adolescents. *Eating Behaviors, 9*, 218–227. doi:10.1016/j.eatbeh.2007.09.004

Rayworth, B. B., Wise, L. A., & Harlow, B. L. (2004). Childhood abuse and risk of eating disorders in women. *Epidemiology, 15*, 271–278. doi:10.1097/01.ede.0000120047.07140.9d

Ricciardelli, L. A., & McCabe, M. P. (2001). Children's body image concerns and eating disturbance: A review of the literature. *Clinical Psychology Review, 21*, 325–344. doi:10.1016/S0272-7358(99)00051-3

Richard, M., Bauer, S., & Kordy, H. (2005). Relapse in anorexia and bulimia nervosa: A 2.5 year follow up study. *European Eating Disorders Review, 13*, 180–190. doi:10.1002/erv.638

Richard B. Russell National School Lunch Act of 1946. 79 Pub. L. No. 396, 60 Stat. 230 (1946).

Ridgeway, R. T., & Tylka, T. L. (2005). College men's perceptions of ideal body composition and shape. *Psychology of Men & Masculinity, 6*, 209–220. doi:10.1037/1524-9220.6.3.209

Roberts, A., Cash, T. F., Feingold, A., & Johnson, B. T. (2006). Are Black-White differences in females' body dissatisfaction decreasing? A meta-analytic review. *Journal of Consulting and Clinical Psychology, 74*, 1121–1131. doi:10.1037/0022-006X.74.6.1121

Roberts, S. L. (2002). School food: Does the future call for new food policy or can the old still hold true? *Drake Journal of Agricultural Law, 7*, 587.

Robinson, S. (2006). Victimization of obese adolescents. *The Journal of School Nursing, 22*, 201–206. doi:10.1177/10598405050220040301

Roehrig, M., Thompson, J. K., & Cafri, G. (2008). Effects of dieting-related messages on psychological and weight control variables. *International Journal of Eating Disorders, 41*, 164–173. doi:10.1002/eat.20470

Rolls, B. J., Engell, D., & Birch, L. L. (2000). Serving portion size influences 5-year-old but not 3-year-old children's food intakes. *Journal of the American Dietetic Association, 100*, 232–234. doi:10.1016/S0002-8223(00)00070-5

Roseman, M. G., Riddell, M. C., & Haynes, J. N. (2011). A content analysis of kindergarten-12th grade school-based nutrition interventions: Taking advantage of past learning. *Journal of Nutrition Education and Behavior, 43*, 2–18. doi:10.1016/j.jneb.2010.07.009

Rosen, J. C., Silberg, N., & Gross, J. (1988). Eating Attitudes Test and Eating Disorder Inventory: Norms for adolescent girls and boys. *Journal of Consulting and Clinical Psychology, 56*, 305–308. doi:10.1037/0022-006X.56.2.305

Rothschild-Yakar, L., Levy-Shiff, R., Fridman-Balaban, R., Gur, E., & Stein, D. (2010). Mentalization and relationships with parents as predictors of eating disordered behavior. *Journal of Nervous and Mental Disease, 198*, 501–507. doi:10.1097/NMD.0b013e3181e526c8

Rozin, P., Fischler, C., Imada, S., Sarubin, A., & Wrzesniewski, A. (1999). Attitudes to food and the role of food in life in the USA, Japan, Flemish Belgium and France: Possible implications for the diet-health debate. *Appetite, 33*, 163–180. doi:10.1006/appe.1999.0244

Rukavina, P. B., & Li, W. (2008). School physical activity interventions: Do not forget about obesity bias. *Obesity Reviews, 9*, 67–75.

Rutter, M. (1985). Resilience in the face of adversity: Protective factors and resistance to psychiatric disorder. *The British Journal of Psychiatry, 147*, 598–611. doi:10.1192/bjp.147.6.598

Rutters, F., Nieuwenhuizen, A. G., Lemmens, S. G., Born, J. M., & Westerterp-Plantenga, M. S. (2009). Acute stress-related changes in eating in the absence of hunger. *Obesity, 17*, 72–77. doi:10.1038/oby.2008.493

Safer, D. L., Couturier, J. L., & Lock, J. (2007). Dialectical behavior therapy modified for adolescent binge eating disorder: A case report. *Cognitive and Behavioral Practice, 14*, 157–167. doi:10.1016/j.cbpra.2006.06.001

Sallis, J. F., Conway, T. L., Prochaska, J. J., McKenzie, T. L., Marshall, S. J., & Brown, M. (2001). The association of school environments with youth physical activity. *American Journal of Public Health, 91*, 618–620. doi:10.2105/AJPH.91.4.618

Sallis, J. F., McKenzie, T. L., Alcaraz, J. E., Kolody, B., Faucette, N., & Hovell, M. E. (1997). The effects of a 2-year physical education program (SPARK) on physical activity and fitness in elementary school students. *American Journal of Public Health, 87*, 1328–1334. doi:10.2105/AJPH.87.8.1328

Sallis, J. F., McKenzie, T. L., Elder, J. P., Broyles, S. L., & Nader, P. R. (1997). Factors parents use in selecting play spaces for young children. *Archives of Pediatrics & Adolescent Medicine, 151*, 414–417. doi:10.1001/archpedi.1997.02170410088012

Salmon, J., Booth, M. L., Phongsavan, P., Murphy, N., & Timperio, A. (2007). Promoting physical activity participation among children and adolescents. *Epidemiologic Reviews, 29*, 144–159. doi:10.1093/epirev/mxm010

Satter, E. (1986). The feeding relationship. *Journal of the American Dietetic Association, 86*, 352–356.

Satter, E. (1995). Feeding dynamics: Helping children to eat well. *Journal of Pediatric Health Care, 9*, 178–184. doi:10.1016/S0891-5245(05)80033-1

Satter, E. (2005). *Your child's weight: Helping without harming.* Madison, WI: Kelcy Press.

Schachter, S. (1971). Some extraordinary facts about obese humans and rats. *American Psychologist, 26*, 129–144. doi:10.1037/h0030817

Schachter, S., & Rodin, J. (1974). *Obese humans and rats.* Washington, DC: Erlbaum/Halsted.

Schneider, M., & Cooper, D. M. (2011). Enjoyment of exercise moderates the impact of a school-based physical activity intervention. *International Journal of Behavioral Nutrition and Physical Activity, 8*, 64. Retrieved from http://www.ijbnpa.org/content/8/1/64 doi:10.1186/1479-5868-8-64

Schonert-Reichl, K. A., & Lawlor, M. S. (2010). The effects of a mindfulness-based education program on pre- and early adolescents' well-being and social and emotional competence. *Mindfulness, 1*, 137–151. doi:10.1007/s12671-010-0011-8

Schwartz, M. B., Novak, S. A., & Fiore, S. (2009). The impact of removing snacks of low nutritional value from middle schools. *Health Education & Behavior, 36*, 999–1011. doi:10.1177/1090198108329998

Schwimmer, J. B., Deutsch, R., Kahen, T., Lavine, J. E., Stanley, C., & Behling, C. (2006). Prevalence of fatty liver in children and adolescents. *Pediatrics, 118*, 1388–1393. doi:10.1542/peds.2006-1212

Scime, M., & Cook-Cottone, C. (2008). Primary prevention of eating disorders: A constructivist integration of mind and body strategies. *International Journal of Eating Disorders, 41*, 134–142. doi:10.1002/eat.20480

Scime, M., Cook-Cottone, C. P., Kane, L., & Watson, T. (2006). Group prevention of eating disorders: Impact on body dissatisfaction, drive for thinness, and media influence. *Eating Disorders: The Journal of Treatment & Prevention, 14*, 143–155. doi:10.1080/10640260500403881

Scrinis, G. (2008). On the ideology of nutritionism. *Gastronomica, 8*, 39–48. doi:10.1525/gfc.2008.8.1.39

Seligman, M. E., & Csikszentmihalyi, M. (2000). Positive psychology. An introduction. *American Psychologist, 55*, 5–14. doi:10.1037/0003-066X.55.1.5

Serwacki, M., & Cook-Cottone, C. P. (2012). Yoga in the schools: A review of the literature. *International Journal of Yoga Therapy, 22*, 101–109.

Shapiro, S. L., & Carlson, L. E. (2009). *The art and science of mindfulness: Integrating mindfulness into psychology and the helping professions.* Washington, DC: American Psychological Association. doi:10.1037/11885-000

Shapiro, S. L., Oman, D., Thoresen, C. E., Plante, T. G., & Flinders, T. (2008). Cultivating mindfulness: Effects on well-being. *Journal of Clinical Psychology, 64*, 840–862. doi:10.1002/jclp.20491

Sharma, M. (2011). Dietary education in school-based childhood obesity prevention programs. *Advances in Nutrition, 2*, 207S-216S. Retrieved from http://advances.nutrition.org/content/2/2/207S.full

Shomaker, L. B., Tanofsky-Kraff, M., Zocca, J. M., Courville, A., Kozlosky, M., Columbo, K. M., . . . Ali, A. H. (2010). Eating in the absence of hunger in adolescents: Intake after a large-array meal compared with that after a standardized meal. *The American Journal of Clinical Nutrition, 92*, 697–703. doi:10.3945/ajcn.2010.29812

Shouse, S. H., & Nilsson, J. (2011). Self-silencing, emotional awareness, and eating behaviors in college women. *Psychology of Women Quarterly, 35*, 451–457. doi:10.1177/0361684310388785

Shunk, J. A., & Birch, L. L. (2004). Girls at risk for overweight at age 5 are at risk for dietary restraint, disinhibited overeating, weight concerns, and greater weight gain from 5 to 9 years. *Journal of the American Dietetic Association, 104*, 1120–1126. doi:10.1016/j.jada.2004.04.031

Siegel, D. J. (2010). *The mindful therapist: A clinician's guide to mindsight and neural integration.* New York, NY: WW Norton & Company.

Simon, J., Schmidt, U., & Pilling, S. (2005). The health service use and cost of eating disorders. *Psychological Medicine, 35*, 1543–1551. doi:10.1017/S0033291705004708

Sjostrom, L. A., & Steiner-Adair, C. (2005). Full of ourselves: A wellness program to advance girl power, health and leadership. *Journal of Nutrition Education and Behavior, 37*, S141–S144. doi:10.1016/S1499-4046(06)60215-7

Skårderud, F. (2009). Bruch revisited and revised. *European Eating Disorders Review, 17*, 83–88. doi:10.1002/erv.923

Slaney, R. B., Rice, K. G., Mobley, M., Trippi, J., & Ashby, J. S. (2001). The revised Almost Perfect Scale. *Measurement & Evaluation in Counseling & Development*, *34*, 130–145.

Smith, A., & Cook-Cottone, C. P. (2011). A review of family therapy as an effective intervention for anorexia nervosa in adolescents. *Journal of Clinical Psychology in Medical Settings*, *18*, 323–334.

Smith, T. S., & Hawks, S. R. (2006). Intuitive eating, diet composition, and the meaning of food in healthy weight promotion. *American Journal of Health Education*, *37*, 130–136.

Smitham, L. (2008). *Evaluating an intuitive eating program for binge eating disorder: A benchmarking study*. Unpublished doctoral dissertation, University of Notre Dame, South Bend, IN.

Smolak, L., & Levine, M. P. (1994). Psychometric properties of the Children's Eating Attitudes Test. *International Journal of Eating Disorders*, *16*, 275–282. doi:10.1002/1098-108X(199411)16:3<275::AID-EAT2260160308>3.0.CO;2-U

Smolak, L., Levine, M. P., & Gralen, S. (1993). The impact of puberty and dating on eating problems among middle school girls. *Journal of Youth and Adolescence*, *22*, 355–368. doi:10.1007/BF01537718

Snyder, C. R., & Lopez, S. J. (2007). *Positive psychology: The scientific and practical explorations of human strengths*. Thousand Oaks, CA: Sage.

Stahl, B., & Goldstein, E. (2010). *A mindfulness-based stress reduction workbook*. Oakland, CA: New Harbinger Publications.

Steiner-Adair, C., & Sjostrom, L. (2006). *Full of ourselves: A wellness program to advance girl power, health, and leadership*. New York, NY: Teachers College Press.

Steiner-Adair, C., Sjostrom, L., Franko, D. L., Pai, S., Tucker, R., Becker, A. E., & Herzog, D. B. (2002). Primary prevention of risk factors for eating disorders in adolescent girls: Learning from practice. *International Journal of Eating Disorders*, *32*, 401–411.

Stice, E. (2001). A prospective test of the dual-pathway model of bulimic pathology: Mediating effects of dieting and negative affect. *Journal of Abnormal Psychology*, *110*, 124–135. doi:10.1037/0021-843X.110.1.124

Stice, E. (2002). Risk and maintenance factors for eating pathology: A meta-analytic review. *Psychological Bulletin*, *128*, 825–848. doi:10.1037/0033-2909.128.5.825

Stice, E., & Agras, W. S. (1998). Predicting onset and cessation of bulimic behaviors during adolescence: A longitudinal grouping analysis. *Behavior Therapy*, *29*, 257–276. doi:10.1016/S0005-7894(98)80006-3

Stice, E., Mazotti, L., Weibel, D., & Agras, W. S. (2000). Dissonance prevention program decreases thin-ideal internalization, body dissatisfaction, dieting, negative affect, and bulimic symptoms: A preliminary experiment. *International Journal of Eating Disorders*, *27*, 206–217. doi:10.1002/(SICI)1098-108X(200003)27:2<206::AID-EAT9>3.0.CO;2-D

Stice, E., & Presnell, K. (2007). *The body project: Promoting body acceptance and preventing eating disorders: Facilitator's guide*. New York, NY: Oxford University Press.

Stice, E., Presnell, K., & Spangler, D. (2002). Risk factors for binge eating onset in adolescent girls: A 2-year prospective investigation. *Health Psychology, 21*, 131–138. doi:10.1037/0278-6133.21.2.131

Stice, E., Rohde, P., Gau, J., & Shaw, H. (2009). An effectiveness trial of a dissonance-based eating disorder prevention program for high-risk adolescent girls. *Journal of Consulting and Clinical Psychology, 77*, 825–834. doi:10.1037/a0016132

Stice, E., & Shaw, H. (2004). Eating disorder prevention programs: A meta-analytic review. *Psychological Bulletin, 130*, 206–227. doi:10.1037/0033-2909.130.2.206

Stice, E., Shaw, H., & Marti, C. N. (2006). A meta-analytic review of obesity prevention programs for children and adolescents: The skinny on interventions that work. *Psychological Bulletin, 132*, 667–691. doi:10.1037/0033-2909.132.5.667

Stice, E., Trost, A., & Chase, A. (2003). Healthy weight control and dissonance-based eating disorder prevention programs: Results from a controlled trial. *International Journal of Eating Disorders, 33*, 10–21. doi:10.1002/eat.10109

Stiegler, L. N. (2005). Understanding pica behavior. *Focus on Autism and Other Developmental Disabilities, 20*, 27–38. doi:10.1177/10883576050200010301

Stock, S., Miranda, C., Evans, S., Plessis, S., Ridley, J., Yeh, S., & Chanoine, J. P. (2007). Healthy buddies: A novel, peer-led health promotion program for the prevention of obesity and eating disorders in children in elementary school. *Pediatrics, 120*, e1059–e1068. doi:10.1542/peds.2006-3003

Story, M. (2009). The school food environment, children's diets, and obesity: Findings from the Third School Nutrition Dietary Assessment Study. *Journal of the American Dietetic Association, 109*(Suppl.2), S3–S135.

Story, M., Kaphingst, K. M., Robinson-O'Brien, R., & Glanz, K. (2008). Creating healthy food and eating environments: Policy and environmental approaches. *Annual Review of Public Health, 29*, 253–272. doi:10.1146/annurev.publhealth.29.020907.090926

Story, M., Nanney, M. S., & Schwartz, M. B. (2009). Schools and obesity prevention: Creating school environments and policies to promote healthy eating and physical activity. *Milbank Quarterly, 87*, 71–100. doi:10.1111/j.1468-0009.2009.00548.x

Strasburger, V. C. (2011). Children, adolescents, obesity, and the media. *Pediatrics, 128*, 201–208. doi:10.1542/peds.2011-1066

Striegel-Moore, R. H., & Bulik, C. M. (2007). Risk factors for eating disorders. *American Psychologist, 62*, 181–198. doi:10.1037/0003-066X.62.3.181

Striegel-Moore, R. H., Fairburn, C. G., Wilfley, D. E., Pike, K. M., Dohm, F. A., & Kraemer, H. C. (2005). Toward an understanding of risk factors for binge-eating disorder in Black and White women: A community-based case-control study. *Psychological Medicine, 35*, 907–917. doi:10.1017/S0033291704003435

Striegel-Moore, R. H., Leslie, D., Petrill, S. A., Garvin, V., & Rosenheck, R. A. (2000). One year use and cost of inpatient and outpatient services among female and male patients with an eating disorder: Evidence from a national database of health insurance claims. *International Journal of Eating Disorders, 27*, 381–389. doi:10.1002/(SICI)1098-108X(200005)27:4<381::AID-EAT2>3.0.CO;2-U

Strober, M., Freeman, R., Lampert, C., Diamond, J., & Kaye, W. (2000). Controlled family study of anorexia nervosa and bulimia nervosa: evidence of shared liability and transmission of partial syndromes. *The American Journal of Psychiatry, 157*, 393–401.

Stunkard, A. J., Harris, J. R., Pedersen, N. L., & McClearn, G. E. (1990, May 24). The body-mass index of twins who have been reared apart. *The New England Journal of Medicine, 322*, 1483–1487. doi:10.1056/NEJM199005243222102

Sullivan, P. F., Bulik, C. M., Fear, J. L., & Pickering, A. (1998). Outcome of anorexia nervosa: A case-control study. *The American Journal of Psychiatry, 155*, 939–946.

Sundgot-Borgen, J., & Torstveit, M. K. (2010). Aspects of disordered eating continuum in elite high-intensity sports. *Scandinavian Journal of Medicine & Science in Sports, 20*, 112–121. doi:10.1111/j.1600-0838.2010.01190.x

Swahn, M. H., Reynolds, M. R., Tice, M., Miranda-Pierangeli, M. C., Jones, C. R., & Jones, I. R. (2009). Perceived overweight, BMI, and risk for suicide attempts: Findings from the 2007 Youth Risk Behavior Survey. *Journal of Adolescent Health, 45*, 292–295. doi:10.1016/j.jadohealth.2009.03.006

Sweetingham, R., & Waller, G. (2008). Childhood experiences of being bullied and teased in the eating disorders. *European Eating Disorders Review, 16*, 401–407. doi:10.1002/erv.839

Tanofsky-Kraff, M., Ranzenhofer, L. M., Yanovski, S. Z., Schvey, N. A., Faith, M., Gustafson, J., & Yanovski, J. A. (2008). Psychometric properties of a new questionnaire to assess eating in the absence of hunger in children and adolescents. *Appetite, 51*, 148–155. doi:10.1016/j.appet.2008.01.001

Thein-Nissenbaum, J. M., & Carr, K. E. (2011). Female athlete triad syndrome in the high school athlete. *Physical Therapy in Sport, 12*, 108–116. doi:10.1016/j.ptsp.2011.04.002

Thompson, J. K., Heinberg, L. J., Altabe, M., & Tantleff-Dunn, S. (1999). *Exacting beauty: Theory, assessment, and treatment of body image disturbance*. Washington, DC: American Psychological Association. doi:10.1037/10312-000

Thompson, J. K., van den Berg, P., Roehrig, M., Guarda, A. S., & Heinberg, L. J. (2004). The Sociocultural Attitudes Towards Appearance Scale-3 (SATAQ-3): Development and validation. *International Journal of Eating Disorders, 35*, 293–304. doi:10.1002/eat.10257

Tomeo, C. A., Field, A. E., Berkey, C. S., Colditz, G. A., & Frazier, A. L. (1999). Weight concerns, weight control behaviors, and smoking initiation. *Pediatrics, 104*, 918–924. doi:10.1542/peds.104.4.918

Trasande, L., Liu, Y., Fryer, G., & Weitzman, M. (2009). Effects of childhood obesity on hospital care and costs, 1999–2005. *Health Affairs, 28*, w751–w760. doi:10.1377/hlthaff.28.4.w751

Treasure, J., Murphy, T., Szmukler, T., Todd, G., Gavan, K., & Joyce, J. (2001). The experience of caregiving for severe mental illness: A comparison between anorexia nervosa and psychosis. *Social Psychiatry and Psychiatric Epidemiology, 36*, 343–347. doi:10.1007/s001270170039

Tribole, E., & Resch, E. (1995). *Intuitive eating*. New York, NY: St. Martin's Press.

Tribole, E., & Resch, E. (2003). *Intuitive eating* (2nd ed.). New York, NY: St. Martin's Press.

Tribole, E., & Resch, E. (2012). *Intuitive eating* (3rd ed.). New York, NY: St. Martin's Press.

Tucker, T. (2008). *The great starvation experiment: Ancel Keys and the men who starved for science*. Minneapolis, MN: University of Minnesota Press.

Tylka, T. L. (2004). The relation between body dissatisfaction and eating disorder symptomatology: An analysis of moderating variables. *Journal of Counseling Psychology, 51*, 178–191. doi:10.1037/0022-0167.51.2.178

Tylka, T. L. (2006). Development and psychometric evaluation of a measure of intuitive eating. *Journal of Counseling Psychology, 53*, 226–240. doi:10.1037/0022-0167.53.2.226

Tylka, T. L. (2011a). Positive psychology perspectives on body image. In T. F. Cash & L. Smolak (Eds.), *Body image: A handbook of science, practice, and prevention* (2nd ed., pp. 56–64). New York, NY: Guilford Press.

Tylka, T. L. (2011b). Refinement of the tripartite influence model for men: Dual body image pathways to body change behaviors. *Body Image, 8*, 199–207. doi:10.1016/j.bodyim.2011.04.008

Tylka, T. L., & Andorka, M. J. (2012). Support for an expanded tripartite influence model with gay men. *Body Image, 9*, 57–67. doi:10.1016/j.bodyim.2011.09.006

Tylka, T. L., & Augustus-Horvath, C. L. (2011). Fighting self-objectification in prevention and intervention contexts. In R. M. Calogero, S. Tantleff-Dunn, & J. K. Thompson (Eds.), *Self-objectification in women: Causes, consequences, and counteractions* (pp. 187–214). Washington, DC: American Psychological Association. doi:10.1037/12304-009

Tylka, T. L., Bergeron, D., & Schwartz, J. P. (2005). Development and psychometric evaluation of the Male Body Attitudes Scale (MBAS). *Body Image, 2*, 161–175. doi:10.1016/j.bodyim.2005.03.001

Tylka, T. L., & Hill, M. S. (2004). Objectification theory as it relates to disordered eating among college women. *Sex Roles, 51*, 719–730. doi:10.1007/s11199-004-0721-2

Tylka, T. L., & Kroon Van Diest, A. M. (2012). *The Intuitive Eating Scale-2: Item refinement and psychometric evaluation with college women and men*. Manuscript submitted for publication.

Tylka, T. L., & Subich, L. M. (2004). Examining a multidimensional model of eating disorder symptomatology among college women. *Journal of Counseling Psychology, 51*, 314–328. doi:10.1037/0022-0167.51.3.314

Tylka, T. L., & Wilcox, J. A. (2006). Are intuitive eating and eating disorder symptomatology opposite poles of the same construct? *Journal of Counseling Psychology, 53*, 474–485. doi:10.1037/0022-0167.53.4.474

USDA Team Nutrition. (2004). *The Child Nutrition and WIC Reauthorization Act (P.L. 108-265). Nutrient standards for foods in schools: Leading the way to healthier youth.* Retrieved from http://www.fns.usda.gov/tn/healthy/108-265.pdf

U.S. Department of Agriculture. (2010). *2010 dietary guidelines for Americans.* Retrieved from http://www.cnpp.usda.gov/dietaryguidelines.htm

U.S. Department of Agriculture. (2011). *My plate.* Retrieved from http://www.choosemyplate.gov/

U.S. Department of Education. (2010). *A blueprint for reform: The reauthorization of the Elementary and Secondary Education Act.* Washington, DC: Author.

U.S. Department of Health and Human Services. (2008). *Physical activity guidelines advisory committee report.* Retrieved from http://www.health.gov/paguidelines/report/

U.S. Prevention Services Task Force (2010). Screening for obesity in children and adolescents: Recommendation statement. *Pediatrics, 125*, 361–367.

van den Berg, P. A., Mond, J., Eisenberg, M., Ackard, D., & Neumark-Sztainer, D. (2010). The link between body dissatisfaction and self-esteem in adolescents: Similarities across gender, age, weight status, race/ethnicity, and socioeconomic status. *Journal of Adolescent Health, 47*, 290–296. doi:10.1016/j.jadohealth.2010.02.004

Van Wijnen, L. G. C., Wendel-Vos, G. C. W., Wammes, B. M., & Bemelmans, W. J. E. (2009). The impact of school-based prevention of overweight on psychosocial well-being of children. *Obesity Reviews, 10*, 298–312. doi:10.1111/j.1467-789X.2008.00549.x

Ventura, A. K., & Birch, L. L. (2008). Does parenting affect children's eating and weight status? *The International Journal of Behavioral Nutrition and Physical Activity, 5*, 15. http://www.ijbnpa.org/content/5/1/15 doi:10.1186/1479-5868-5-15

Wall, M. I., Carlson, S. A., Stein, A. D., Lee, S. M., & Fulton, J. E. (2011). Trends by age in youth physical activity: Youth media campaign longitudinal survey. *Medicine and Science in Sports and Exercise, 43*, 2140–2147. doi:10.1249/MSS.0b013e31821f561a

Wanden-Berghe, R. G., Sanz-Valero, J., & Wanden-Berghe, C. (2010). The application of mindfulness to eating disorders treatment: A systematic review. *Eating Disorders: The Journal of Treatment & Prevention, 19*, 34–48. doi:10.1080/10640266.2011.533604

Ward, D. S., Saunders, R., Felton, G. M., Williams, E., Epping, J. N., & Pate, R. R. (2006). Implementation of a school environment intervention to increase physical activity in high school girls. *Health Education Research, 21*, 896–910. doi:10.1093/her/cyl134

Warner, J. (2010). Junking junk food. *New York Times Magazine.* Retrieved from http://www.nytimes.com/2010/11/28/magazine/28FOB-wwln-t.html

Weiss, C. C., Purciel, M., Bader, M., Quinn, J. W., Lovasi, G., Neckerman, K. M., & Rundle, A. G. (2011). Reconsidering access: Park facilities and neighborhood disamenities in New York City. *Journal of Urban Health, 88*, 297–310. doi:10.1007/s11524-011-9551-z

Whetstone, L. M., Morrissey, S. L., & Cummings, D. M. (2007). Children at risk: The association between perceived weight status and suicidal thoughts and attempts in middle school youth. *The Journal of School Health, 77*, 59–66. doi:10.1111/j.1746-1561.2007.00168.x

Wilksch, S. M., Tiggemann, M., & Wade, T. D. (2006). Impact of interactive school-based media literacy lessons for reducing internalization of media ideals in young adolescent girls and boys. *International Journal of Eating Disorders, 39*, 385–393. doi:10.1002/eat.20237

Wilksch, S. M., & Wade, T. D. (2009a). Reduction of shape and weight concern in young adolescents: A 30-month controlled evaluation of a media literacy program. *Journal of the American Academy of Child & Adolescent Psychiatry, 48*, 652–661. doi:10.1097/CHI.0b013e3181a1f559

Wilksch, S., & Wade, T. (2009b). School-based eating disorder prevention. In S. J. Paxton & P. J. Hay (Eds.), *Treatment approaches for body dissatisfaction and eating disorders: Evidence and practice* (pp. 7–22). Melbourne, Australia: IP Communications.

Wilksch, S. M., & Wade, T. D. (2010). Risk factors for clinically significant importance of shape and weight in adolescent girls. *Journal of Abnormal Psychology, 119*, 206–215. doi:10.1037/a0017779

Wilksch, S. M., & Wade, T. D. (2012). Examination of the Sociocultural Attitudes Towards Appearance Questionnaire-3 in a mixed gender young adolescent sample. *Psychological Assessment, 24*, 352–364. doi:10.1037/a0025618

Willett, W. C., & Skerrett, P. J. (2005). *Eat, drink, and be healthy: The Harvard Medical School guide to healthy eating.* New York, NY: Free Press.

Wilson, G. T., Grilo, C. M., & Vitousek, K. M. (2007). Psychological treatment of eating disorders. *American Psychologist, 62*, 199–216. doi:10.1037/0003-066X.62.3.199

Wood-Barcalow, N. L., Tylka, T. L., & Augustus-Horvath, C. L. (2010). "But I like my body": Positive body image characteristics and a holistic model for young adult women. *Body Image, 7*, 106–116. doi:10.1016/j.bodyim.2010.01.001

World Health Organization. (2011). *Preamble to the constitution of the World Health Organization as adopted by the International Health Conference, New York, 19–22 June 1946.* Retrieved from http://www.who.int/bulletin/bulletin_board/83/ustun11051/en/

Yager, Z., & O'Dea, J. (2005). The role of teachers and other educators in the prevention of eating disorders and child obesity: What are the issues? *Eating Disorders: The Journal of Treatment & Prevention, 13*, 261–278. doi:10.1080/10640260590932878

Yager, Z., & O'Dea, J. A. (2008). Prevention programs for body image and eating disorders on university campuses: A review of large, controlled interventions. *Health Promotion International, 23*, 173–189. doi:10.1093/heapro/dan004

Young, S. K. (2011). *Promoting healthy eating among college women: Effectiveness of an intuitive eating intervention.* Unpublished doctoral dissertation, Iowa State University, Ames, IA.

Zipfel, S., Lowe, B., Reas, D. L., Deter, H. C., & Herzog, W. (2000, February 26). Long-term prognosis in anorexia nervosa: Lessons from a 21-year follow-up study. *The Lancet, 355*, 721–722. doi:10.1016/S0140-6736(99)05363-5

INDEX

Eating disorder treatment, 194–198
  academic support as part of, 196, 198
  research on, 42–43
  role of school personnel in, 196–198
  support during meals for, 198
  teams for, 195–196
Eating in the absence of hunger (EAH)
  assessment and screening tools for, 187–189
  and dieting, 30
  prevention strategies for, 148, 170, 176
  and promoting health, 83
  as risk factor for overeating and obesity, 5, 37, 46, 100
Eating in the Absence of Hunger Questionnaire for Children (EAH-C), 188–189
EDAP (National Eating Disorders Awareness and Prevention), 236
Eddy, K. T., 13
EDNOS (eating disorder not otherwise specified), 10, 16–17
EDs. See Eating disorders
Elementary and Secondary Education Act (ESEA), 207
Elementary schools, 118–119
Ellyn Satter's Reproducible Education Resources, 232
Emotional eating, 124, 126–127, 160
Emotional regulation, 64, 137–140
  benefits of, 123–124
  defined, 123
  and eating in the absence of hunger, 188
  future directions for applications of, 141
  in healthy eating, 125
  school-based applications of, 140–141
  self-care practices as foundation of, 137–138
  training for children, 138–140
Emotional-regulation theory, 126–127
Emotions. See also Emotional regulation
  and food, 31–32
  in mindfulness-based eating awareness training, 131
  and psychological well-being, 38–39
  and the self, 63–64
  wholesome, 129–130

Empowerment, 148
Energy availability, 220
Energy intake, 211–212, 220
Environmentally-based physical activity, 125
ESEA (Elementary and Secondary Education Act), 207
Ethnoculture, 52. See also Race and ethnicity
Everybody's Different intervention program
  delivery of, 183
  effectiveness of, 188
  overview, 149, 162–166
  resources, 232
  transcontextual approach of, 71
Exacting Beauty (J. K. Thompson, L. J. Heinberg, M. Altabe, & S. Tantleff-Dunn), 193
Exercise. See Physical activity
Exosystem, 52–54
External eating rules, 27, 28, 30, 176
Externality theory, 176

Fairburn, C. G., 16
Faith M. S., 19
Family. See also Parents and caregivers
  in healthy student approach, 70, 72
  influence of, 40
  and the self, 54–55
Family meals
  intuitive eating during, 72
  positive outcomes with, 77
Family therapy, 196
Farm-to-school programs, 73, 213–214
Farrow, C. V., 40
Fat talk, 79–80, 217
Federal nutrition programs, 3
Federal school food programs, 205–208
Feeding disorder of infancy or early childhood, 220
Feelings. See Emotions
Feingold, A., 61
Female athlete triad, 219–221
The Female Athlete Triad Coalition, 235
The Female Athlete Triad Position Stand (ACSM report), 231
Females
  body ideals for, 190
  intuitive eating in, 38
  physical activity levels of, 111

ABOUT THE AUTHORS

Catherine Cook-Cottone, PhD, is an associate professor at the University at Buffalo, State University of New York. She has published over 45 research articles and book chapters and has made numerous national and international presentations. Her primary research trajectory is in the area of eating disorders. She is also a certified school psychologist, licensed psychologist, and certified yoga teacher with a private practice that serves patients with eating disorders.

Evelyn Tribole, MS, RD, is an award-winning registered dietitian, with a nutrition counseling practice, specializing in eating disorders and intuitive eating in Newport Beach, California. She has written seven books, including *Intuitive Eating* (coauthored with Elyse Resch).

Tracy Tylka, PhD, is an associate professor at The Ohio State University. She has published 29 empirical articles and book chapters on body image and eating behavior, often exploring how they intersect. She studies both positive and negative body image as well as adaptive and maladaptive eating. She has made numerous national and international presentations and she is an associate editor for *Body Image: An International Journal of Research* and a guest editor for three special issues on gendered body image that will appear in *Sex Roles: A Journal of Research*.